The
WILEY
advantage

D1312273

Dear Valued Customer,

We realize that you're a busy professional with deadlines to hit. Whether your goal is to learn a new technology or solve a critical problem, we want to be there to lend you a hand. Our primary objective is to provide you with the insight and knowledge you need to stay atop the highly competitive and ever-changing technology industry.

Wiley Publishing, Inc., offers books on a wide variety of technical categories, including security, data warehousing, software development tools, and networking — everything you need to reach your peak. Regardless of your level of expertise, the Wiley family of books has you covered.

- For Dummies – The *fun* and *easy* way to learn
- The Weekend Crash Course –The *fastest* way to learn a new tool or technology
- Visual – For those who prefer to learn a new topic *visually*
- The Bible – The *100% comprehensive* tutorial and reference
- The Wiley Professional list – *Practical* and *reliable* resources for IT professionals

The book you hold now, *XMLSPY Handbook*, is the official guide to Altova's award-winning XML development suite. If you are an XML newbie, or even if you are an expert, *XMLSPY Handbook* is everything you need to master this incredible tool. Starting with detailed installation instructions, one of Altova's very own XML "spies" guides you through building and editing XML documents, DTDs and Schemas, XSL and XSLT, and even SOAP and Web services. Top it all off with tips and sample questions to help you pass the XML Developer Certification exam, and you have everything you need to get into the XMLSPY game.

Our commitment to you does not end at the last page of this book. We want to open a dialog with you to see what other solutions we can provide. Please be sure to visit us at www.wiley.com/compbooks to review our complete title list and explore the other resources we offer. If you have a comment, suggestion, or any other inquiry, please locate the "contact us" link at www.wiley.com.

Thank you for your support. We look forward to hearing from you and serving your needs again in the future.

Sincerely,

Richard K. Swadley
Vice President & Executive Group Publisher
Wiley Technology Publishing

15 HOUR WEEKEND CRASH COURSE

V™ Visual

Bible

DUMMIES

WILEY
Wiley Publishing, Inc.

XMLSPY Handbook

Larry Kim

Wiley Publishing, Inc.

XMLSPY Handbook

Published by
Wiley Publishing, Inc.
10475 Crosspoint Boulevard
Indianapolis, IN 46256
www.wiley.com

Copyright © 2003 by Wiley Publishing, Inc., Indianapolis, Indiana

Published simultaneously in Canada

ISBN: 0-7645-4964-2

Manufactured in the United States of America.

10 9 8 7 6 5 4 3 2 1

For general information on our other products and services or to obtain technical support, please contact our Customer Care Department within the U.S. at (800) 762-2974, outside the U.S. at (317) 572-3993, or fax (317) 572-4002.

Wiley also publishes its books in a variety of electronic formats. Some content that appears in print may not be available in electronic books.

Library of Congress Control Number: 2002110288

This book is dedicated to my good friend, Kay Lee Park.

About the Author

Larry Kim is a technical director with Altova, Inc., producer of the industry-leading XML development environment, XMLSPY. He works out of Altova's U.S. offices on the North Shore of Boston, Massachusetts, and writes various XML developer resources, such as the XMLSPY newsletter.

Larry has coauthored several books on Java programming and co-wrote the XMLSPY – XML Developer Certification exam, which is offered by Prometric in the U.S. and Canada.

Prior to his association with Altova, Larry was the product manager for Macromedia's JRun Server, a popular J2EE Server. He is a frequent speaker at industry conferences, including the XML 2001 Conference & Expo and JavaOne, the official Sun Microsystems Java Developer's Conference. Larry has an undergraduate degree in electrical engineering from the University of Waterloo, in Canada, and is currently pursuing a graduate degree in computer science.

Credits

EXECUTIVE EDITOR
Chris Webb

SENIOR PROJECT EDITOR
Jodi Jensen

TECHNICAL REVIEW
Altova, Inc.

COPY EDITOR
Mary Lagu

EDITORIAL MANAGER
Mary Beth Wakefield

VICE PRESIDENT AND EXECUTIVE GROUP PUBLISHER
Richard Swadley

VICE PRESIDENT AND EXECUTIVE PUBLISHER
Bob Ipsen

VICE PRESIDENT AND PUBLISHER
Joseph B. Wikert

EXECUTIVE EDITORIAL DIRECTOR
Mary Bednarek

PROJECT COORDINATOR
Cindy Phipps

GRAPHICS AND PRODUCTION SPECIALISTS
Sean Decker
Clint Lahnen
Mary Virgin

PROOFREADING
Kim Cofer

INDEXING
Johnna VanHoose Dinse
Tom Dinse

Foreword

If you are holding this book in your hands, chances are pretty good that you are a Web developer, programmer, database architect, or IT professional and that you've already heard about XML or Web services in some form or the other. Who hasn't, with all the buzz and marketing hype surrounding these topics lately? But wait. Is it really hype that we are dealing with here? Consider for a moment that Microsoft and Sun, Oracle and IBM are all releasing product after product built on XML. Such common ground among competitors is, indeed, highly unusual. Might there actually be some interesting technology behind all that hype?

You bet! XML is the foundation of all these new products for a good reason: It is simple, it is powerful, it is extensible, and it is here to stay. XML – the Extensible Markup Language defined by the World Wide Web Consortium (W3C) in 1998 – has already been called the *lingua franca* of the Internet by many. That is certainly true: No other language has the expressive power to describe texts from the *Digital Dictionary of Buddhism* (www.acmuller.net/ddb) as well as from the genome sequence of *Drosophila melanogaster* – the common fruit fly (www.fruitfly.org/sequence). XML owes this flexibility to the elegant, yet simple concept of *markup* – the idea that documents are comprised of text, which can be *tagged* to give it meaning.

Based on this foundation, XML has grown over the past years and is now widely used in diverse applications ranging from document management to business-to-business (B2B) communication. In these applications, XML is usually augmented by related technologies, such as XML Schema for expressing content models, XSLT for transforming data, and Web services for communicating between systems.

To take advantage of all these XML-related technologies, you need one environment, where all of them can be brought into perspective – and with XMLSPY 5, Altova has created just that: the ultimate tool for all things XML. Multiple views let you see XML documents in a whole new light and drill right down to the core of XML! Edit XML Schema content models in a graphical view, debug XSLT stylesheets step-by-step, create definitions for Web services, connect from XML to databases, create Java or C++ source code automatically, or migrate old-style HTML Web sites to XML.

Part of the new v5 Altova product line, XMLSPY 5 is the premier XML development environment and builds on the success of previous XMLSPY versions. Both XMLSPY 5 and its previous versions have won numerous industry awards, including *PC Magazine*'s Editors' Choice Award, *Java Developer Journal*'s Readers' Choice Award for best XML Tool, and *Visual Studio Magazine*'s Best XML and XSLT Software.

The *XMLSPY Handbook* is your secret decoder ring to the entire world of XML and XMLSPY 5. With Larry Kim as your guide, you will master XML, namespaces, XML Schema, XSLT, WSDL, and many other acronyms that may seem daunting at first. You will discover a whole new level of productivity provided with these new technologies. Larry's long-term experience in the development–tools market and his insight into XML enables him to present these fundamental concepts in an easy-to-understand way. With the XMLSPY 5 software provided with this book, you can try out everything immediately. As you progress to the more advanced topics, Larry explains even the most complex aspects of XML Schema through his very structured, yet easy-to-read style. In no time, you will find yourself as a true Master of XML.

May the journey begin!

Alexander Falk
President & CEO
Altova, Inc.

Preface

XML technologies are finding their way into all aspects of modern software development projects, from configuration files to remote procedure calls. Diverse programming languages, platforms, operating systems, and vendors are all adopting XML technologies. XML is changing the way software applications are built. It is a huge leap forward in computing technologies, similar in magnitude to the recent advent of the Web. In order to build XML applications, you must become proficient at creating, editing, and debugging XML technologies using XML development tools. This book is about gaining experience with XML technologies with the help of XMLSPY – the world's leading XML development environment, currently used by more than one million developers.

Who Should Read This Book

Today, hundreds of universities and training companies use XMLSPY to teach XML technologies. The XMLSPY development environment provides a hands-on, concrete means for learning XML faster. XML technologies, such as XML Schema, DTDs, XSL, XSLT, SOAP, and WSDL are, in general, quite abstract and complex. This book differs from other XML books in that it uses the XMLSPY editing environment as it introduces various XML technologies, allowing you to easily create any XML documents and immediately visualize the results as you type. It is the first book dedicated to learning all core XML technologies with the help of the XMLSPY development environment. If you are new to XML, this book reduces the learning curve, providing you with a solid understanding of XML technologies. If you are already familiar with XML technologies, this book's focus on hands-on examples will accelerate your development productivity using the various advanced XML editing features of XMLSPY. If you fall into one of the following categories, this book is a must for you:

◆ **Microsoft and Java developers:** Both the Microsoft .NET framework and Sun Microsystems's J2EE platform use XML and Web services technologies to communicate among applications. This book covers building Web Service Description Language documents, using the XMLSPY WSDL Editor, and testing and debugging SOAP applications.

◆ **Web developers:** XSLT enables you to separate a Web page's content from its presentation markup, enabling Web developers to tackle such issues as internationalization of Web sites, content aggregation, and multiple output formats (for Web, wireless, and so on). This book covers XSLT in detail and includes coverage of XMLSPY's XSLT debugger and XPath analyzer, both of which greatly facilitate XSLT development. Differentiate yourself from the millions of other Web developers by learning the intricacies of XSLT and becoming proficient with XMLSPY's XSLT editing facilities!

◆ **Database administrators:** XML is rapidly finding its way into the leading databases. Today, both Microsoft SQL Server 2000 and Oracle 9i support XML Schema, XML column types, XML views on relational data, relational views on XML data, and XML-based query or transformation languages. In fact, XML Schema may soon become the preferred data modeling language, replacing more abstract techniques such as entity-relationship diagrams. SQL is currently being extended to support XPath expressions and much more. This book includes comprehensive coverage of XML data modeling with XML Schema, XML Schema data types, and data conversion between XML and relational database formats. These topics are requirements for database administrators seeking to stay current with the latest developments in XML technologies in the database.

XML is one of the few technologies that pervades programming languages, platforms, operating systems, and the different technological tiers (Web, middleware, database) that all software vendors support. If your current project does not involve XML technologies, chances are that your next one will. So this book is for you!

Hardware and Software Requirements

To follow along with the examples presented in this book, you need a PC with a Pentium (or equivalent) processor running at 120 MHz or faster, with Windows 9x, Windows 2000, Windows NT4 (with SP 4 or later), Windows Me, or Windows XP. You need at least 32MB of total RAM installed on your computer. For best performance, I recommend at least 64MB. You also need a CD-ROM drive, an Internet connection to obtain a software key code, and an e-mail address to which the key code can be mailed. (An Internet connection is not required after you obtain the key code).

How This Book Is Organized

Chapter 1, "The XMLSPY Game," introduces XML technologies and how they are used to solve various programming challenges in industry today. It also provides an overview of the XMLSPY development environment and tells you how to obtain and install XMLSPY 5.

Chapter 2, "Editing XML Documents with XMLSPY 5," covers XML 1.0 syntax and how to build XML documents using the XMLSPY editing environment. In addition, I present various common editing operations including converting documents or databases to XML format, or the reverse.

Chapter 3, "DTD Editing and Validation," is about using DTDs and XMLSPY to build content models that structure XML documents. I also cover document validation using XMLSPY.

Chapter 4, "Editing XML Schemas with XMLSPY," is the first of two chapters on XML Schema development. It discusses viewing XML Schemas using the XMLSPY Schema Editor. The chapter includes designing and building your first XML Schema, which you then use to validate XML documents. All basic XML Schema syntax and language constructs are covered.

Chapter 5, "Advanced XML Schema Development," covers building modular, reusable XML Schemas. It discusses advanced topics including XML namespaces, object-oriented XML Schema design techniques, and other advanced XMLSPY schema-editing features.

Chapter 6, "Introduction to XSLT," is the first of two chapters on XSLT (Extensible Stylesheet Transformations). This chapter is a departure from the other chapters in the book in that it shows how to programmatically write XSLT programs, which are XML documents with a specific XML Schema definition. In this chapter, I cover the basics of XSLT, starting with the process of XSLT, using XMLSPY to debug an XSLT document. Other topics include the various programmatic constructs included in XSLT.

Chapter 7, "Advanced XSLT," goes beyond the XSLT basics covered in Chapter 6. Specific topics, such as how to work with XSLT templates and the available XSLT functions are discussed. More complex examples are provided to show how you can use XSLT to solve common problems. Also covered is a simple example of how you can combine an XMLSPY plugin with another technology to produce HTML content.

Chapter 8, "Introduction to SOAP and WSDL," covers the essential concept of Web services. Web services is a new technology that enables computer-to-computer communication with XML. WSDL (Web Services Description Language) and SOAP (Simple Object Access Protocol) are two XML technologies used in Web services. I show you how a SOAP call can be debugged using XMLSPY and how to build a WSDL file using XMLSPY.

Chapter 9, "Altova XML Developer Certification," provides an overview of the XMLSPY Developer Certification exam offered through Prometric. It includes sample questions, tips, and strategies for taking and passing the exam.

The appendixes include detailed coverage of XMLSPY technical resources, important XML standards and references, an overview of regular expressions, and a detailed description of what's on the CD-ROM.

Companion CD-ROM

This book offers a companion CD-ROM that includes an exclusive 90-day evaluation copy of XMLSPY 5 Enterprise Edition. When you run the installer for this special version of XMLSPY 5, all example files used in this book are installed as the default project when you launch the application. If you happen to already have XMLSPY installed on your system, you can still access the example files by locating the XMLSPY Handbook.spp file (a project file) from the CD and copying it (and the subsequent subdirectories) to your local file system. Then open the project file by choosing Project → Open Project. The CD also contains various related XML software programs, including various XSLT processors and XML processing APIs that can enhance the capabilities of the XMLSPY editing environment. See Appendix D for a complete listing of third-party software included on the CD-ROM.

Conventions

Here are some conventions that I use throughout to help you use this book more efficiently:

- *Italics* indicate a new term that I'm defining, represent placeholder text (especially when used in code), or add emphasis.
- **Bold** text indicates something that you should type.
- A special `monofont` typeface is used throughout the book to indicate code, a filename or pathname, or an Internet address.

Navigating This Book

If you're completely new to XML, start at the beginning and work your way through to the end. Each chapter assumes that you're familiar with the concepts included in the chapters that precede it. Intermediate to advanced developers should skim Chapters 1 and 2 and then read the chapters and sections that appeal to you, based on the table of contents and introductory text in all chapters. I suggest that you use the index to find the appropriate bits of information that you need.

Icons appear in the text to indicate important or especially helpful items. Here's a list of the icons and their functions:

Notes provide additional or critical information and technical data on the current topic.

Tip icons point you to useful techniques and helpful hints.

Cross-Reference icons point you to another chapter where you can find more information on a particular topic.

The Caution icon is your warning of a potential problem or pitfall.

The On the CD-ROM icon indicates that the companion CD contains a related file or additional information.

Further Information

If you have any feedback about the book, you can reach me by e-mail at larry@altova.com. I will try my best to respond. For more general inquiries about XMLSPY and related XML technologies, please post a message to the Altova User Forums at: http://altova.com/forum/forums/index.asp.

Acknowledgments

I would like to acknowledge Alexander Falk, president and CEO of Altova, Inc., for his inspiration and leadership. Alex, you are a great person to work for! I would also like to say thanks to my coworkers at Altova who have made showing up for work quite enjoyable for me: Christina, Allyson, Tina, Andrea, Chris, Nancy, Gerry, Trace, Steve, Jon, Liz, and Amberlee. A special thanks to Christian Gross for writing Chapters 6, 7, and 8. Finally, thanks to Chris Webb and Jodi Jensen for their help and patience with me when deadlines were looming.

Contents at a Glance

Contents

Chapter 1

The XMLSPY Game

IN THIS CHAPTER

◆ Understanding XML and XML Schemas

◆ Examining XML in the industry

◆ Looking at the Software Development Lifecycle Model

◆ Finding out how to obtain XMLSPY 5 and how to install it

THE ABILITY TO WORK WITH XML TECHNOLOGIES is an important requirement for programmers, Web developers, and database administrators today. Because of the explosive growth of many different (yet interrelated) XML technologies employed across so many different software application platforms, however, it is a challenge to become well-versed enough to design and program XML-based applications.

This hands-on book is about accelerating the XML learning curve and enabling you to become technically proficient at actually editing and working with all kinds of XML documents with the help of XMLSPY – a powerful XML Integrated Development Environment (IDE) used by a community of over one million developers world-wide. In this chapter, I present an overview of the key XML technologies, how they are used in industry today, and I tell you how to install and get started using XMLSPY 5.

 If you are already familiar with XML technologies and know how to obtain and install XMLSPY, you might want to jump to Chapter 2, which covers XML editing with XMLSPY 5.

Got XML?

XML (Extensible Markup Language) in its broadest form can be regarded as a universal language for describing structured information. *Structured information* can be anything that contains both *content* (words, images, tables, and so on) and *markup*, which is the additional information that describes the content and gives it a definite meaning (table header, quantity, price, and so on). XML defines a standard syntax for describing a document's content through the use of *markup tags*, as shown in the following code snippet:

1

```
<?xml version="1.0" encoding="UTF-8"?>
<person>
<first-name>Larry</first-name>
<last-name>Kim</last-name>
</person>
```

As the preceding code snippet illustrates, XML is unique in comparison to other information storage formats (for example, word processor, text, and spreadsheet files) in that it contains both the content (Larry Kim) and additional markup describing the semantics of the document's content (first-name, last-name). As you can see in the preceding example, the document's content and markup are interwoven within the code.

XML markup resembles HTML syntax to some extent; but unlike HTML, XML has no pre-defined tag set (such as Title, H1, Head, and Body). Instead, XML provides a general facility and syntax for defining tags and the structural relationships between them. The idea is that developers can then use this general form to create customized XML-based tag sets (also known as *markup languages* or custom XML *vocabularies*) for describing documents specific to their organization or industry. XML can be used as a flexible way to create common information formats and share content and information on the Internet.

There are many different kinds of XML documents currently used in the software industry. In addition, new XML document standards are being developed by various industry consortiums to address increasingly advanced functionality across virtually any vertical industry.

The vast majority of XML documents (or XML technologies) can be categorized as either a core XML infrastructure technology or as providing an XML-based vocabulary for a particular application or industry. This book focuses on core XML infrastructure technologies: XML Schemas, XSL/XSLT, SOAP, and WSDL, which are introduced in the following sections. Later chapters are entirely dedicated to designing and editing documents in each technology.

The important concept to grasp is that XML Schemas, XSL/XSLT, and SOAP are all simply XML documents. IT professionals, like you, must eventually design and edit these types of documents. Having a solid understanding of the core XML infrastructure technologies can give you a clear picture of what XML is and how the various technologies work together to solve a wide variety of technical challenges.

XML Schemas

An XML Schema is the World Wide Web Consortium's (W3C) official XML document definition language. It addresses many shortcomings associated with Document Type Definitions (DTD) and has industry support from all major software corporations. An XML Schema is an XML document that defines the structure and allowable permutations that other XML documents can adopt in order to be considered a member of the common family of XML documents. Think of an XML Schema as *metadata* (essentially, data that describes data). As an analogy, think of how, in any object-oriented programming language, a class definition defines a family of objects or a relational database schema defines the data types and constraints to which a dataset must adhere to exist in a particular table. In both analogies, the class definition and relational database schema merely lay out some basic ground rules for restricting structure and data ranges, which in turn can be used in any application.

As previously mentioned, industry consortiums are joining together to develop XML Schemas that define common file formats for describing mathematical formulas, research documents, news articles, credit card transactions, accounting audits, medical prescriptions, and much more. Development of industry-standard XML Schemas enhances software application interoperability through the use of common XML-based file formats to express data and content. Using a common XML Schema, software applications can exchange information as an XML document that conforms to a particular XML Schema.

An XML Schema is most commonly used by an XML processor to validate XML documents. *Validation* is the process of verifying that an XML document conforms to the rules defined within the XML Schema. An XML processor that can perform XML Schema-based document validation (that is, an XML Schema validator) enables a developer to offload the burden of code validation from the application to the XML processor.

I discuss DTDs in Chapter 3. DTDs, however, have clearly been marked for obsolescence by the W3C.

A complete discussion of applied XML Schema design is provided in Chapters 4 and 5.

XSL/XSLT

The Extensible Stylesheet Language (XSL) and the Extensible Stylesheet Language Transformations (XSLT) are standardized XML-based vocabularies (markup languages) for changing the content and data stored in an XML document into a different output form. Using XSL, you can take content saved in an XML format and transform it into any output media (HTML, WML, PDF, PostScript, plain text) by applying a special XML *stylesheet* document written using XSL or XSLT. The XSLT transformation process is illustrated in Figure 1-1.

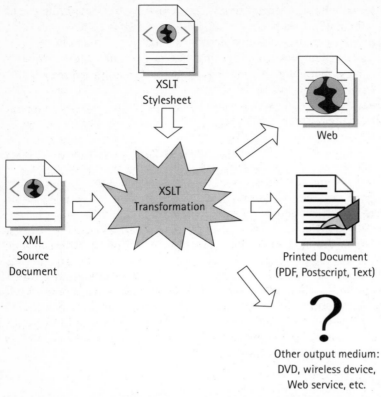

Figure 1–1: Transforming XML into a variety of output formats using XSLT.

Simple Object Access Protocol

Any networked computing environment must be able to invoke methods across both process and physical machine boundaries. This capability requires a means for locating a remote process, serializing method parameters, invoking the remote method, and deserializing the return value – all in a secure manner. Many protocols currently provide this functionality including DCE, Microsoft's DCOM, CORBA's IIOP, Java RMI and EJB, and many others. However, they all require proprietary class libraries to be loaded on both the client and remote host in order to inter-communicate. This requirement has greatly restricted distributed application interoperability.

Simple Object Access Protocol (SOAP) is a natural evolution of existing distributed technologies. SOAP is an encoding of a remote method invocation (method parameters, return type, and error codes) within an XML document that can be easily understood by any client using an XML parser. (XML parsers are freely available in every programming language and platform combination.) The SOAP document is typically sent over HTTP, the core protocol of the Web. HTTP enables greater interoperability because firewalls typically don't block HTTP traffic, and it

provides greater security because encryption is readily available through the use of
Secure Sockets Layer (SSL).

XML in Today's Software Industry

The adoption of XML technologies is primarily being driven by *enterprise* applications, which are loosely defined as mission-critical, business-class software applications, as opposed to desktop applications geared for home users. Now that I've
introduced the core technologies, this section provides an overview of the various
industry focus areas that are being overhauled thanks to new XML technologies.

Web services

By using SOAP, XML Schema, and other related technologies (collectively referred
to as *Web services*), companies can expose programmatic access to business logic
over the Web. This business logic can subsequently be accessed by any device,
remote process, desktop application, or Web application. Web services are transforming the World Wide Web from simple business-to-consumer applications,
which require human interaction, to a distributed federation of loosely coupled
services. A key area for growth will be enhancing business-to-business (B2B) application infrastructure, enabling the creation of virtual marketplaces, as well as
streamlined order processing and back-office operations.

The World Wide Web

The Web in its current form is growing at an astounding rate, with an estimated
base of 3 billion HTML documents distributed across the world. These documents
are primarily intended to be read by people through a browser. Because it could
take thousands of years to manually read through these documents, it becomes
increasingly important to preserve a document's semantics. The *semantics* provide
the context or meaning of a document, allowing you to better understand it.
Contrast this to brute force search engines that determine a document's relevancy
to a particular subject simply by calculating the number of times a keyword occurs.

  Although search engines such as Google.com and Alltheweb.com have developed impressive algorithms for making sense of the vast amount of data on the
Web, computers in general have quite a tough time deciphering the billions of
documents out there. The challenge comes from all the miscellaneous things that
clutter the actual document content: navigation bars, graphics, advertisements,
applets, Flash files, and other things meant to enhance the human user experience
but that don't count as actual page content as far as a Web-bot is concerned.

  XSL/XSLT stylesheets are commonly used by Web developers to separate data
from presentation markup on a Web page. This separation can greatly simplify the
indexing, sharing, and retrieving of data on the Web by both people and Web-bots.
XSLT also enables the internationalization and localization of Web sites and the

delivery of personalized Web site content to Web-enabled mobile devices. XSLT has the potential to radically change Web development. It's likely to become a critical skill of future Web developers.

XML publishing and document management

The publishing and news industries regularly work with volumes of documents, typically published in multiple output forms, most commonly in print and Web-based media. The goal has long been a single document source from which all derivative output could be generated. XML has many benefits as a storage format for the rich, structured content represented in printed publications and Web articles. Industry standard XML vocabularies such as DocBook (an XML vocabulary for describing technical publications) and NewsML (an XML vocabulary for describing news articles) facilitate the preservation of the semantics and context of information and allow for efficient retrieval and repurposing of content. Using XSLT, an XML document can be transformed into several XML-based document-layout languages including PDF, PostScript, Scalable Vector Graphics (SVG), and XHTML.

Document management refers to storing a company's documents in a document repository, thereby preserving the knowledge of a company. Document management systems have been around for a while — long before the relatively recent standardization of the XML specification. Historically, these systems have been both proprietary and costly to implement. Today, XML technologies make document management systems far easier to implement through the use of one or more industry-standard XML languages (or tag sets) for storing a particular type of information, an XML editor, and a database or XML server capable of storing XML documents. This standards-based approach to document management has the potential to unlock proprietary content management systems.

Database and application integration

The back-end processing systems of large companies are a heterogeneous mix of various distributed application platforms (J2EE, CORBA, DCOM, and so on). These applications are written in different programming languages, run on different operating systems, and use different data repositories. XML is being used in many areas to integrate enterprise applications. Most commonly, an XML document is employed as an intermediary format (or adaptor) between two or more systems. For example, an Electronic Data Interchange (EDI) message may be encoded into an XML format and then sent off to another application or database that processes the XML message. Software vendors such as Microsoft and Oracle have been adding support to their database product offerings to deal with such scenarios.

Microsoft .NET Framework

Microsoft, the world's largest software company, produces hundreds of products, Web-based services, and server applications. The challenge for the recently released .NET Framework is to make all these pieces work together and expose the combined functionality through Web services. The Microsoft .NET product vision encompasses various application servers, SQL Server 2000, the Windows operating system, multiple programming languages, mobile devices, and more. SOAP and XML Schema bring all the pieces together, allowing tremendous application interoperability. XML development skills are likely to become an essential requirement for Microsoft developers wanting to access the various .NET products and services.

Java and XML

The Java platform enables platform interoperability at a binary level. Java programs are compiled into an intermediate language and subsequently executed on any operating system through a native Java Virtual Machine. The combination of Java and XML has the potential to improve interoperability by further decoupling the application from the underlying data storage format and opening up the application's communication protocol; these are important milestones in realizing true application portability. At the time of this writing, Sun has just recently released several powerful new standards for Web services, XML bindings, and XML messaging, which will greatly improve application interoperability.

XML technologies are interrelated and are pervasive across a wide spectrum of industry applications. Figure 1-2 graphically summarizes some of the most common uses and their relationships.

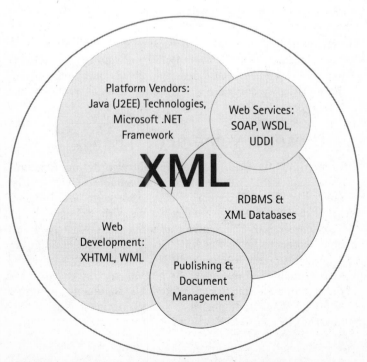

Figure 1-2: Common use of XML technologies in the enterprise.

It's safe to say that any IT professional writing any kind of code has had (or will eventually have) the need to effectively edit and work with XML documents at some level. Clearly the ability to develop using XML is a critical skill in today's job market!

The Software Development Lifecycle Model

This section compares the classic software development process and the XML software development process to explore the overall effect of the introduction of XML technologies on the software development process.

Classic software development (before XML)

Classic software development refers to the process of developing applications using procedural programming languages such as C/C++, Java, C#, COBOL, and Perl. The classic software development process typically begins with a high-level architecting process that includes modeling the software objects and their interactions. Next, an editor is used to write the source code according to the proper syntax, and the compiler is invoked to translate and link the software to an executable binary format. Finally, a debugger is used to catch any errors, thereby ensuring correct program behavior.

Classic IDEs, such as Microsoft's Visual Studio or Borland's JBuilder, have revolutionized the software development process by providing enhanced tool support for editing source code, as well as modeling and debugging tools that have enabled developers to produce higher quality software while simultaneously reducing the required effort.

Modern XML software development

XML technologies differ significantly from classic procedural programming languages in structure, syntax, and nature. Therefore, it's reasonable to expect that XML application development is also different from classic software development. You begin XML application development by developing the XML Schema, which defines a family of XML documents to be used in the application. Next, you edit and validate XML documents according to the XML Schema. Finally, a language binding must be programmed to enable the XML document to be consumed or processed by some XML-enabled framework. As previously discussed, XML document operations typically include transforming the XML document to another format, saving the XML document to a database, or transmitting the XML document to a remote process. The XML software development process is illustrated in Figure 1-3.

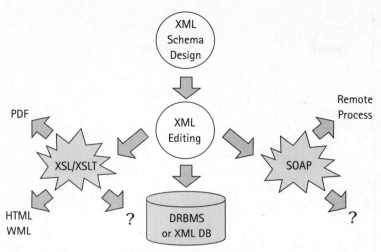

Figure 1-3: The XML software development process.

The important point here is that you must develop proficiency with XML development tools. These important tools, all covered in this book, include XML Schema modeling tools to define XML content; XML editing and validation tools to author XML documents; XSL/XSLT development and debugging tools for transforming XML; XML-to-database mapping tools for database integration applications; and SOAP development and debugging tools for building Web services.

The Spy Who Loved XML

Once there was a spy on a very important assignment. The mission: To build advanced XML and Web services applications. In order to help ensure a successfully completed mission, Spy Headquarters, which typically equips field agents with state-of-the-art gadgets like cars with ejection seats and wrist watches with laser beams, has provided the spy with an XML integrated development environment, codename: XMLSPY.

An XML IDE is a collection of tools that provides support for the development of critical XML technologies: XML Schemas and DTDs, XSL/XSLT, SOAP, and Web services, as well as XML editing and validation. XMLSPY 5 is an XML IDE. It's not meant to replace an existing classic software programming IDE, Web-development tool, or database programming/administration tool. Instead, XMLSPY 5 complements and enhances an external developer tool by providing comprehensive support for the XML development component of any potential application. XMLSPY 5 also provides tools and features to help cross the boundary from a pure XML technology to a particular language binding, server runtime environment, or database. Figure 1-4 illustrates how an XML IDE complements existing software development tools.

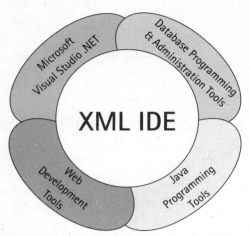

Figure 1–4: An XML IDE, such as XMLSPY 5, provides XML development support and complements other software development tools.

Just as classic IDEs have revolutionized the software development process over the past two decades, XML IDEs — in particular, XMLSPY 5 — are modernizing XML and Web services development by providing editing support for all XML technologies. As for the spy's secret identity and the outcome of the mission? You are the spy, and your mission will be accomplished with the help of XMLSPY and the *XMLSPY Handbook* as your secret guide to the intricacies of XML.

License to XML

XMLSPY 5 is developed by Altova, Inc. (www.altova.com) and is available in Enterprise, Professional, and Home Editions that vary in price and feature-set. The CD-ROM that accompanies this book includes a special 90-day trial version of the XMLSPY 5 Enterprise Edition. This special version differs from the version that you can download from the XMLSPY Web site (www.altova.com) in that it enables you to obtain a 90-day evaluation key code to ensure that you have more than enough time to complete all the exercises in this book. The regular downloadable version from the Altova site operates as a 30-day evaluation copy.

XMLSPY 5 system requirements

To install and use XMLSPY 5, your system should have the following minimum specifications:

- Windows 95/98/ME/NT4/2000/XP

- 64MB of memory

- 30MB free disk space

- Internet Explorer 5.5 or higher

Additional memory resources will allow you to parse and process larger documents.

Installing XMLSPY 5

Insert the CD-ROM into your disk drive and the InstallShield application is automatically launched. If for some reason the installer does not automatically launch, manually execute the XMLSPYHandbook.exe file on the CD-ROM. Select the Install XMLSPY 5 Enterprise Edition option and follow the installation instructions, choosing all the default values, which will place an XMLSPY shortcut button on the Windows taskbar and on the desktop. After installation, when you open XMLSPY 5 for the first time (by clicking either the shortcut or the program icon), a dialog box appears and prompts you to enter a valid license key-code, as shown in Figure 1-5.

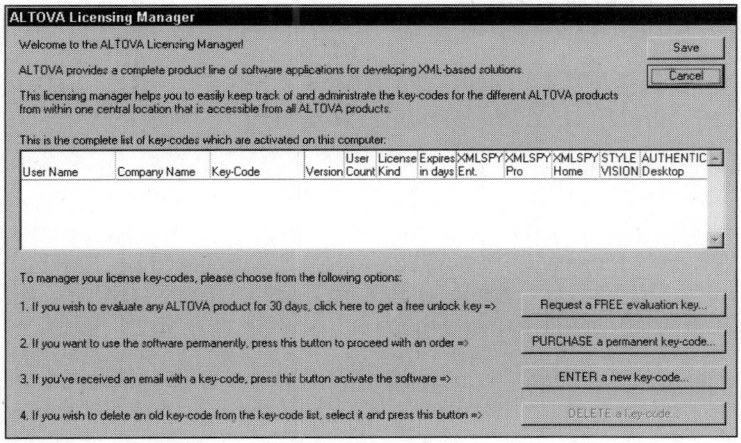

Figure 1-5: The Altova Licensing Manager.

To obtain a free key-code, click the Request a FREE Evaluation Key button and fill out the dialog box shown in Figure 1-6. Click the Request Now! button, and an e-mail containing your key-code will be sent to the address you provided. Please note that requesting and obtaining a key-code requires a working Internet connection. Copy and paste your key-code into the Key-Code field and click OK. You have now completed installing and registering XMLSPY.

Ignore the message that says ... `to evaluate XMLSPY for 30 days for free press this button ...` ".The key-code that will be e-mailed to you is valid for 90 days.

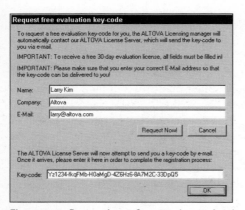

Figure 1–6: Requesting a free 90–day evaluation code requires a working Internet connection.

Updating the XMLSPY 5 Suite

Altova, Inc. periodically issues service packs containing bug fixes and other updates. The software updates are put on the Web for free download at `www.altova.com/download`. Be sure to visit this site periodically to check for updates. Valid evaluation key-code holders or customers who have purchased an XMLSPY license may upgrade to the newest version for free by uninstalling XMLSPY (using the Windows Control Panel and choosing Add/Remove Programs) and reinstalling the new version. An XMLSPY 5 key-code works for any XMLSPY service pack update, provided that the key-code has not expired.

Summary

In this chapter, I introduced XML as a language that describes structured documents in a such a way that the document is easily understood by any person or computer. This chapter covered these points:

 ◆ XML is a standard syntax for creating tag-based vocabularies, such as XML Schema, XSL/XSLT, and SOAP. These vocabularies provide a way to express a document's structure, as well as to transform and transmit the information contained within that XML document.

- ◆ XML technologies are employed in a wide variety of software development applications, yet they are all expressed using XML syntax in the form of XML documents, which in turn need to be designed and edited.

- ◆ XMLSPY 5 is an XML IDE that makes editing XML documents easy, including XML Schemas, XSL/XSLT stylesheets, and SOAP documents.

- ◆ How to obtain and install XMLSPY 5.

In the next chapter, you find out how to edit XML documents in XMLSPY 5.

Chapter 2

Editing XML Documents with XMLSPY 5

IN THIS CHAPTER

- ◆ Reviewing basic XML syntax constructs
- ◆ Examining the rules for writing XML documents
- ◆ Using enhanced Grid view
- ◆ Converting data to XML by using XMLSPY
- ◆ Creating and managing XMLSPY projects
- ◆ Examining XMLSPYs other editing features

NOW THAT YOU HAVE INSTALLED **XMLSPY 5**, it's time to take a closer look at the structure and syntax of an XML document.

In this chapter, you use XMLSPY 5 to create and edit XML documents – both from scratch and by converting documents from several different file formats (such as Microsoft Word or Microsoft Access). By the end of this chapter, you'll have hands-on experience working with XML files and will be sufficiently familiar with XMLSPY 5 to easily navigate its editing environment in order to tackle more advanced topics.

 See Chapter 1 if you need help installing XMLSPY 5.

Creating Your First XML Document with XMLSPY 5

Launch XMLSPY 5 from the Windows taskbar by choosing Start → Program Files → XMLSPY 5 Enterprise Edition → XMLSPY 5. Upon installation, XMLSPY 5 optionally becomes the default resource associated for various XML-related file types

15

(`.xml`, `.xsl`, `.xsd`, `.xhtml`, `.wsdl`, `.fo`, and so on). Simply double-clicking any of these associated file types from the Microsoft Windows Explorer automatically launches XMLSPY 5. After you have launched XMLSPY 5, you see the screen shown in Figure 2-1.

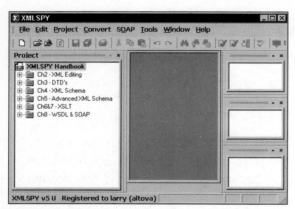

Figure 2-1: XMLSPY 5 upon start-up.

By default, the special XMLSPY 5 version included on the CD-ROM that accompanies this book opens a project folder with example files corresponding to the chapters of this book. The Project window has several folders: `Ch2`, `Ch3`, `Ch4`, and so on. You can find these example files in `C:\Program Files\Altova\XMLSPY\Examples\xmlspyhandbook`. If the version of XMLSPY that you are using is not the same as the one included on the CD (for example, if you downloaded it from the Web), you can still follow along by copying the `XMLSPY Handbook.spp` file and all subdirectories (such as `Ch2`, `Ch3`, and so on) from the CD to your local file system. Then choose Project → Open Project and select the `XMLSPY Handbook.spp` file. XMLSPY's project management features are covered toward the end of this chapter.

To create a new XML file, choose File → New, and the Create New Document dialog box appears as shown in Figure 2-2. Choose XML Document from the list and click OK.

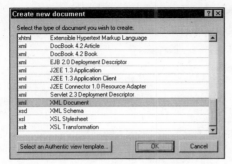

Figure 2-2: The Create New Document dialog box.

 XMLSPY 5 supports editing of any XML document. As a convenience, XML-SPY includes built-in menu options for creating some of the most common types of XML documents, including Mathematical Markup Language, Wireless Markup Language, various Java configuration files, and many other popular XML document types.

When you click the OK button in the Create New Document dialog box, another New File dialog box (see Figure 2-3) appears, asking whether the new XML document is intended to be validated based on a Document Type Definition (DTD) or an XML Schema. The XML documents are generally used in conjunction with a content model, which is defined in either a DTD or an XML Schema. I discuss XML Schemas and DTDs in Chapter 3, so for now simply click Cancel.

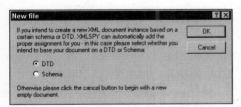

Figure 2-3: XMLSPY can assign a DTD or an XML Schema to an XML document.

By default, the newly created XML file is displayed in Enhanced Grid view as shown in Figure 2-4. For more details, see the section "Enhanced Grid View" later in this chapter.

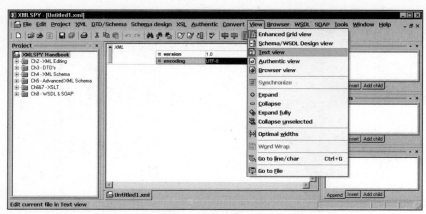

Figure 2–4: Creating a new XML document in XMLSPY.

The principal benefit of using XMLSPY over a regular text editor is that it offers multiple views for editing XML documents. I'll start with Text view, which is the most basic of all available XML editing views. To view an XML document in Text view, you need to switch views either by choosing View → Text view (refer to Figure 2-4) or by clicking the Text View icon on the main toolbar (see Figure 2-5).

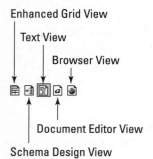

Figure 2–5: The main toolbar contains buttons
to quickly switch between different views.

After switching to Text view, you should see the newly created XML document as shown in Figure 2-6. In the next few sections, you learn the basic XML constructs using Text view.

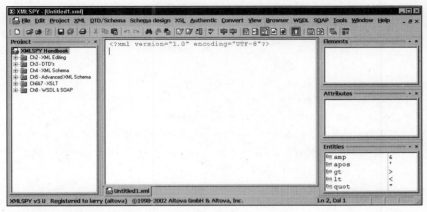

Figure 2-6: A new XML document in Text view.

Elements and attributes

XML uses basic constructs: elements, attributes, and their associated values to form an XML document. An *XML element* (or just *element*) is the most basic building block of an XML document. An element's body can contain either one or more nested elements or text-based content. Element occurrences are specified by opening and closing tags — also referred to as *start tags* and *end tags*, respectively. *Opening tags* begin with the less-than sign (<), followed by the element name, and terminate with a greater-than sign (>). *Closing tags* look very similar to opening tags, except that a closing tag has a forward slash (/) immediately after the (<) of the closing tag. This is illustrated in Figure 2-7. An element name can be just about anything (although clear, descriptive names make the most sense), provided that the following naming guidelines are met:

◆ Element names must begin with a letter or underscore character, and can be preceded by any number of additional letters, digits, underscores, hyphens, and periods.

◆ Unlike HTML, element and attribute names are case-sensitive; this is a common source of errors.

An element's *content* (also referred to as its *value*) appears nested between the opening and closing tags, as shown in Figure 2-7. To start your first XML document, use Text view to type the document fragment shown in Figure 2-7 into the new XML document, which you have just created.

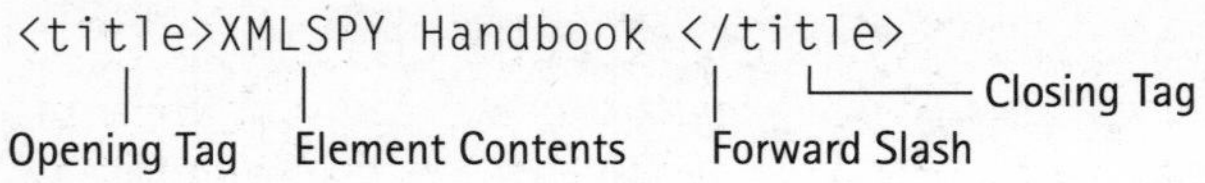

```
<title>XMLSPY Handbook </title>
   |        |              |    └─────── Closing Tag
Opening Tag  Element Contents  Forward Slash
```

Figure 2-7: An XML element.

 XMLSPY's Text view has numerous editing features that can help you write XML documents. For example, XMLSPY automatically inserts the closing tag for any XML element that you define. It also color codes XML elements and attributes to make them more readable.

XML attributes (or simply, *attributes*) provide additional descriptive information about an element and are contained within an element's opening tag. Attributes are specified by stating the name of the attribute, followed by an equal sign (=) and the attribute value within quotation marks (as shown in Figure 2-8). You can use either double quotation marks (") or single quotation marks (') to delimit attribute values, provided that they are used in pairs. In other words, you cannot use a double quotation mark at the beginning of the attribute and a single quotation mark at the end. There is no limit to the number of attributes that an XML element can have; however, every attribute must have a unique name. The rules for naming attributes are the same as the rules for naming elements. Add an attribute to your XML document using Text view as shown in Figure 2-8. This figure is shown here in black and white, but on your screen, notice that XMLSPY applies a different color to attributes to distinguish them from elements.

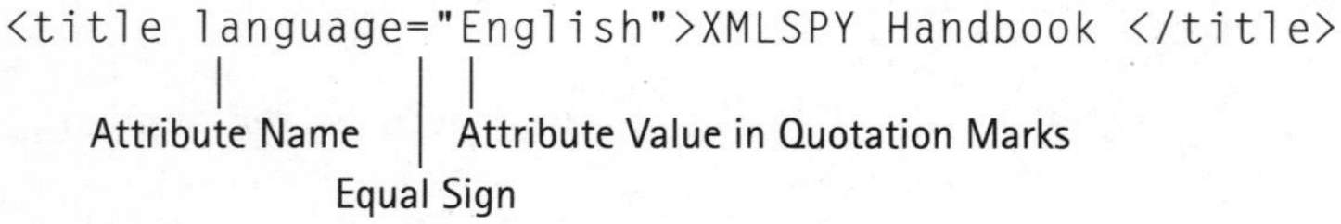

```
<title language="English">XMLSPY Handbook </title>
      |               |
  Attribute Name    Attribute Value in Quotation Marks
            Equal Sign
```

Figure 2-8: A sample attribute declaration.

XML syntax guidelines

In Chapter 1, I defined XML as a standardized language for describing structured information. The standardized syntax guidelines of an XML documents allow it to be easily processed and understood by computer applications. The minimum requirement for an XML document to be used in an XML-processing environment is that the XML document must be *well-formed*, which means it must adhere to the constraints described in the following sections.

EVERY XML DOCUMENT MUST HAVE A ROOT ELEMENT

All XML documents must contain exactly one element, called the *root* element, which contains all other elements within the XML document (it is the parent of all child elements). This concept is illustrated in Figure 2-9.

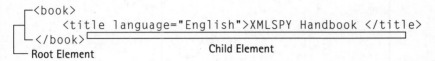

```
<book>
    <title language="English">XMLSPY Handbook </title>
</book>
```
Root Element   Child Element

Figure 2–9: The root element (<book>) contains all the child elements.

The only things in an XML document that may appear outside the root element are *comments* and *processing instructions*, both of which will be discussed shortly.

 Because the structure of an XML document is hierarchical, I use the terms *parent* and *child* to describe an element with respect to another element. For example, in Figure 2-9, <book> is the parent element of <title>; conversely, <title> is a child element of <book>.

EVERY ELEMENT MUST HAVE A CLOSING TAG

Every element must have a corresponding closing tag; in the case of empty elements (that is, an element containing no element content and zero-to-any number of attributes), you can optionally use a shorthand, equivalent notation of the closing tag as shown in Figure 2-10.

Forward Slash (abbreviated Closing Tag)
                                |
```
<logo file="xmlspy.gif"/>
```
              Empty Element

Figure 2–10: An empty element whose closing
tag uses a shorthand notation.

ELEMENTS MUST BE PROPERLY NESTED

Simply put, this means that if element A contains element B, you must close element B before you close element A (see Figure 2-11).

```
<firstname>Larry<lastname>
</firstname>Kim</lastname>
```

Illegal: Element opening and closing tags are out of sequence.

```
<firstname>Larry</firstname>
  <lastname>Kim</lastname>
```

Legal: Element opening and closing tags are in the correct order.

Figure 2-11: Illegal and well-formed XML fragments.

ATTRIBUTES MUST BE ENCLOSED WITHIN QUOTATION MARKS
Unlike HTML, XML strictly requires that all attribute values be enclosed in quotation marks – most commonly, a pair of double quotation marks (") is used to delimit attribute values; however, a pair of single quotation marks (') is also acceptable.

Checking well-formedness with XMLSPY

XMLSPY can help you check whether the XML document you are working on is well-formed. Simply click the yellow check-mark button on the main toolbar or choose XML → Check Well-Formedness. Now type into a single XML document all the XML document fragments that I just discussed and verify that it is, indeed, well-formed (as illustrated in Figure 2-12). Congratulations! Using XMLSPY, you have just completed an XML document that meets the criteria for being well-formed. You can save the newly created XML file by choosing File → Save, by clicking the Save button on the main toolbar, or by pressing Ctrl+S.

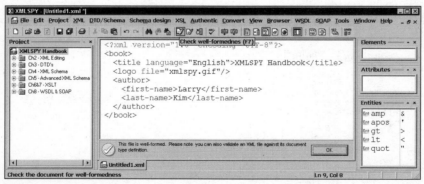

Figure 2-12: Using XMLSPY's well-formedness checker in Text view.

You can also invoke the well-formedness checker by pressing the F7 key. If XMLSPY determines that an XML document is not well-formed, XMLSPY places the cursor on the line immediately after the line containing the error and provides an error message at the bottom of the main editing window. XMLSPY does a well-formedness check automatically whenever you open or save a file.

Declaring the XML version

As I previously mentioned, XMLSPY automatically inserts the *XML declaration*, which states the XML version number and character encoding information for the current document, as in the following:

```
<?xml version="1.0" encoding="UTF-8"?>
```

In general, a tag that begins with `<?` and ends with `?>` is called a *processing instruction*. These tags are used to specify document-processing variables to configure the behavior of the XML parser or application that is processing the XML document. For example, you could use a processing instruction to specify the filename of the XSLT stylesheet associated with the current document (see Chapters 6 and 7 to find out more about XSLT stylesheets). After you type the opening tag for a processing instruction (`<?`), XMLSPY auto-inserts the closing tag (`?>`).

At the time of this writing, the most current XML version is 1.0, which was adopted as an official W3C recommendation in October 2000. XML 1.1 currently exists as a candidate draft, but it may become a recommendation sometime in 2003. The default character encoding used in XMLSPY is Unicode (UTF-8), a preferred character encoding that supports many international character sets and is backward compatible with environments originally designed entirely around ASCII.

Whitespace

XML processors, as well as applications that use XML documents, ignore whitespace (extra spaces, line breaks, and tabs) — just as Internet Explorer or Netscape browsers both ignore any whitespace in HTML code. You can have XMLSPY *pretty-print* your XML document by automatically eliminating any extra whitespace and nicely formatting it if you choose Edit → Pretty Print-XML Text. This feature works only for well-formed documents.

XMLSPY's pretty-printer also automatically substitutes for any empty elements. As an example: `<image></image>` is substituted with the equivalent shorthand-notation, `<image/>`. You can disable this automatic concatenation of empty elements on a per–file-type basis if you choose Tools → Options → File Types.

XML comments

Although you may think that your XML document is easy to understand, it is always helpful to annotate XML documents by using XML comments to improve the readability of your work. An XML *comment* works the same as an HTML comment: you type `<!--` to begin your comment and `-->` to end the comment. Whatever you type inside the body of a comment is completely ignored by an XML parser. Although a double dash (`--`) is used to delimit the start and end of comment tags, a double dash is forbidden within the comment itself. The XML processor would read the second set of dashes as the beginning of the end-of-comment delimiter.

XMLSPY automatically changes the appearance of XML comments to a light shade of gray to prevent the reader from mistaking it for an XML element. You can easily customize the look of comments by choosing Tools → Options → Text Fonts.

Entities

By default, XML includes five *entities*, which are substitute notations for the special characters shown in Figure 2-13.

Figure 2-13: Default XML entity definitions and values are displayed in XMLSPY Text view.

Here are some reasons why you may need to use an entity:

◆ An element or attribute's value requires a quotation mark (") that an XML parser could confuse with a string delimiter

◆ An element or attribute's value requires an angle bracket (< or >) that an XML parser could confuse with an opening or closing tag delimiter

◆ An element or attribute's value contains an ampersand character (&) that an XML parser could confuse with an entity declaration (the ampersand is the character used to specify an entity)

To use an entity, simply type the ampersand character &. XMLSPY provides a drop-down box displaying the list of defined entities. Select the desired entity using the up and down arrow keys and press the Enter key. Remember to terminate the entity with a semicolon (;). As an example, the entity for an ampersand character, when expressed using an identity, should look like &. Entities are also often used as a macro or a substitute for text that frequently occurs throughout an XML document.

 In Chapter 3, you learn how to define custom entities.

Character Data (CDATA)

Sometimes, you may need to write out sections of an XML document as plain text. In this case, you don't want the XML parser to process the section as it regularly would. Suppose that you are writing a book on XML and saving the chapters as an XML document. You may want to treat the sample XML files in the book as plain text, despite the fact that the sample files contain XML markup. You can do this easily by enclosing that portion of the XML document within a Character Data (CDATA) section, which instructs the XML parser to simply treat the section as meaningless raw character data regardless of any markup inside. To start a CDATA section, simply type

```
<![CDATA[
```

and terminate the section by typing

```
]]>
```

Within a CDATA section you can type just about anything as long as you don't break these rules:

◆ Do not use XML entities within a CDATA section. Entities are special characters that must be processed and interpreted by the XML processor in order to work properly. Special characters (entities, elements, attributes, comments, CDATA sections, and so on) have no special meaning inside a CDATA section as far as the XML processor is concerned; therefore, they do not work.

◆ Do not nest CDATA sections, for example:

```
<![CDATA[ ignore this text
   <![CDATA[ illegal nested cdata section ]]>
]]>
```

Not only is it redundant to tell the XML processor to "ignore" the special meaning of a block of text that is already being treated that way due to the first CDATA section block, but the closing]]> of the nested CDATA section has the unintentional effect of terminating the CDATA section.

Enhanced Grid View

In the preceding section, you have been working with XML documents exclusively using XMLSPY's Text view, which is ideal for manually editing any XML document at the code level. Although it is important to understand the basics and be able to work with XML documents at code level, as XML documents become bigger and increasingly more complex in their structure, working with XML can quickly become a laborious task. As previously mentioned, XMLSPY can greatly simplify your work with XML documents by providing various powerful graphical views of a document. In this chapter, you learn to use the Enhanced Grid view, which I henceforth refer to as simply Grid view.

Viewing XML documents in Grid view

After you have opened an XML document within the XMLSPY editing environment, you can easily switch back and forth between Text view and Grid view (or any view for that matter) at any time, simply by choosing View → Enhanced Grid View (as shown in Figure 2-14). Alternatively, you can click the Enhanced Grid View button on the main toolbar. Note that you cannot switch from one view to another unless the focus is on the main editing window. For example, if the focus is on the Project window, the various view menu options and toolbar buttons will be grayed out. Simply clicking the main editing window returns the focus to that window and enables you to switch views.

Figure 2-14: Switching from Text view to Enhanced Grid view using the View menu.

How XML documents are rendered in Grid view

For this section, you need to use a slightly more advanced XML sample file than the basic XML file you built previously. Open the OrgChart.xml sample file located in the C:\Program Files\Altova\XMLSPY\Examples directory. Choose either File → Open or click the Open File button on the main toolbar and then switch to Grid view. You should see something similar to the screenshot in Figure 2-15. The OrgChart.xml file is one of the default sample files included with XMLSPY.

Click to expand root element

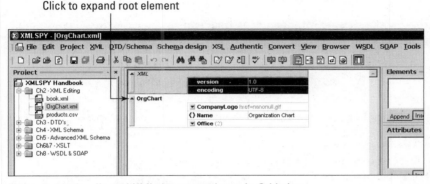

Figure 2–15: A collapsed XML document shown in Grid view.

Figure 2-15 shows the OrgChart.xml file collapsed into two rows (a *processing instruction,* and the *root element*). To further expand the contents of the XML document, toggle the two gray arrow buttons (CompanyLogo and Office) that appear to the right of the OrgChart element. After expanding the OrgChart element, you will find more nested elements that you also must expand. Practice expanding and collapsing the entire document tree by toggling the arrow buttons.

The Grid view, as its name suggests, is a tabular (or grid-like) view of an XML document, which in some respects is similar to a spreadsheet or relational database view of data. The main difference between Grid view and a Microsoft Excel spreadsheet or Microsoft Access database table is that databases and spreadsheets both have fairly rigid, tabular data sources. An XML document, on the other hand, has a very extensible underlying tree-like structure. Grid view displays repeating patterns of elements and/or attributes within an XML document as rows in a table; the columns of the table are determined by the sequence of repeated elements and/or attributes. This graphical rendering methodology is applied recursively throughout an entire XML document, nesting tables within tables, all of which can be expanded or collapsed by toggling the arrow button. This nested table structure is referred to as a *semantic table.* Semantic tables represent a very important principle that you need to understand in order to effectively work with XML documents in Grid view.

In Grid view, for each repeating pattern of XML elements and/or attributes, Grid view builds a table. Each time the repeated pattern is encountered, Grid view builds a new row in the table. The columns of the table are determined by the sequence of elements and attributes within one instance of the repeating pattern. Repeating patterns within a repeating pattern are represented as a nested table within a table. Each table structure in Grid view is referred to as a *semantic table*.

Figure 2-16 shows an XML document fragment displayed as a semantic table in Grid view; it is the result of expanding the `OrgChart`, `Office`, and `Department` elements.

() Department	
⊟ **Department** (4)	
() **Name**	() **Person**
1 Administration	☒ **Person** (3)
2 Marketing	☒ **Person** (2)
3 Engineering	☒ **Person** (6)
4 IT & Technical Support	☒ **Person** (4)

Figure 2-16: A section of the OrgChart.xml document displayed in Grid view.

The `Department` table of Figure 2-16 has two columns (the sequence of repeated elements `Name` and `Person`), and four rows (`Administration`, `Marketing`, `Engineering`, `IT & Technical Support`). Note that the number in parentheses, (4), corresponds to the number of rows in the current table. (In general, a number in parentheses to the right of any element name indicates the number of times a pattern is encountered, also corresponding to the number of rows in the semantic table.) The `<>` indicates that both the `Name` and `Person` columns are XML elements. `Name` is a single-valued element, so the content of the `Name` column corresponds to the content of the `<Name>` element. The content of the `<>` `Person` column is actually a *complex element*, which is simply an element that contains one or more child elements. The complex element `Person` appears in the `Department` table as an unexpanded, nested-table structure (denoted by an unexpanded arrow button). Take a look at the `OrgChart.xml` file listing in Figure 2-17 to see what is happening here.

Figure 2-17 is a decomposition of a section of the `OrgChart.xml` file, which was graphically displayed as a semantic table in Grid view in Figure 2-16. Notice that some `<Person>` elements have been omitted for the sake of brevity. Figure 2-17 has several repeating patterns; the outermost pattern is the four-time repeating sequence of `<Department>` elements. The semantic table of Figure 2-16 has exactly four rows, corresponding to each of the four repeating `<Department>` elements. The two columns of Figure 2-16 correspond to `<Department>`'s two child elements, `<Name>` and `<Person>`, respectively.

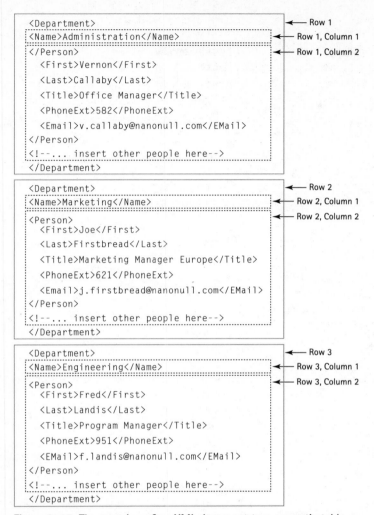

```
<Department>                                    ←— Row 1
<Name>Administration</Name>                     ←— Row 1, Column 1
</Person>                                        ←— Row 1, Column 2
  <First>Vernon</First>
  <Last>Callaby</Last>
  <Title>Office Manager</Title>
  <PhoneExt>582</PhoneExt>
  <Email>v.callaby@nanonull.com</EMail>
</Person>
<!--... insert other people here-->
</Department>
```

```
<Department>                                    ←— Row 2
<Name>Marketing</Name>                          ←— Row 2, Column 1
                                                ←— Row 2, Column 2
<Person>
  <First>Joe</First>
  <Last>Firstbread</Last>
  <Title>Marketing Manager Europe</Title>
  <PhoneExt>621</PhoneExt>
  <Email>j.firstbread@nanonull.com</EMail>
</Person>
<!--... insert other people here-->
</Department>
```

```
<Department>                                    ←— Row 3
<Name>Engineering</Name>                        ←— Row 3, Column 1
                                                ←— Row 3, Column 2
<Person>
  <First>Fred</First>
  <Last>Landis</Last>
  <Title>Program Manager</Title>
  <PhoneExt>951</PhoneExt>
  <EMail>f.landis@nanonull.com</EMail>
</Person>
<!--... insert other people here-->
</Department>
```

Figure 2-17: The mapping of an XML document to a semantic table
in Grid view.

To continue the analysis of the Grid view, expand the nested <Person> elements
of Figure 2-16 (represented as nested semantic tables) by toggling the arrow buttons
adjacent to the Person nodes, as shown in Figure 2-18. Notice that the highlighted
Person (3) table has exactly three rows (Vernon, Frank, and Loby). So again, the
(3) represents the number of rows in the current table.

Let's analyze the highlighted semantic table of Figure 2-18 in more detail by
looking at its corresponding XML document fragment from OrgChart.xml file — the
XML source is listed in Figure 2-19.

Three repeating Person elements rendered as a semantic table in Grid view

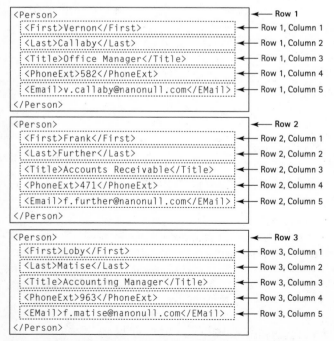

		() Name	() Person					
	1	Administration	Person (3)					
				() First	() Last	() Title	() PhoneExt	() EMail
			1	Vernon	Callaby	Office Manager	582	v.callaby@nanonull.com
			2	Frank	Further	Accounts Receivable	471	f.further@nanonull.com
			3	Loby	Matise	Accounting Manager	963	l.matise@nanonull.com
	2	Marketing	Person (2)					
				() First	() Last	() Title	() PhoneExt	() EMail
			1	Joe	Firstbread	Marketing Manager Europe	621	j.firstbread@nanonull.com
			2	Susi	Sanna	Art Director	753	s.sanna@nanonull.com
	3	Engineering	Person (6)					
				() First	() Last	() Title	() PhoneExt	() EMail
			1	Fred	Landis	Program Manager	951	f.landis@nanonull.com
			2	Michelle	Butler	Software Engineer	654	m.landis@nanonull.com
			3	Dilip	Ogale	Software Engineer	852	d.ogale@nanonull.com
			4	Kay	Park	Medical Doctor	951	k.park@nanonull.com
			5	Liz	Gardner	Software Engineer	753	l.gardner@nanonull.com
			6	Paul	Smith	Software Engineer	334	p.smith@nanonull.com
	4	IT & Technical Support	Person (4)					
				() First	() Last	() Title	() PhoneExt	() EMail
			1	Alex	Martin	IT Manager	778	a.martin@nanonull.com
			2	George	Hammer	Web Developer	223	g.hammer@nanonull.com
			3	Jessica	Bander	Support Engineer	241	j.band@nanonull.com
			4	Lui	King	Support Engineer	345	l.king@nanonull.com

Figure 2-18: Expanding a nested Person table of the Department table, from the OrgChart.xml document, using Grid view.

```
<Person>                                           ← Row 1
  <First>Vernon</First>                            ← Row 1, Column 1
  <Last>Callaby</Last>                             ← Row 1, Column 2
  <Title>Office Manager</Title>                    ← Row 1, Column 3
  <PhoneExt>582</PhoneExt>                         ← Row 1, Column 4
  <Email>v.callaby@nanonull.com</Email>           ← Row 1, Column 5
</Person>
```

```
<Person>                                           ← Row 2
  <First>Frank</First>                             ← Row 2, Column 1
  <Last>Further</Last>                             ← Row 2, Column 2
  <Title>Accounts Receivable</Title>              ← Row 2, Column 3
  <PhoneExt>471</PhoneExt>                         ← Row 2, Column 4
  <Email>f.further@nanonull.com</Email>           ← Row 2, Column 5
</Person>
```

```
<Person>                                           ← Row 3
  <First>Loby</First>                              ← Row 3, Column 1
  <Last>Matise</Last>                              ← Row 3, Column 2
  <Title>Accounting Manager</Title>               ← Row 3, Column 3
  <PhoneExt>963</PhoneExt>                         ← Row 3, Column 4
  <EMail>f.matise@nanonull.com</EMail>            ← Row 3, Column 5
</Person>
```

Figure 2-19: Mappings from the XML source listing to the semantic table highlighted in Figure 2-18.

This three-time repeating sequence of <Person> elements in the OrgChart.xml file is represented in Grid view as a Person table with columns: First, Last, Title, PhoneExt, Email. These columns are child elements of <Person>. The Person table has exactly three rows, corresponding to each of the three repeating <Person> elements. In summary, XMLSPY's Grid view, through the use of semantic tables, enables you to easily visually analyze the contents of an entire XML document. For example, the OrgChart.xml file is over 200 lines in length, yet by toggling just a few arrow buttons, you can quickly zoom in or out of any section of the XML document.

Working with Grid view

Grid view's semantic tables enable you to perform editing operations on an XML document as a whole, as opposed to editing only one line at a time using Text view. This will make more sense in the next few subsections, as you cover some of the most common XML editing operations: inserting and deleting elements or attributes, moving elements and attributes, switching elements and attributes, and importing and exporting data. You can accomplish all of this easily by using Grid view.

 The XMLSPY Grid view (as well as all other views) supports unlimited Undo (Ctrl+Z) and Redo (Ctrl+Y). So if you make a mistake at any time when you're in Grid view, you can easily recover from the error by using these features.

INSERTING AND DELETING ELEMENTS AND ATTRIBUTES

Grid view is ideal for modifying the structure of an existing XML document. You can, for example, change every <Person> element to include an additional attribute, emp-id, which contains an employee identification number. You can also add an additional sub-element called <middle> that corresponds to a person's middle name. The desired output would look similar to the XML document shown in Listing 2-1.

Listing 2-1: Modifying the Person Element

```
<Person emp-id="127">
  <First>Vernon</First>
  <Middle>James</Middle>
  <Last>Callaby</Last>
  <Title>Office Manager</Title>
  <PhoneExt>582</PhoneExt>
  <EMail>v.callaby@nanonull.com</EMail>
</Person>
```

Of course you could simply type this additional information manually for each <Person> element throughout the document; however, using Grid view, it is possible to insert attributes for all the <Person> elements simultaneously. Simply select a column header within the <Person> semantic table (such as the <> First column), right-click the column, and choose Insert → Attribute, as shown in Figure 2-20.

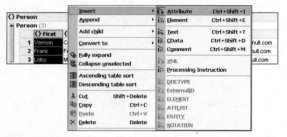

Figure 2–20: Adding a new attribute to every <Person> element within the current semantic table.

In Grid view, you can easily add additional elements and attributes to any semantic table simply by right-clicking a table column header adjacent to where you would like the new element to be inserted and choosing Insert → Element. XMLSPY auto-inserts the new element. Be sure to name the new columns emp-id and Middle, respectively. Next, type some sample values into the new emp-id attribute and <Middle> element fields so that you get a result similar to the one shown in Figure 2-21.

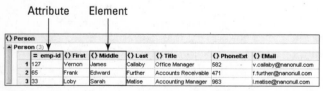

Figure 2–21: Inserting an attribute and an element into a table. Columns starting with = correspond to attributes, and columns starting with greater< > correspond to elements.

It is important to remember that any change you make to an XML document in Grid view is automatically synchronized with any other view in XMLSPY. This behavior can be verified by switching to Text view by choosing View → Text View and examining the XML source document for the section of the OrgChart.xml file just edited. The XML document fragment is shown in Listing 2-2 with the newly inserted attributes and elements shown in bold.

Listing 2-2: Modified Semantic Table

```
<Person emp-id="127">
   <First>Vernon</First>
   <Middle>James</Middle>
   <Last>Callaby</Last>
   <Title>Office Manager</Title>
   <PhoneExt>582</PhoneExt>
   <EMail>v.callaby@nanonull.com</EMail>
</Person>
<Person emp-id="65">
   <First>Frank</First>
   <Middle>Edward</Middle>
   <Last>Further</Last>
   <Title>Accounts Receivable</Title>
   <PhoneExt>471</PhoneExt>
   <EMail>f.further@nanonull.com</EMail>
</Person>
<Person emp-id="33">
   <First>Loby</First>
   <Middle>Sarah</Middle>
   <Last>Matise</Last>
   <Title>Accounting Manager</Title>
   <PhoneExt>963</PhoneExt>
   <EMail>l.matise@nanonull.com</EMail>
</Person>
```

In the following subsections, you make changes to an XML document in Grid view. After making the changes, try switching back to Text view to verify that XMLSPY has updated the underlying XML document source.

MOVING ELEMENTS AND ATTRIBUTES

Using Grid view, it is easy to change the ordering of attributes or elements in an XML document. Practice selecting any column of a semantic table by clicking the column header. Drag over the silhouette of the column to its new location and release the mouse button. Figure 2-22 shows the dragging and dropping of a <Title> column so that it appears as the first sub-element of its parent, the <Person> element.

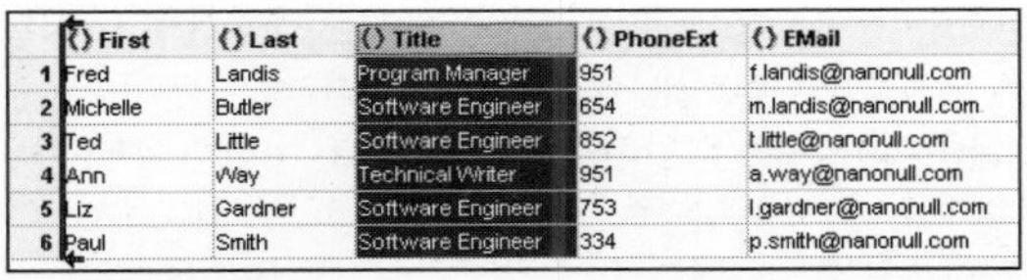

	() First	() Last	() Title	() PhoneExt	() EMail
1	Fred	Landis	Program Manager	951	f.landis@nanonull.com
2	Michelle	Butler	Software Engineer	654	m.landis@nanonull.com
3	Ted	Little	Software Engineer	852	t.little@nanonull.com
4	Ann	Way	Technical Writer	951	a.way@nanonull.com
5	Liz	Gardner	Software Engineer	753	l.gardner@nanonull.com
6	Paul	Smith	Software Engineer	334	p.smith@nanonull.com

Figure 2-22: Changing the ordering of child elements in Grid view.

After you switch back to Text view, you see that the <Title> element appears before the <First> element for all six <Person> elements in this particular XML document fragment.

SWITCHING ELEMENTS AND ATTRIBUTES

Changing an XML element into an XML attribute, or the reverse – changing an XML attribute into an XML element – is a very common XML editing task. This situation arises frequently because there isn't a universally accepted guideline dictating exactly if information should be represented as an XML element or XML attribute. (In practice, you generally try out a few different possibilities!) As an example, try changing the <EMail> element so that it appears as an attribute of <Person>. In Grid view, you can switch content represented as XML elements to XML attributes by first selecting a column of elements to operate on. Clicking a semantic table's column header highlights the entire column, as shown in Figure 2-23. Then, right-click the selected column and choose Convert to → Attribute from the submenu.

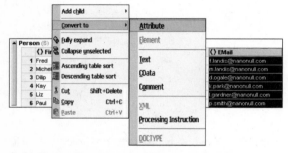

Figure 2-23: Changing the <Email> Element to an attribute using Grid view.

Similarly, you convert an XML attribute to an XML element by selecting a column of attributes in Grid view, right-clicking the selected column, and then choosing Convert to → Element from the submenu.

RENAMING ELEMENTS AND ATTRIBUTES

Using Grid view, it is easy to simultaneously rename multiple occurrences of elements or attributes throughout an XML document. Double-click the column header of any semantic table, which places an active cursor in the column header. (*Note*: You can also simply select a column header and press the F2 key.) Editing the header field renames all elements or attribute names in the selected column. Figure 2-24 shows an XML element being renamed from <Title> to <Job-Title>.

	{} First	{} Last	{} Job-Title	{} PhoneExt	{} EMail
1	Vernon	Callaby	Office Manager	582	v.callaby@nanonull.com
2	Frank	Further	Accounts Receivable	471	f.further@nanonull.com
3	Loby	Matise	Accounting Manager	963	l.matise@nanonull.com

Figure 2-24: Renaming an element from <Title> to <Job-Title>.

SORTING XML DOCUMENTS

XMLSPY's Grid view supports the sorting of any semantic table by any XML element or attribute field. For example, suppose that you want to sort a sequence of six <Person> elements, alphabetically by last name. In Grid view, you do this by selecting the sort column (in this example, the <Last> element), right-clicking the selected column, and then choosing Ascending Table Sort from the menu (see Figure 2-25). Conversely, to reverse-alphabetize the sequence of <Person> elements by last name, right-click the <Last> column and select Descending Table Sort.

Figure 2-25: Sorting a sequence of <Person> elements by last name.

IMPORTING AND EXPORTING DATA WITH MICROSOFT EXCEL

Grid view is ideally suited to copy and accept content from Microsoft Office applications such as Microsoft Excel, Microsoft Access, Microsoft Word, or Microsoft PowerPoint. You export content from an XML document to Microsoft Excel by selecting a region of a semantic table in Grid view, right-clicking the selected region, and choosing Copy as Structured Text from the menu (see Figure 2-26). This copies the selected data to the Clipboard as tab-delimited data.

Next, launch Microsoft Excel (or any other Windows program) and place the cursor in the top-left corner of where you want to insert the previously selected information. Choose Edit → Paste or press Ctrl+V (the keyboard shortcut for the Paste command). The result is shown in Figure 2-27.

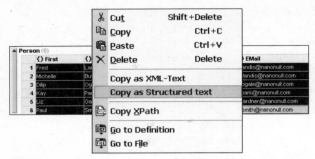

Figure 2-26: Exporting data from Grid view for use with any
external Windows application.

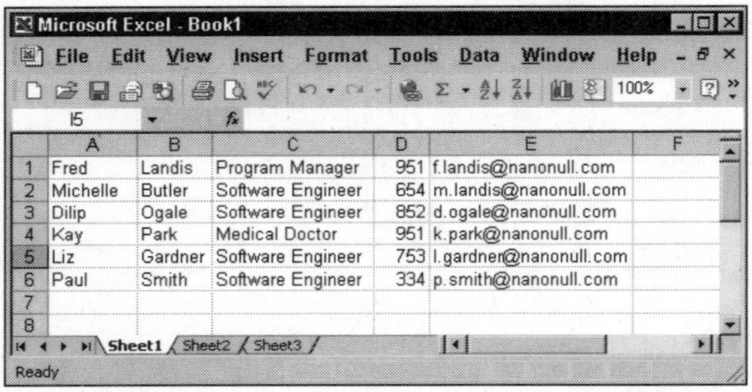

Figure 2-27: Exporting XML data from XMLSPY's Grid
view to Microsoft Excel.

Similarly, you can import data from a Microsoft Office application, such as
Excel, into XMLSPY by reversing what you just did to import data. Select the fields
in Excel that you want to copy and place them on the Clipboard by choosing Edit
→ Copy or by pressing Ctrl+C. Open an XML document in Grid view and place the
cursor in the top-left corner of a semantic table where the data is to be inserted.
Choose Edit → Paste or press Ctrl+V. The Grid view automatically converts the
tabular data into an XML format.

Converting a Data Source to an XML Document Using XMLSPY

A popular use of XML in industry today is that of an intermediary format to enable
information sharing between software applications. Data and content stored somewhere in a native format can be converted to an XML format. After it is in XML
format, any other external program that understands XML can use the data, possibly
converting it back to its own native format if required. To help make this conversion

possible, XMLSPY includes data conversion utilities that can help you move information stored in text files and databases and various other formats into XML documents. Conversely, XMLSPY can convert XML documents into text file or databases formats. You can access all XMLSPY data conversion utilities from the Convert menu. In this section, you experience first-hand how Grid view can be very helpful for performing data conversions.

Text files

With XMLSPY, you can import text files to an XML document, as well as export XML documents to text files. To convert a text file into an XML document, choose Convert → Import Text file, which opens the Text Import dialog box.

As an example, configure the Text Import dialog box by following these steps:

1. Click the Choose File button, select C:\Program Files\Altova\XMLSPY\ Examples\xmlspyhandbook\ch2\products.csv, and then click Open. XMLSPY loads the file and returns you to the Text Import dialog box. The configurable options become editable.

2. In the File Encoding field, choose Codepage 1252 (Western).

3. In the Field Delimiter section, choose the Comma option button.

4. In the Text Enclosed In section, click the double quotation mark (") option button.

5. Click to select the First Row Contains Field Names check box.

Before finishing the import operation, suppose that you would like the ProductID field to appear as an XML attribute rather than an XML element. Click the ProductID header so that an equal sign (=) instead of empty brackets (<>) appears adjacent to the ProductID field. Finally, click the OK button. The imported data, now in XML format, is displayed to the screen in Grid view. Notice that as you change the various options in the Text Import dialog box, a preview of the output is displayed in real time, in the bottom pane, as shown in Figure 2-28.

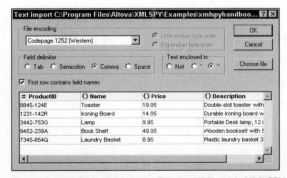

Figure 2-28: Converting text files to XML with XMLSPY.

Now, examine the XML document that was created by XMLSPY as a result of this import from text file operation. By default, the imported XML document has a root element called <Import>, and each imported row is called <Row>. As previously discussed, you can rename these fields simply by double-clicking the table headers in Grid view. You can then give the imported data more meaningful element names, such as Catalog and Product, as shown in Figure 2-29.

Rename table headers (from <Import> and <Row>)

Figure 2-29: Modifying the newly imported XML data in Grid view.

The resulting well-formed XML document is shown in Listing 2-3. You can see that the Text File Import utility combined with Grid view makes for a very powerful combined data integration tool.

Listing 2-3: Generated XML File from the Import Text File Operation

```
<Catalog>
   <Product ProductID="8845-124E">
      <Name>Toaster</Name>
      <Price>19.95</Price>
      <Description>Double-slot toaster.</Description>
   </Product>
   <Product ProductID="1231-142R">
      <Name>Ironing Board</Name>
      <Price>14.95</Price>
      <Description>Durable ironing board.</Description>
   </Product>
   <Product ProductID="3442-753G">
      <Name>Lamp</Name>
      <Price>9.95</Price>
      <Description>Portable Desk lamp.</Description>
   </Product>
   <!-- ... Products omitted for brevity. -->
</Catalog>
```

Exporting an XML file to a text file is a slightly more involved process than importing a text file to an XML format. This is because a text file typically requires a tabular structure, whereas an XML document is tree-like in nature. To overcome this potential issue, XMLSPY (as you probably guessed by now) makes use of semantic tables to (optionally) generate multiple output files, each corresponding to a semantic table from the Grid view. In this next example, you export the OrgChart.xml file, which you can find in the Ch2 folder in the Project window or on your system at C:\Program Files\Altova\XMLSPY\Examples\xmlspyhandbook\OrgChart.xml, to several text files. Choose Convert → Export to Text Files/Database. Notice that this menu option is unavailable unless you have an open XML document within the XMLSPY editing environment.

Choosing Convert → Export to Text Files/Database causes the Export to Text Files/Database dialog box to appear (see Figure 2-30).

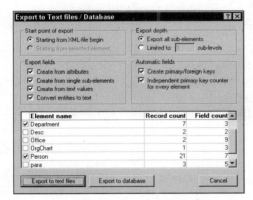

Figure 2–30: The Export to Text Files/Database dialog box.

Exporting an XML document to a text file is a highly configurable process in XMLSPY. The configuration options are explained in the following list:

◆ **Start Point of Export:** Using Grid view, you can highlight a section of an XML document to be exported to a text file as opposed to exporting the entire XML document.

◆ **Export Depth:** Specify the number of nodes deep you wish to export, relative to the starting point.

◆ **Export Fields:** Allows you to specify the appearance of Export Fields.

◆ **Automatic Fields:** XMLSPY will optionally generate primary and foreign keys for each row exported to the text file. A *primary key* is a field whose value uniquely identifies a row in a table; a *foreign key* is a field that refers to the primary key of an external table. XMLSPY determines the value of the primary and foreign key fields by determining the row's position within its semantic table representation. Primary and foreign keys are commonly used in relational database theory.

In this example, you want to export data only from the Department and Person elements. You can do this by unselecting all the other elements in the list displayed in the bottom pane of Figure 2-30. Next, click the Export to Text Files button to open the Export to Text Files dialog box shown in Figure 2-31.

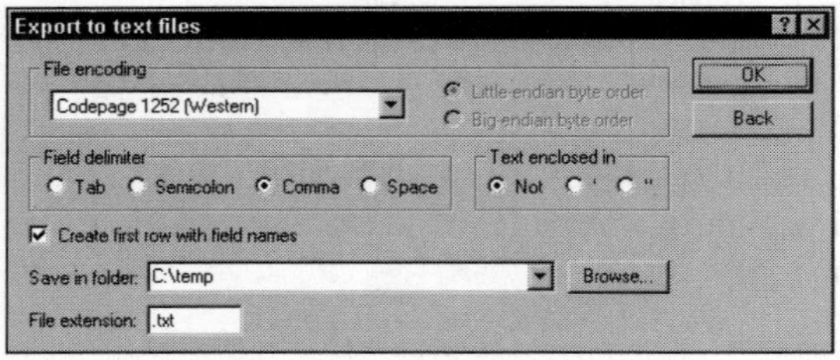

Figure 2–31: The Export to Text Files dialog box.

In this example, you are using the default file encoding. Specify tabs to be the field delimiter. Do not enclose text in quotation marks. Insert the field names in the first row. Then specify the output folder and click OK. This should generate two files — Department.txt and Person.txt. The Department.txt file is shown in Listing 2-4.

Listing 2–4: The Department.txt File

```
PrimaryKey,ForeignKey,Name,
1,1,Administration,
2,1,Marketing,
3,1,Engineering,
4,1,IT & Technical Support,
5,2,Administration,
6,2,Marketing,
7,2,IT & Technical Support,
```

The PrimaryKey field shown in Listing 2-4 has been determined by the position of the Department element relative to the other Department elements. The ForeignKey field has been calculated by determining the relative position of a Department's parent element (that is, its corresponding Office element). For example, the first four Department elements belong to the first Office. Therefore, they have a ForeignKey equal to one; the last three Department elements belonged to the second Office element, and so their foreign key is equal to two.

Relational databases

XML technologies, compared to a conventional relational database, can potentially improve information reuse for certain forms of structured content. But don't forget that the vast majority of corporate information and data (by most estimates, in excess of 80%) is stored in relational databases. Relational databases are extremely well-suited for storing and working with tabular data and will remain very widely used regardless of how successful XML technologies are. Therefore, it is important to have data conversion utilities that can work directly with relational databases to convert relational data into XML and also convert XML back into relational data.

XMLSPY's data conversion utilities can import database tables into an XML document, as well as export XML documents to relational databases. It does this for all commercial databases including Oracle, Microsoft SQL Server, IBM DB2 — or any other database that supports Open Database Connectivity (ODBC), a widely supported means for programmatic database access. In this section, I assume that you have Microsoft Access installed on your computer. Microsoft Access, a widely installed database product, is easy to use and is ideal for demonstrating XMLSPY's database import/export capabilities. Look at a sample Microsoft Access database called `Altova.mdb`, located in `c\Program Files\Altova\XMLSPY \Examples\Import`. The database tables and their primary and foreign key relationships, as well as the degree (or cardinality) of the relationships, are displayed in Figure 2-32.

Figure 2-32: A sample database schema showing relationships and cardinality.

To convert any one of the database tables of Figure 2-32 to an XML document, choose Convert → Import Database Data.

The Database Import dialog box appears as shown in Figure 2-33. Click Choose File, select the `Altova.mdb` file located in `C:\Program Files\Altova\XMLSPY\ Examples\Import`, and click Open. Next, click the Choose Table button and select the `Person` table. A default query (`SELECT * FROM [Person]`) appears in the Selection Statement section. Click the Preview button.

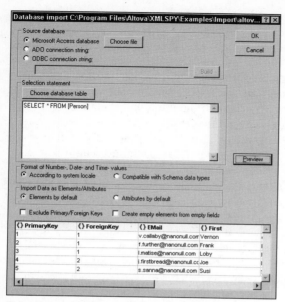

Figure 2–33: The Database Import window.

The process of importing database tables is highly configurable in XMLSPY. The options are shown in the following list:

◆ **Format of Number:** Allows you to specify how imported database data (in particular, date and time values) should be formatted. For now, choose According to System Locale. With this option selected, whatever setting you have set in the Windows Control Panel is used.

◆ **Import Data as Elements/Attributes:** Allows you to specify how imported data should be represented in an XML document by default. Choose Elements by Default. Of course, you can represent imported data as a mix of both elements and attributes by manually clicking a column header in the preview window. For example, convert the `PrimaryKey` and `ForeignKey` fields to attributes by clicking their respective column headers, which toggles the element symbol (<>) to an attribute symbol (=).

◆ **Exclude Primary/Foreign Keys:** You can choose to exclude the importing of primary and foreign keys because this information is often implied if you examine the element's location within an XML document. In this example, simply leave the option box unchecked so that primary and foreign keys are included.

◆ **Create Empty Elements from Empty Fields:** A database table might specify that a particular row was allowed to have null values. This option box allows you to specify if an empty or null value should be represented as an empty element or empty attribute value. For this example, leave it unchecked.

By default, the imported XML document has a root element called `<Import>`, and each imported row is called `<Row>`, as was the case when you imported data from text files in the previous section. Again, you can rename these fields simply by double-clicking the table headers in Grid view and giving the imported data more meaningful element names, such as `<Person>` (see Figure 2-34).

≡ PK	≡ FK	() EMail	() First	() Last	() Ext	() Title	
1 1	1	v.callaby@nanonull.com	Vernon	Callaby	582	Office Manager	
2 2	1	f.further@nanonull.com	Frank	Further	471	Accounts Receivable	
3 3	1	l.matise@nanonull.com	Loby	Matise	963	Accounting Manager	
4 4	2	j.firstbread@nanonull.com	Joe	Firstbread	621	Marketing Manager Europe	
5 5	2	s.sanna@nanonull.com	Susi	Sanna	753	Art Director	
6 6	3	f.landis@nanonull.com	Fred	Landis	951	Program Manager	
7 7	3	m.landis@nanonull.com	Michelle	Butler	654	Software Engineer	
8 8	3	t.little@nanonull.com	Ted	Little	852	Software Engineer	
9 9	3	a.way@nanonull.com	Ann	Way	951	Technical Writer	
10 10	3	l.gardner@nanonull.com	Liz	Gardner	753	Software Engineer	
11 11	3	p.smith@nanonull.com	Paul	Smith	334	Software Engineer	
12 12	4	a.martin@nanonull.com	Alex	Martin	778	IT Manager	
13 13	4	g.hammer@nanonull.com	George	Hammer	223	Web Developer	
14 14	4	j.band@nanonull.com	Jessica	Bander	241	Support Engineer	
15 15	4	l.king@nanonull.com	Lui	King	345	Support Engineer	
16 16	5	s.meier@nanonull.com	Steve	Meier	114	Office Manager	
17 17	5	t.bone@nanonull.com	Theo	Bone	331	Accounts Receivable	
18 18	6	m.nafta@nanonull.com	Max	Nafta	122	PR & Marketing Manager US	
19 19	7	v.bass@nanonull.com	Valentin	Bass	716	IT Manager	
20 20	7	c.franken@nanonull.com	Carl	Franken	147	Support Engineer	
21 21	7	m.redgreen@nanonull.com	Mark	Redgreen	152	Support Engineer	

Figure 2-34: Data imported from a relational database table.

XMLSPY can convert XML documents into relational database tables, but this is a slightly more involved process than importing a database table into an XML document. It is, however, virtually the same process as exporting XML to a text file that was discussed in the previous section. The only differences are that after you make all your selections in the Convert → Export to Text Files/Database window, you must remember to unselect Create Primary/Foreign Keys in the Automatic Fields section if the data you are exporting already has an explicitly specified primary key field. Of course, you must also press the Export to Database button instead of the Export to Text File button. This causes the Export to Database window (shown in Figure 2-35) to appear.

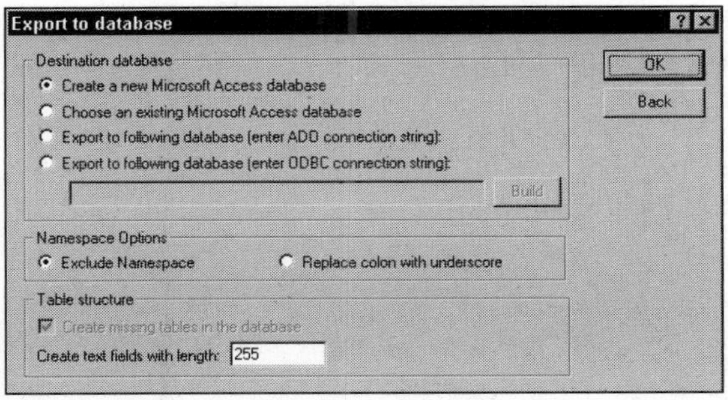

Figure 2-35: The Export to Database window.

Now, you have the option of inserting the exported data into an existing database or having XMLSPY automatically create new database files. Choose Create a New Microsoft Access Database and click OK. You are prompted to specify a filename and a directory in which to save the database files. XMLSPY automatically generates new Microsoft Access files, as shown in Figure 2-36.

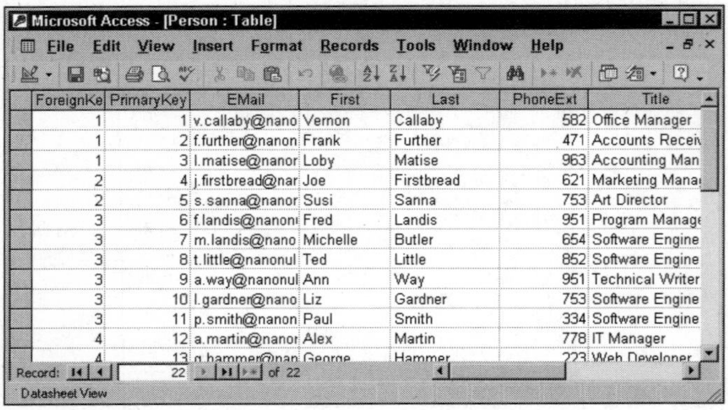

Microsoft Access - [Person : Table]

ForeignKe	PrimaryKey	EMail	First	Last	PhoneExt	Title
1	1	v.callaby@nano	Vernon	Callaby	582	Office Manager
1	2	f.further@nanon	Frank	Further	471	Accounts Receiv
1	3	l.matise@nanor	Loby	Matise	963	Accounting Man
2	4	j.firstbread@nar	Joe	Firstbread	621	Marketing Mana
2	5	s.sanna@nanor	Susi	Sanna	753	Art Director
3	6	f.landis@nanon	Fred	Landis	951	Program Manage
3	7	m.landis@nano	Michelle	Butler	654	Software Engine
3	8	t.little@nanonul	Ted	Little	852	Software Engine
3	9	a.way@nanonul	Ann	Way	951	Technical Writer
3	10	l.gardner@nano	Liz	Gardner	753	Software Engine
3	11	p.smith@nanon	Paul	Smith	334	Software Engine
4	12	a.martin@nanor	Alex	Martin	778	IT Manager
4	13	g.hammer@nan	George	Hammer	223	Web Developer

Record: 22 of 22

Datasheet View

Figure 2-36: Exporting the OrgChart.xml file to a Microsoft Access database table.

Converting Microsoft Word documents to XML

XML is not limited to representing data stored in text files and database tables. In fact, one of XML's greatest strengths is as a format for storing content such as books, encyclopedias, stories, poems, newspaper articles, and research papers. In this section, you look at converting Microsoft Word documents to XML by using XMLSPY. Follow these steps:

1. Choose Convert → Import Microsoft Word Document. A file explorer appears asking you to choose a Microsoft Word document.
2. Choose any Word document on your system. XMLSPY imports the contents of the Word document into XML format. Listing 2-5 shows the format of the converted Microsoft Word document.

Listing 2-5: Converted Microsoft Word Document

```
<Word-Document>
   <HTML:STYLE>
   ... <!--Abbreviated -->
   </HTML:STYLE>
   <Normal>
      <p>xmlspy urgently needs your vote</p>
      <p>best editor for xml, schema, xslt</p>
```

```
      <p>new features include debugging soap</p>
      <p>please vote for xmlspy asap</p>
   </Normal>
</Word-Document>
```

In addition to the poem's content, XMLSPY has also imported the stylesheet associated with this Word document (abbreviated in the preceding listing). If you are wondering about the context of the poem, it was a plea for votes in the Web Services Journal Readers' Choice Awards, which originally appeared in the June 2002 Altova *Developer Connection* newsletter.

Creating and Managing XMLSPY Projects

Because building an XML application is likely to involve many files of varying types, XMLSPY includes a Project window to help you effectively organize and work with multiple files in a team environment. The benefits of using the XMLSPY Project window include the capability to organize files into folders and the capability to set folder properties that specify a certain behavior to be applied to all files within the folder. Examples of folder properties include specifying that a particular XSLT stylesheet or XML Schema be used on all files in a particular folder, or performing a document validation or well-formedness check on all files in a folder as a batch operation. In this section, you learn the important aspects of working with XMLSPY projects, including creating projects and folders, adding files to projects, specifying folder or project properties, and configuring XMLSPY for use with external source code version control systems.

The special version of XMLSPY included on the accompanying CD opens the XMLSPY Handbook project by default. This project is also accessible from the Project window located at the top-left corner of the XMLSPY editing environment. If you did not install XMLSPY from the accompanying CD, make a local copy of the XMLSPY Handbook.spp file from the CD, along with all subdirectories (Ch2, Ch3, Ch4, and so on). You handle all project operations, including opening, closing, saving, and creating new XMLSPY projects, from the Project menu (see Figure 2-37).

To create a new project, choose Project → New Project. A new Project window (shown in Figure 2-38) automatically appears. The Project window, like most other XMLSPY windows, is a completely dockable window that you can move anywhere within in the XMLSPY editing environment. You can also toggle its visibility on or off by choosing Window → Project Window. All project settings are stored in an XMLSPY project file (.spp), which is an XML-based configuration file that normally you should not edit manually.

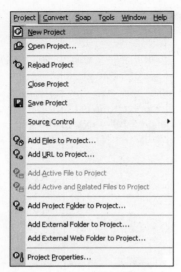

Figure 2–37: The XMLSPY Project menu.

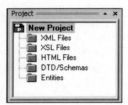

Figure 2–38: A new XMLSPY project
displayed in the Project window.

After you create a new XMLSPY project, that project becomes the current project. By default, the project includes some basic project folders. You can easily delete folders that you don't need by clicking the folder and pressing the Delete key.

Adding files to a project

To add files to a project, right-click the project folder to which you want to add files and choose Project → Add Files. A file explorer appears. Choose the file that you want to add and click OK. XMLSPY also supports adding files located on an external server, provided that the server supports access through HTTP, WebDAV, or FTP (most servers do this, of course). To add files from an external server, choose Project → Add URL to Project, and type the file URL in the resulting dialog box. You can also add the active document (the document that you are working on) from the main editing window to the current project by choosing Project → Add Active File to Project. Remember that you must save your work to a file before you can add it to a project.

Folder types and adding folders to a project

XMLSPY's Project window allows you to create three different types of folders: Project folders, External folders, and Web folders. You can insert or nest them anywhere within an XMLSPY project. These folders are described in more detail in the following list:

◆ **Project folders:** Internal to XMLSPY only, they do not exist or have any meaning anywhere outside of the XMLSPY Project window.

◆ **External folders:** Correspond to a Microsoft Windows operating system folder on either the local file system (such as the `My Documents` directory) or on the local area network.

◆ **Web folders:** Folder located on an external server, accessible via HTTP, FTP, or WebDAV file access protocols. In the case of HTTP, you will most likely be editing a copy of the file. Upon saving, XMLSPY attempts to save the file back to the Web server, but it likely will fail. You are then prompted to save the file to the local file system. In the case of FTP or WebDAV access, however, your edits are saved back to the server from which the document originated.

To add any of the preceding types of folders to a project, open the Project menu and choose the Add Folder option that corresponds to the type of folder you want to add to your project. In the case of a Web folder, you must specify the URL, as well as a username and password, to access the remote server (see Figure 2-39).

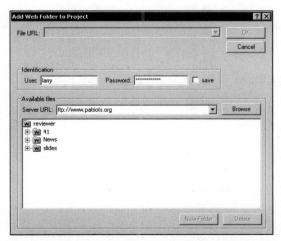

Figure 2-39: Add a Web folder to the Project window.

WebDAV stands for Web-based Distributed Authoring and Versioning. It is a connectionless distributed file-sharing protocol developed by the Internet Engineering Task Force (IETF) that is intended to be a replacement for FTP. Using a WebDAV-enabled editor such as XMLSPY, however, you can access and edit files located on external (WebDAV-compliant) Web servers, data-bases, or file systems and make changes to the documents as though they reside on the local file system. Upon saving, the updated files are sent back to the server from which they originated.

Setting folder properties

Files residing on the local file system, as well as external file URLs can be grouped into folders by common file extensions or by any other criteria you choose. After arranging your files, you can perform batch processing on specific folders or on the project as a whole. Here are some examples:

◆ You can assign DTD or XML Schemas to specific folders allowing any XML file within the folder to be validated with a single click.

◆ You can assign an XSLT stylesheet to specific folders, allowing for any XML file within the folder to be transformed with a single click.

◆ You can specify the output directory of an XSL transformation.

You can define the settings for a project by choosing Project → Project Properties to open the Properties dialog box. Alternatively, you can apply settings to a single folder by right-clicking the folder and choosing Properties from the drop-down list. The Properties dialog box is the same for both projects and folders (see Figure 2-40).

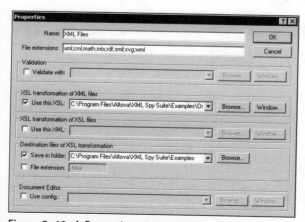

Figure 2-40: A Properties window for either a project folder or the entire project.

Source control integration

A source code repository and versioning system is a centralized server for storing all of a company's source code files, including both the most current version and a history of all previous changes made to the source code files. Using a repository and versioning system, a company's software engineering group can collectively store all source code files in such a manner that multiple developers can safely work together on the same project. To understand the value of a source code and versioning system, consider the potential problems of developing a large software project in a team environment:

◆ Two developers may accidentally work on the same file simultaneously and when they save back their work to a regular file server, one developer's work is over-written.

◆ Changes to one file may cause adverse side effects to other parts of the software program.

Repository and versioning systems such as Microsoft Visual SourceSafe (VSS) overcome these problems by disallowing concurrent access to files. If you want to make a change to a file, you must first check out the file from VSS. While you are working on the files, VSS places a lock on the files that blocks any attempt to access them. When you are finished editing the file, you must check the file back in to VSS. VSS maintains a change log that shows the differences of the file before and after your edits.

XML files edited using XMLSPY can be edited in conjunction with an external source code repository and version control system, such as Microsoft VSS. In this section, I cover how to configure XMLSPY to work with Microsoft VSS.

CONFIGURING XMLSPY BY USING A MICROSOFT VISUAL SOURCESAFE DATABASE

Be sure that you have installed the Microsoft VSS client software on your local computer. Then make sure that you have a username and password that enables you to access a Microsoft VSS database installation from your computer. To obtain a copy of Visual SourceSafe, ask your IT department if they have a Microsoft Developers Network (MSDN) Universal Subscription or visit http://msdn.microsoft.com/ssafe/.

XMLSPY projects differ from VSS projects and should not be confused with one another. Consider that XMLSPY projects support three different types of folders: Project, External, and Web folders. VSS supports only one type of folder, which also happens to be named Projects, and which is essentially Microsoft Windows directories on a file system. One immediate consequence is that Web folders cannot be used in conjunction with Microsoft VSS. Follow these steps to integrate XMLSPY with Microsoft VSS:

1. Open the XMLSPY project file (.spp) that you would like to use in conjunction with Microsoft VSS. In this example, I have created a hypothetical project called myproject and have added two files as previously explained. Click the .spp project file that appears at the top of the Project View window, as shown in Figure 2-41.

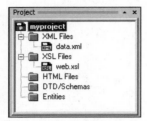

Figure 2–41: A project to be used in conjunction with Microsoft Visual SourceSafe.

2. Choose Project → Source Control → Add to Source Control. The Microsoft VSS Client Software Login dialog box appears, prompting you to log in to a VSS database.

3. Type your username and password and click OK. The Microsoft VSS client software's Add to SourceSafe Project dialog box appears.

4. Select an existing VSS project to add the file(s) to or create a new VSS project by typing a project name. Click OK. In Figure 2-42, there are no existing projects in the VSS Database, therefore, you simply type the new project name in the Project field. When you click OK, VSS asks Project $/myproject Does Not Exist. Would You Like to Create It? Select Yes.

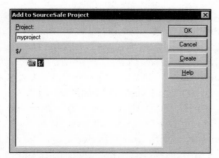

Figure 2–42: The Add to Microsoft SourceSafe Project window.

5. Microsoft VSS prompts you to select which files you want to add to the project. In this example, I have the option to add `data.xml` and `web.xsl`, in addition to the `myproject.spp` file (see Figure 2-43). Those files happen to be in the same folder as the `.spp` file. Select the files you want to add and then click OK. (*Note*: You can add more files to Microsoft VSS at any later time.)

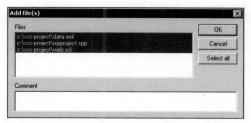

Figure 2–43: The Microsoft VSS Add File(s) window.

You have now configured your XMLSPY project to work in conjunction with Microsoft VSS. Note that the file icons in the Project window should now have tiny little locks on the top-right corner, as shown in Figure 2-44. These locks indicate that the files are read-only because they are checked into Microsoft VSS.

Figure 2–44: XMLSPY's Project window, integrated with Microsoft VSS.

6. In order to edit a file in your project, you must first check out the file from the Microsoft VSS database, thus placing an exclusive lock on the file and preventing other people from working on the file while you are making edits. Right-click the file that you would like to edit and choose Check Out from the menu.

Notice that when a file is checked out from Microsoft VSS (that is, you have locked the file and have exclusive write-access to it), the file icon displays a little red check-mark on the top-right corner, as shown in Figure 2-45.

Figure 2–45: XMLSPY's Project window indicates
when a file has been checked out.

7. When your edits are complete, right-click the file icon and choose Check-
In from the menu.

OTHER VERSION CONTROL SYSTEMS

In addition to Microsoft Visual SourceSafe, XMLSPY can work with other repository and version control systems – in particular, Concurrent Versioning System
(CVS), a widely used open-source product. Connectivity with CVS and other version
control systems is achieved through a third-party driver called Jalindi Igloo. For
more information, see the Web page for the product at www.jalindi.com/igloo/.

Other Helpful Editing Features

XMLSPY includes a multitude of miscellaneous editing features to make your work
as easy as possible. This section highlights four of these features.

Online Help

XMLSPY includes an indexed and fully searchable online Help to assist you with
any XMLSPY feature. Although this book covers all the important features and
technologies related to XMLSPY, it is not a reference manual. If you need assistance
with something not covered in this book, refer to the online Help, which you can
access directly from the Help menu. In addition, most windows in XMLSPY have a
small question mark button in the top-right corner, adjacent to the Close button.
The question mark indicates a context-sensitive Help button, which automatically
pops open the online Help manual for the relevant section. The most current
version of the online Help manual is maintained at the www.xmlspy.com Web site,
and a printed version of the product documentation (currently over 700 pages) is
available either directly from the U.S. publisher at www.iuniverse.com or through
international resellers such as www.amazon.com.

Spell checking in XMLSPY

XMLSPY includes spell checking for both Grid view and Text view. To spell-check a document, simply click the Spell Check button on the main toolbar, press Shift+F7, or choose Tools → Spelling. Spell checking an XML document is a little different from checking a Microsoft Word document. You specify certain regions of the XML document that you want to ignore, such as within certain elements or attributes, comments, or CDATA sections. The spell checker supports 16 languages, including English, German, French, and Italian, and includes both Medical and Legal dictionaries. To change spell checking options, simply click the Options button in the Spell Checking dialog box.

Customizing the XMLSPY editing environment

XMLSPY has a completely customizable editing environment. To access the configuration panel, choose Tools → Options. The Options panel, shown in Figure 2-46, has multiple panes that specify everything from associated file types, editing preferences, fonts, and colors to character encoding and more.

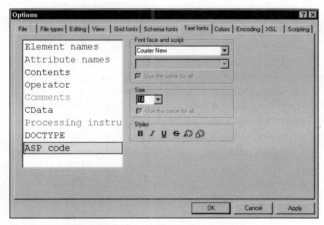

Figure 2-46: The Options configuration panel.

Customizing XMLSPY toolbars

XMLSPY has many features, and so there are toolbars for every functional group of features. You can enable or disable toolbars by choosing Tools → Customize.

Summary

This chapter covered the following topics:

- A review of basic XML syntax constructs and how to edit them in Text view

- The various rules for writing XML documents, including well-formedness and how to test for well-formedness using XMLSPY

- Grid view as a powerful, higher-level view for performing editing operations on XML documents as a whole, rather than editing on a line-by-line basis in Text view

- How Grid view's semantic tables represent repeating patterns in XML documents as rows within tables, which is ideal for performing higher-level editing operations

- Data conversion of XML to and from text files and databases, as well as Microsoft Word documents

- How to use XMLSPY's Projects window and configure it to work with the Microsoft Visual SourceSafe, a code repository and versioning system

- Help menus, spell-checking, and customizing the XMLSPY editing environment to get the most out of the XMLSPY editing environment

In the next chapter, I introduce content model development, including building Document Type Definitions with XMLSPY.

Chapter 3

DTD Editing and Validation

IN THIS CHAPTER

- ◆ Building content models for XML documents
- ◆ Editing DTDs with XMLSPY
- ◆ Validating XML documents with XMLSPY
- ◆ Converting XML documents with XMLSPY

THIS CHAPTER IS ALL ABOUT BUILDING YOUR VERY OWN, customized markup languages using XMLSPY. You can use XML to describe anything imaginable – purchase orders, books, scientific data, medical records, literally anything! When you build a custom markup language, you define all the allowable XML structures – elements, attributes, and entities – along with any restrictions or constraints on those structures.

Your custom markup language has to be expressed in a schema language, and historically, the most common schema language has been a Document Type Definition (DTD). In this chapter, I cover DTD syntax in detail. You learn how to develop a DTD and then use it to validate your own XML documents within the XMLSPY editing environment. I discuss various DTD design strategies and some of XMLSPY's helpful DTD editing functionality, such as the capability to automatically generate a DTD. Finally, I offer some tips on how to make a modular DTD, and I highlight some of the differences between DTDs and XML Schemas (the technological successor of DTDs). I also provide the pros and cons of using DTDs and XML Schemas.

XML Content Models

The first step in building your own custom markup language is to lay down the ground rules to which all XML documents belonging to your custom markup language must adhere. Specifically, you need to design a model of which elements, attributes, and entities can appear in your XML documents, in what order, and how many times. I refer to the model of a custom markup language as an *XML content model* or simply as a *content model*. A content model is the blueprint or schema for your own custom family of XML documents. You use it similarly to the way you use a database schema, which defines a data model for tabular data, or a class definition, which defines a model for software objects. The ground rules of a content model must be expressed in a schema language such as DTD or XML Schema, and in this chapter, I show you how to build content models by using DTDs.

As it turns out, the XML documents you worked with in Chapters 1 and 2 were *document fragments* – well-formed snippets of XML code. They didn't belong to any particular class of document. In the book example in Chapter 2, you expressed a book's description using an XML format, but you never explicitly specified any rules for how a book's information should be represented. In this chapter, however, you build a content model for describing books – a book markup language – that lets you create XML documents that describe other books in a clear, consistent, and structured manner. By defining a content model for your books, you can differentiate your book XML documents from any other XML document and determine whether the information contained within the XML document is valid (that is, it abides by all the rules and restrictions specified in the content model). I should note that content models are also sometimes referred to as simply *schemas* for short. In this book, I use *content model* to avoid any potential confusion with XML Schemas.

Here are some of the reasons why you should develop a content model for your XML documents:

◆ **Improved interoperability:** If everyone created individual markup languages *without* creating associated content models, the overall world-wide level of application interoperability would be practically the same as if no one used XML in the first place. Software application interoperability requires informing others (both programmers and applications) about the kind of input and output required to work with your application. All this information must be expressed in a content model.

◆ **Enhanced editing support:** By working with XMLSPY and a content model (typically expressed in either a DTD or an XML Schema), you can automate application development support including visual editing, code completion, code generation, and database schema generation.

◆ **Good programming practice:** A content model is your data interface. Any distributed Internet application will likely require programming of clients (consumers) and servers (producers) of data. If you specify a data interface (content model) prior to developing the client and server applications, different programming teams can independently implement their respective programming contracts, resulting in reduced development times.

It is necessary, but not sufficient, to simply write out information and data encoded within angle brackets as specified by the XML syntax. In order for XML-encoded information to have meaning and be understood, you must first design a conceptual model of the information being conveyed and clearly specify the set of permissible data elements and the structure to which an XML document must conform to be considered a member of a particular markup language.

This chapter explains how to use a DTD to build a straightforward content model for books. In industry today, the development of XML content models to describe business processes is of great interest to all companies. Global consortiums, such as the World Wide Web Consortium (W3C) and the Organization for the Advancement of Structured Information Standards (OASIS), bring together a diverse group of products, services, and systems integration companies. These drive the development, convergence, and adoption of XML content models to describe business processes such as purchase orders, stock quotations, research reports — essentially any information communicated from one source to another. A listing of the most widely used XML content models (both DTDs and XML Schemas) in industry is included in Appendix B.

Instance Documents and Validation

An XML content model defines a technical blueprint for a family or class of XML documents. An XML document that is intended to belong to a particular family of documents (that is, it is meant to conform to all the rules defined within a content model) is called an *instance document*. This differentiation is required to demonstrate that the document is just one instance member of a particular family of documents (for example, a particular markup language). The distinction between an instance document and its associated content model is analogous to the relationship between an object and its class definition in object-oriented programming languages, or to a database table's schema definition and a row of data within the table. Both a class definition and a database schema define a template or model, which is subsequently used to create objects or data that share the same characteristics. Suppose that you want to convey, in XML format, the information contained in a collection of books. You first must design a general content model to describe a book; then, you can create several XML instance documents that correspond to each book in your collection.

Although the content model is an optional feature of XML, it is an extremely powerful feature. A content model is a necessary requirement for performing document *validation*; the process by which an XML instance document is systematically checked and verified to be in conformance with the all the rules and restrictions defined within a content model. Having a content model is a necessary requirement for document validation. In the absence of a content model, there are no rules to enforce upon an XML document. XML, by itself, does not enforce or place any restrictions on what kinds of data elements may be included or a document's structure outside the basic rules for constructing XML documents (such as the requirements that a document be well-formed and adhere to certain naming conventions and other rules described in Chapter 2).

Document validation is an automatic process as far as the developer is concerned. All major commercial-grade XML *parser*s (also called XML *processors*) today are validating XML parsers. This means that they have both a parser, which reads an XML document, and an XML *validator*, which is a software component that can understand and enforce content models expressed in one of the major schema languages, such as DTD or XML Schema. You only have to specify an instance document to be validated and a content model containing the rules to be validated against, and then you simply instruct the XML parser to perform the document validation. Typically, the processor's XML validator either reports a success message, if your instance document is determined to be valid, or provides some kind of error message in the event that the XML processor's validator catches a violation of one of the constraints specified in your content model. Indeed, the XML processor included in XMLSPY's parser includes an XML validator that can accept any content model (expressed either as a DTD or an XML Schema), as well as an XML instance document to be validated. It will validate the document against all the rules defined in the content model. In the following section, I show you how to use a DTD to validate XML documents within the XMLSPY editing environment.

Using content models to validate XML instance documents is important for the following reasons:

- ◆ **Consistent program behavior:** As a general rule, data input to any software application should be validated for reasons of security and to ensure proper program behavior. By using a content model, you eliminate the fear of unexpected input, so your software application (which uses XML documents) is less likely to crash and more likely to produce consistent, meaningful results — obviously a highly desirable result!

- ◆ **Less validation code:** The use of a content model to restrict program input and output offloads the burden of writing and maintaining vast amounts of validation code from the application developer by passing off this responsibility to the XML validator. By using an XML validator, programmers can write applications that create or consume XML documents without fear of encountering an unexpected input. One of the most common problems of implementing and maintaining separate application data validation modules is that any change of program input or output must be reconciled with the data validation module. Any desynchronization of the application's external interface from the validation module will result in errors. As an application grows in complexity, so do the number of possible program inputs and the potential for errors.

For the reasons just stated, it's not a good idea to use XML documents without an associated content model. Content model development should take precedence over editing XML instance documents in the XML application development process. Only after having spent at least some time developing and refining a content model for a family of XML documents should you start editing instance documents.

Document Type Definitions

Historically, DTDs have been widely used to specify content models for XML documents. DTD syntax was predominantly inherited from Structured Generalized Markup Language (SGML), the technological predecessor of both HTML and XML. You can place a DTD at the top of every XML document that is meant to conform to it (an *internal declaration*), or you can save the DTD in a separate file and reference it by a special instruction near the top of the XML document (an *external declaration*). I highly recommend the use of external DTDs because they are reusable and are much less susceptible to versioning problems than internal declarations. If fact, internal declarations are so often problematic that I focus primarily on externally declared DTDs in this section.

In this section, you create a book markup language — a content model to describe books — and you express the content model as an external DTD. You then use the book DTD that you build to validate the book XML files, similar to the book file that you built in Chapter 2.

To create a new DTD in XMLSPY, choose File → New or click the New File button on the main toolbar and choose Document Type Definition from the Create New Document dialog box. Save the file to your local file system as book.dtd. You build this empty DTD file so that you can use it for validating book instance documents.

For your convenience, all the files that you build in this chapter (and throughout the book) are included on the accompanying CD-ROM. The exclusive version of XMLSPY included on the CD automatically specifies the XMLSPY Handbook project as the default project. If the version of XMLSPY that you are using is *not* the one that came on this book's CD (that is, you downloaded it from the Web or elsewhere), you can still access the example files. Simply copy the XMLSPY Handbook.spp file and all subdirectories (Ch2, Ch3, Ch4, and so on) from the CD to your local hard drive.

Figure 3-1 shows where — on the CD that accompanies this book — you can find all the files that you build in this chapter.

If you ever happen to inadvertently lose your default project settings, you can recover them by opening the XMLSPY Handbook project files from the Project menu. To do this, choose Project → Open Project and locate the XMLSPY Handbook.spp file located in the Program files\Altova\XMLSPY\Examples\xmlspyhandbook directory. Here are the files you will use in the next few sections:

book.dtd: The book content model expressed as an external DTD

bookinstance.xml: A book instance document, similar to the book XML files
                         you built in Chapter 2

Figure 3-1: The project files for XMLSPY Handbook.

These files are the completed versions. However, I recommend that you manually re-create the files in a separate directory and refer to the completed files only in the event that you get stuck. You get more from the experience if you manually type the DTD and XML instance document as you go along. The following listing provides the code for the `bookinstance.xml` document. Create and save a new `bookinstance.xml` file to your local file system with the contents of this listing:

```xml
<?xml version="1.0" encoding="UTF-8"?>
<book isbn="5-2341-9384-2" language="English">
   <title>The XMLSPY Game</title>
   <logo file="cover.gif"/>
      <author-list>
         <author>
            <firstname>David</firstname>
            <lastname>Smith</lastname>
         </author>
      </author-list>
   <copyright>1999</copyright>
</book>
```

 If you are looking for the DTD specification, you might be surprised to find that there isn't an official standalone DTD specification. However, DTDs are discussed as part of the XML 1.0 specification, and in a few other places here and there, such as the XHTML and HTML specifications. Appendix B provides a listing of important XML grammars and standards.

A DTD example

In this example, I define a DTD for describing books, such as the one described in `bookinstance.xml`. The first step in content model development is to list the design requirements. For this example, I have determined that a book has the following characteristics:

- A required ISBN number

- A required language attribute — either English, French, German, or Russian

- Exactly one book title

- An author list, containing at least one or possibly more authors, with each author having his or her respective first and last names

- An optional logo file (multiple logos are permitted)

- Optional copyright information

Figure 3-2 shows a tree representation of the preliminary design requirements for the book structure. Elements are shown as ovals, and attributes are shown as rectangles. A line joining two elements indicates a nested element, and a line joining an attribute and an element indicates that the attribute appears inside the indicated element. The numbers on the connecting lines indicate the cardinality or multiplicity of the relationship. For example, if both ends are labeled with a *1*, it is a required element or attribute. You should design your DTD so that it matches your design criteria.

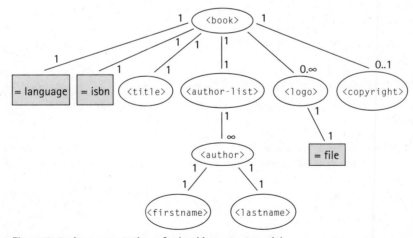

Figure 3-2: A representation of a book's content model.

Here we take a quick peek at the DTD for the book sketched out in Figure 3-2. The following listing shows all the elements and attributes and one entity we just described. Don't worry if it doesn't all make sense yet because everything will be explained in the next few sections.

```
<?xml version="1.0" encoding="UTF-8"?>
<!ELEMENT book (title, logo*, author-list, copyright?)>
<!ATTLIST book
         isbn NMTOLKEN #REQUIRED
         language (English | French | German | Russian ) #REQUIRED
>
<!ELEMENT title (#PCDATA)>
<!ELEMENT author-list (author+)>
<!ELEMENT author (firstname, lastname)>
<!ELEMENT firstname (#PCDATA)>
<!ELEMENT lastname (#PCDATA)>
<!ELEMENT logo EMPTY>
<!ATTLIST logo
         file CDATA #REQUIRED
>
<!ELEMENT copyright (#PCDATA)>
<!ENTITY copy "&#xA9;">
```

Defining elements

DTDs have a very concise syntax for element declarations. Before declaring an element, you must determine how and what kind of information the element will represent. Typically, element declarations fall into one of these categories:

- ◆ **Empty element:** Can contain optional attributes but no body content; essentially a placeholder

- ◆ **Text-only element:** Contains only plain text content within the body of the element.

- ◆ **Container element:** Contains nested child elements only

- ◆ **Mixed content element:** Contains a mix of both child elements and textual content

- ◆ **Unspecified element:** Content structure is unspecified; this element can cause errors and should be avoided

Table 3-1 provides a syntax example for each of the element declaration types just listed.

TABLE 3-1 SAMPLE ELEMENT DEFINITIONS USING DTDS

Type of Element	Example
Empty element	`<!ELEMENT myelement EMPTY>`

Type of Element	Example
Text-only element	`<!ELEMENT myelement (#PCDATA)>`
Container element	`<!ELEMENT myelement (child1, child2, child2)>`
Mixed content element	`<!ELEMENT myelement (#PCDATA | child)*>`
Unspecified element	`<!ELEMENT myelement ANY>`

All element declarations start with `<!ELEMENT myelement`, in which `myelement` is a placeholder that should be replaced with the name of the element you wish to define. Pay special attention to the last part of the element declaration, which specifies the element type.

Defining element type information requires the use of special symbols known as *occurrence operators*. Occurrence operators specify the number of times an element can appear within a document, as well as the sequence in which the element must appear. Table 3-2 lists all the available occurrence operators that you can use inside an element definition to specify an element's type. The type of element determines the number of times an element can appear in an XML document and the kind of information it can contain.

TABLE 3-2 OCCURRENCE OPERATORS THAT SPECIFY THE NUMBER OF TIMES AN ELEMENT CAN APPEAR

Occurrence Operator	Description	Numerical Range
?	Optional — once or not at all	0 or 1
*	Optional and repeatable	0 to ∞
+	At least once, optionally more	1 to ∞
	Required (default behavior, no symbol required)	Exactly once

∞ = *infinity*

As shown in Table 3-3, you can also use occurrence operators to specify the ordering or sequence in which element types can appear.

TABLE **3-3** OCCURRENCE OPERATORS THAT SPECIFY ALLOWABLE
               SEQUENCES OF ELEMENTS

Occurrence Operator	Description
,	Comma indicates that the child elements must appear in the same sequence in which they are defined.
|	Logical OR operator indicates a choice; one of two or more specified elements must appear in the document.

Occurrence operators are used together to define all sorts of possible element structures, for example:

```
<!ELEMENT book (title, logo*, author-list, copyright?)>
```

This code defines a book element that is a container element for a sequence of child elements. Occurrence operators are appended to the right of each child element; otherwise, they are required elements by default. The commas separating the child elements indicate the sequence in which the elements must appear; the child elements are either required, optional, or repeatable depending on the occurrence operator appended to the end of the element name. This example shows several concepts simultaneously, so don't worry if it doesn't make complete sense right now. I revisit this example after I explain the most common cases in a little more detail.

EMPTY ELEMENTS

Empty (placeholder) elements are widely used in HTML, such as in the image and horizontal rule tags: <img ... /> and <hr ... />. *Empty* is a reference to the fact that the element has no body content, although empty elements can and often do contain attributes. To specify an empty element, you do not need to use any of the occurrence operators because an empty element is completely empty! Simply use the special keyword EMPTY as the element type. For example, <!ELEMENT logo EMPTY> defines the logo element as an empty element.

ELEMENTS THAT CONTAIN ONLY TEXT

To define an element that contains only text, you specify the type as (#PCDATA), which stands for Parsed Character Data (which is essentially a plain text string). For example, <!ELEMENT firstname (#PCDATA)> defines the firstname element as containing parsed character data. Remember to include the opening and closing parentheses, or XMLSPY will report that the DTD has a syntax error. There is no way to constrain the contents of the text that appears within a text-only element using a DTD, however you can accomplish this using an XML Schema. Again, occurrence operators are not required because there is no limit to how much text can be contained inside a (#PCDATA) element.

 You find out how to edit XML Schemas in Chapters 4 and 5.

REQUIRED CHILD ELEMENT(S)

To specify one or more required child element(s), type the name of the child element(s), separated by commas as necessary and enclosed in parentheses. By default, the sequence of child elements appearing in an XML instance document must appear in the same sequence as specified in the comma-separated listing in the element type definition in order to be valid. As an example, the author element is defined as a sequence of two required child elements: firstname and lastname:

```
<!ELEMENT author (firstname, lastname)>
```

You know that these are required elements because no occurrence operator is explicitly specified and, therefore, they are required by default. The sequence is indicated by the comma separating firstname and lastname. If, in an instance document, lastname were to appear before firstname, a validating XML processor would report that the document was invalid.

OPTIONAL CHILD ELEMENTS

To make a child element optional, you can append the ? occurrence operator to the right of the optional child element's name, as it appears in the sequence of one or more elements. Type the following to add an optional logo element to the book element:

```
<!ELEMENT book (title, author-list, logo?)>.
```

REQUIRED AND REPEATABLE CHILD ELEMENTS

In the book element, the author-list element requires a minimum of one author, but it can potentially have many other coauthors. To specify this option, you can use the + occurrence operator, as follows:

```
<!ELEMENT author-list (author+)>
```

OPTIONAL AND REPEATABLE

The book element can contain a logo element that is both optional and repeatable. You specify these traits by using the * occurrence operator as follows:

```
<!ELEMENT book (title, author-list, logo*)>
```

CHOICE OF TWO OR MORE ELEMENTS

DTDs support a choice construct that gives the author of an XML instance document the flexibility to choose one element out of several possible allowable elements. To specify a choice of several elements, you type the names of the permissible elements, separated by the logical OR occurrence operator (|), and enclosed in parentheses. For example, to specify an element called *myelement* as a choice between three child elements (*choice1*, *choice2*, and *choice3*), type the following:

```
<!ELEMENT myelement (choice1 | choice2 | choice3)>
```

SPECIFYING MIXED CONTENT

An element that allows both text and child elements is said to have *mixed* content. There is no special operator to specify mixed content. Rather, it is a consequence of specifying a combination of occurrence operators. For example, you can define a paragraph element that allows text, as well as bold and italic child elements, as follows:

```
<!ELEMENT para (#PCDATA | bold |italic )*>
```

In plain English, this element declaration reads like this: The para element can contain either parsed character data, bold, or italic elements, repeatable from zero to an infinite number of times. For example, the following bit of XML code would be valid:

```
<para>Building DTDs is <italic>Easy</italic> with <bold>XMLSPY</bold>.</para>
```

Defining attributes

DTDs offer a concise syntax for defining one or more attributes, and the basic syntax is shown in Figure 3-3.

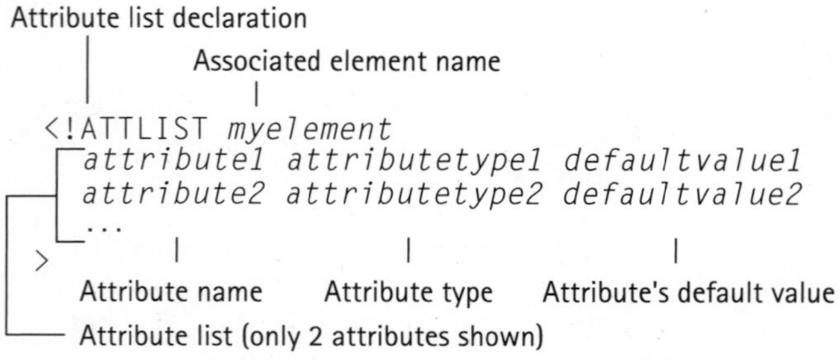

Figure 3-3: Defining a sequence of attributes in a DTD.

As I mentioned in Chapter 2, there are no specific W3C guidelines on what to make an attribute versus an element. In general, however, information contained in an attribute tends to be about the document's content, rather than being part of the content itself. As an example, the `language` attribute in the `book` element describes the information about the `book` but is not a part of the `book` element's content. Of course, because there are no official guidelines, creating an additional language element would also work.

ATTRIBUTE TYPES

DTDs support 10 different types of attributes. The following list describes each type, along with an example of how to use a couple of the most common types:

- **CDATA:** Possibly the most commonly used attribute type. `CDATA` indicates that the attribute value consists of a character data string of arbitrary length, which can include any characters except for single and double quotation marks and angle brackets; entities are permitted. The logo element has a required file attribute of type `CDATA`, which you declare like this:

```
<!ATTLIST logo
        file CDATA #REQUIRED
>
```

- **ENTITY:** Indicates that the attribute value corresponds to the value of an entity declared or referenced elsewhere in the DTD.

- **ENTITIES:** Indicates that the attribute value takes on the value of multiple entity references, separated by whitespace.

- **Enumerated:** Not an actual attribute type. If an attribute value must be equal to one value from a list of possible values, you can specify this behavior by typing

```
(option1|option2|option3| ...)
```

  where `optionx` corresponds to a legal value. Each legal value is separated by the vertical bar (logical OR symbol), and the entire list is enclosed in parentheses.

- **ID:** Specifies that an attribute is of type `identifier`, which implies that each occurrence of this field must have a unique value throughout the XML document. `ID`s are very helpful when you are navigating the XML document, particularly in XSLT stylesheet development.

- ◆ IDREF: Specifies that an attribute is of type *identifier reference*. This type implies that it has a value that is a reference to another ID within the XML document. This is similar to the concept of a foreign key in relational databases.

- ◆ IDREFS: Similar to an IDREF. An attribute of type IDREFS takes on multiple-element IDs as its value, with each ID separated by whitespace. You can use the IDREFS attribute to point to a list of related elements elsewhere in an XML document, or you can use it when performing database imports to an XML file in which a table contains multiple foreign key fields.

- ◆ NMTOKEN: A token, as far as an XML parser is concerned, is a string of characters whose start and end is delimited by a token delimiter such as whitespace or a comma. As an example, the string

```
DTDs aren't difficult
```

  consists of three whitespace delimited tokens: DTDs, aren't, and difficult. An attribute of type NMTOKEN can be any single-string token; however, it must abide by the basic rules of XML elements. Recall that a valid name token in XML consists of one or more alphanumeric characters, hyphens, or underscores. Spaces are not permitted because the parser would interpret the space as a token delimiter signifying the termination of the token. Of the three tokens shown here, only DTDs and difficult could pass as an attribute value of type NMTOKEN. The aren't token contains an apostrophe, which is not a legal character for naming XML elements. NMTOKEN is an ideal candidate for the isbn attribute of the book as shown in the following line:

```
<!ATTLIST book
        isbn NMTOLKEN #REQUIRED
        ...
>
```

- ◆ NMTOKENS: A whitespace-delimited list of NMTOKENS, which means that you can include spaces in the attribute value, but each individual token must still satisfy the rules for naming XML elements. As an example, the string Illegal NMTOKEN value is a completely legal value for an attribute of type NMTOKENS because it consists of three whitespace delimited name tokens.

- ◆ NOTATION: A reference to a notation defined elsewhere in the XML document.

ATTRIBUTE DEFAULTS

Three attribute default options are available and are described in the following list. You specify one of three keywords to explain how the default values should be handled, followed by the desired default value in quotation marks:

◆ **#FIXED:** This reserved word means that the specified attribute value is a fixed constant; if the attribute appears inside an element, the value must equal the default value specified. If an author includes another value, the XML parser will return an error. Even if the attribute were omitted from an element, the parser would assume the default value. For reasons of inflexibility, this construct is seldom used.

◆ **#IMPLIED:** This keyword makes an attribute optional, with a null or undefined value when the attribute is not present. Use an implied attribute if you don't want to force the author to include an attribute and you don't have an option for a default value.

◆ **#REQUIRED:** This keyword requires that an attribute be present inside an element; if the attribute is missing, the document is invalid. Note that you cannot define the actual attribute default value; you may only require that the attribute be present.

TABLE 3-4 EXAMPLE SYNTAX FOR SPECIFYING ATTRIBUTE DEFAULTS

Default Type	DTD Syntax	Explanation	Sample Valid Usage
#FIXED	`<!ATTLIST sender company CDATA #FIXED "Altova">`	Defines a company attribute for the sender element with fixed value "Altova"	`<sender company= "Altova"/>`
#IMPLIED	`<!ATTLIST contact fax CDATA #IMPLIED>`	Defines a fax attribute for the contact element — optional and no default value.	`<contact fax= "978-816- 1606" />`
#REQUIRED	`<!ATTLIST logo file CDATA #REQUIRED >`	Defines a required file attribute for the logo element	`<logo file= "xmlspy.gif"/>`

SIMPLIFIED ATTRIBUTE DECLARATION PROCESS
Follow these steps to declare an attribute:

1. Begin an attribute list declaration with `<!ATTLIST`.

2. Inside the declaration, first specify the associated element name — attributes can only exist within an element's opening tag. Thus, the associated element is the element that is meant to contain the attributes being defined.

3. Define the attribute's name (for example: *attribute1* or *attribute2*).

4. Specify the attribute type – choose from one of the 10 different data types, or simply choose CDATA (character data), which is the most general type, specifying that the attribute will consist of regular character data with no tags but possibly with entities.

5. Enter the default value (defaultvalue in Figure 3-3) – this will be the value for the attribute if none is explicitly set. Use the keywords #FIXED, #REQUIRED, or #IMPLIED to specify additional information about attribute defaults.

6. Repeat this process for as many attributes as there are in a particular element and terminate the attribute list with a closing >. Note that XML attributes are un-ordered, so the order in which you declare your attributes for a particular element makes no difference. An XML validator does not enforce a specific order for attributes.

Defining entities

DTDs offer a concise syntax for defining entities, which fall into two broad categories, *general entities* and *parameter identities*. The editing of both types of entities is supported by XMLSPY and is explained in the following sections.

GENERAL ENTITIES

As you learned in Chapter 2, XML entities are often used to substitute a frequently occurring text string with a unique symbolic representation. Suppose that you are writing a book on XMLSPY 5, and you are saving the book's contents into an industry standard XML-based book format, such as DocBook. To avoid having to write out *XMLSPY 5* hundreds of times, you could define a shorthand notation such as &spy;. Whenever *XMLSPY 5* is supposed to appear in the book text, you can simply type the entity notation instead. The XML processor substitutes the true value, XMLSPY 5, for the entity whenever it is processed.

In addition to letting you type fewer characters, entities have a huge added benefit in that they make a document easier to maintain. Suppose that one year from now, Altova releases a new version of XMLSPY called XMLSPY 2003. To update your book's text files to include this new product name, you only have to change one entity definition, as opposed to searching the entire document to make the change. Other possible uses for general entities include a navigation menu bar for a Web site or header/footer information common to more than one page.

To declare a general entity, type the following line of code into your DTD:

```
<!ENTITY generalentityname "substitute text">
```

For example, the following line of code defines an entity called &spy; that has the value of XMLSPY 5:

```
<!ENTITY &spy; "XMLSPY 5">
```

As shown in the following code, a general entity definition can contain nested entities:

```
<!ENTITY product "XMLSPY 5">
<!ENTITY edition "Enterprise Edition">
<!ENTITY spy "&product; &edition;">
```

In this case, &spy; resolves to XMLSPY 5 Enterprise Edition. *Circular* entity references (when two entity definitions both reference each other) are not permitted, however, and can cause unpredictable results.

General entities are also ideal for representing special symbols such as currency, mathematical, and other symbols that don't fit on a 101-key English keyboard. In your XMLSPY 5 book DTD, you can use the following code to define an entity called copy with a value of "&#xA9", which is the Unicode character reference for the copyright symbol (©):

```
<!ENTITY copy "&#xA9;">
```

General entity definitions can be used in a DTD for sections where you are specifying shortcuts for text that will be later used as document content; they cannot function as part of a DTD's internal structure or markup. The following example makes this point by illegally trying to use the entity &pcd;, whose value is the reserved word, "(#PCDATA)".:

```
<!ENTITY PCD "(#PCDATA)" >
...
<!ENTITY firstname &pcd; >
<!ENTITY lastname &pcd; >
```

It's illegal to use the entity &pcd; in this way as a shortcut for defining an entity. However, you can use &pcd; in a completely different way — inside a paragraph within your document:

```
...
<paragraph>Element content often consists of Parsed Character Data - &pcd;
...
</paragraph>
```

In this case, the &pcd; entity resolves to be part of the instance document's content. Of course, there are often situations in which you might want to define an entity for use in helping defining your DTD; and in this situation, *parameter entities* allow you to define strings of substitutable text within for use in specifying a DTD's internal structure or markup. Parameter entities are the subject of the next section.

PARAMETER ENTITIES

Parameter entities reference data which itself becomes a part of the DTD. They are not meant for substitution of anything that appears in the contents of an XML document. You declare a *parameter entity* by typing the following line of code into your DTD:

```
<!ENTITY % parameterentityname "substitute text">
```

The *parameter entity* declaration is the same as the *general entity* declaration except that it has a percent symbol before the entity name. To reference a parameter entity, simply type the percent sign (%), followed by the parameter entity's name, and terminate with a semicolon. For example, the invalid general entity example of the previous section can be fixed using parameter entities as follows:

```
<!ENTITY % pcd "(#PCDATA)" >
...
<!ENTITY firstname %pcd; >
<!ENTITY lastname %pcd; >
```

The typical use of parameter entities in a DTD usually falls into one of two categories, both of which serve to modularize and increase the reusability of your DTD. The following sections explain these two categories.

SUBSTITUTING FREQUENTLY REOCCURRING MARKUP   If a long string of text is repeated in multiple locations throughout a DTD, it is an ideal candidate for a parameter entity. Creating a parameter entity can save typing and make updating the DTD easier if the string of text happens to change. As an example, suppose that there is an attribute field, states, that is an enumeration of two-letter codes representing U.S. states and territories:

```
<!ENTITY % states "( AL|AR|AZ|CA|CO|CT|DC|DE|FL|GA|GU|HI|IA|ID|
IL|IN|KS|KY|LA|MA|MD|ME|MI|MN|MO|MS|MT|NC|ND|NE|NH|NJ|NM|NV|NY|OH|
OK|OR|PA|PR|RI|SC|SD|TN|TX|UT|VA|VI|VT|WA|WI|WV|WY)">
```

Now suppose that a DTD contains several elements, all of which contain an attribute whose value must correspond to an official U.S. state or territory two-letter abbreviation. Rather than retyping the long enumeration of valid tokens, you could simply do something like this:

```
<!ELEMENT shipping-address ( ... ) >
<!ATTLIST shipping-address state %state; #REQUIRED>

<!ELEMENT billing-address ( ... ) >
<!ATTLIST billing-address state %state; #REQUIRED>
```

```
<!ELEMENT mailing-address ( ... ) >
<!ATTLIST mailing-address state %state; #REQUIRED>
```

In addition to the bonus of less typing, the DTD is more modular. If the company in this example ever expanded to offer services to both Canada and the United States, updating all address-related elements to support the two-letter abbreviations corresponding to Canadian provinces and territories would only require modifying the one parameter entity definition. Another example of this kind of substitution can be found in the HTML specification. The W3C has made extensive use of parameter entities to define attributes common to many elements, including name, title, ID, and various styles.

COMBINING DTDS USING PARAMETER ENTITIES   Another common use of parameter entities is to combine multiple DTDs. Suppose that you need to build a single DTD which draws from externally defined DTDs that are either publicly available or that you have previously made. As an example, a new DTD for an online store might contain the products and address structures from another DTD. Here you could accelerate DTD development by using an *external parameter entity reference* as shown in the following code:

```
<?xml version="1.0" encoding="UTF-8"?>
<!ENTITY % product SYSTEM "c:\dtds\product.dtd">
<!ENTITY % address SYSTEM "c:\dtds\address.dtd">
%product;
%address;
<!-- Define the rest of your DTD here -->
...
```

Again, just as in the DOCTYPE declaration, the use of the SYSTEM keyword here also tells the XML parser to fetch the DTD from an external location.

This usage of parameter entities in this example is similar to how you might use the C/C++ #include preprocessor directive to import a header file containing constants. Although parameter entities do increase the overall modularity of a DTD, if you find yourself making heavy use of parameter entities in your DTDs, I highly recommend the use of XML Schemas to achieve even greater flexibility and modularity.

Declaring a DTD

Now that I've explained all the syntax involved in creating a DTD, including defining elements, attributes, and entities, take a minute to type the contents of the `book.dtd` file (as it was listed earlier in the chapter) into your own `book.dtd` file.

After you complete the `book.dtd` file, you can use it to create and validate other book instance documents. To use an instance document in conjunction with a DTD (for validation or editing purposes), an instance document must tell the XML processor where to find the corresponding DTD. The line of code that does this is called a *document type declaration*.

Be careful not to confuse a *document type declaration* with a *Document Type Definition* — even though they have the same initials. A document type declaration is the line in an XML file that links the file with its document type definition. The document type definition file defines all the rules for that particular class of document.

XMLSPY can associate an instance document (`bookinstance.xml`) with its corresponding DTD (`book.dtd`). To do this, open your `bookinstance.xml` file in the main editing window so that it is the active document in the XMLSPY editing environment. Then choose DTD/Schema → Assign DTD, as shown in Figure 3-4.

Figure 3-4: Assigning a DTD to an XML document.

Note that XMLSPY automatically inserts the required document type declaration into the `bookinstance.xml` file, as shown in Figure 3-5.

```
Document Type Declaration
            DTD Name    External DTD Specifier
              |            |
<!DOCTYPE book SYSTEM
"C:\Program Files\Altova\XMLSPY\Examples\xmlspyhandbook\ch3\book.dtd">
          └─ Path to External DTD
```
Figure 3-5: XMLSPY automatically inserts the DTD at the top of the XML file.

The parts of the document type declaration have been labeled in Figure 3-5. The following list describes these parts in more detail.

- ◆ `<!DOCTYPE:` The special symbol that starts a document type declaration.

- ◆ *book*: The DTD name. The name must correspond to the name of root element for the XML document that contains this document type declaration.

- ◆ `SYSTEM:` The keyword that instructs the XML parser to look for an externally defined DTD at a specified location.

- ◆ **Path to the external DTD:** The path that specifies a DTD location in the form of any Uniform Resource Identifier (URI), such as a path on the local file system or a Web URL.

Validating and editing XML documents using XMLSPY

At this point, you've built both a DTD and an instance document and have associated the instance document with the DTD using a document type declaration. Now, you're ready to create, edit, and validate XML instance documents in XMLSPY.

XMLSPY's editing and validation support applies to any XML document with an associated content model; the content can be expressed as either a DTD or an XML Schema. Therefore, although in this section we show editing and validation XML documents with DTDs, the whole section is also applicable to XML Schemas.

In this section, you start by creating a new document called `newbook.xml`.

1. Choose File → New or press the New File button on the main taskbar. The Create New Document window appears.

2. Select XML Document and click OK. The New File dialog box shown in Figure 3-6 appears. It asks whether the new instance document you are creating should be based on a DTD or an XML Schema.

3. Select the DTD option and click OK. If you want instead to edit and validate an instance document using an XML Schema, you simply choose the XML Schema option.

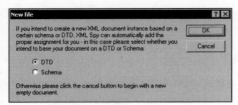

Figure 3-6: The New File dialog box.

4. When XMLSPY asks you to choose the DTD (see Figure 3-7), browse to the `book.dtd` file that you built earlier, click OK, and you're finished!

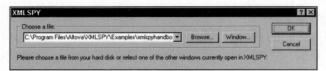

Figure 3-7: Open the DTD that you want to associate with the XML instance document.

When you create a new XML document based on a content model (in this case, a DTD), XMLSPY automatically inspects the DTD or XML Schema and creates all mandatory elements and attributes, filling in default values whenever possible, as shown in the following listing:

```
<?xml version="1.0" encoding="UTF-8"?>
<!DOCTYPE book SYSTEM "C:\Program Files\Altova\XMLSPY\Examples\
xmlspyhandbook\ch3\book.dtd">
<book isbn="" language="">
   <title></title>
   <author-list>
      <author>
         <firstname></firstname>
         <lastname></lastname>
      </author>
   </author-list>
</book>
```

XMLSPY includes several XML editing and XML document validation features that are grouped together into the category of *intelligent editing* and are available in both Text view and Grid view. The following list describes the intelligent editing features:

◆ **Code sensing:** As you type new elements in your XML document, drop-down boxes appear helping you remember which elements are defined in your document (shown in Figure 3-8).

◆ **Auto-completion:** XMLSPY will insert an element's closing tag and mandatory child elements and attributes as you type.

◆ **Entry Helper windows:** Three configurable helper windows showing you the elements, attributes, and entities that are in the scope of the cursor position – that is, elements, attributes and entities that may appear in the document at the present cursor location.

◆ **Document validation:** Single-click document validation with error high-lighting and reporting (shown in the next section).

Figure 3-8: XMLSPY offers intelligent editing support in both Text view and Grid view.

The code sensing and auto-completion features described in the preceding list are very straightforward. Entry Helper windows and document validation require some additional explanation and are discussed in the following sections.

ENTRY HELPER WINDOWS

Entry Helper windows for elements, attributes, and entities appear by default on the right side of the XMLSPY editing environment in both Text view and Grid view. If you click an element or attribute in a Entry Helper window, it is automatically inserted into the current document at the cursor position. One kind of Entry Helper window, the Elements window (shown in Figure 3-9), lists all the elements in the scope of the current XML document.

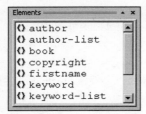

Figure 3-9: The Elements window
displays all available elements.

The Attributes window is context-sensitive. It lists only the attributes that are in scope according to the position of the cursor. Two mandatory elements of the book element are listed in the Attributes window shown in Figure 3-10.

The Entities window displays the five default XML entities, in addition to any general entities declared within your content model. The © general entity defined in the book.dtd file is resolved and displayed in an Entities window shown in Figure 3-11. If you are editing a DTD file, any parameter entities you defined are visible; any other XML document general entities and built-in entities appear in the Entities window.

Figure 3-10: A context-sensitive Attributes
window shows attributes that are in scope.

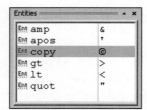

Figure 3-11: The Entities window
displays all available entities.

TIP If you are editing a DTD or an XML Schema while simultaneously working on an associated instance document in XMLSPY, you can force a manual refresh of Entry Helper windows after making changes to the content model. Choose XML → Update Helper Entries and make sure that the contents of the Entry Helper windows reflect your most current content model revision.

Remember, if you accidentally close a Entry Helper window and want to get it back, or if you are editing a big document and want to turn off the entry windows to free up more space, choose Window → Entry Helper. You can control all the functionality of Entry Helper windows with this command.

DOCUMENT VALIDATION

XMLSPY can validate your XML documents for you — simply click the green check mark button on the main toolbar or choose XML → Validate. The validator can also be invoked by pressing the F8 key. If XMLSPY determines that an XML document is invalid, it highlights the line containing the error and provides an error message at the bottom of the main editing window explaining the situation. For example, in Figure 3-12, the validator has found an error and the error message is `Required attribute 'isbn' of parent element "book" is expected before first child element`. Fix the error and click the Revalidate button located on the status bar at the bottom of the main editing area. Continue this process until you get no errors and have validated your XML document.

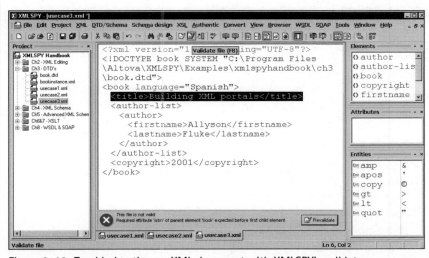

Figure 3-12: Troubleshooting an XML document with XMLSPY's validator.

Editing DTDs with XMLSPY

Earlier in this chapter, I made the case that you should develop your content model (either a DTD or an XML Schema) before editing any XML instance documents. One common question is: What happens if you create various XML document fragments before having formalized a content model, or if you inherited an XML application that doesn't use DTDs or XML Schemas? First, you should write: "I will not create XML documents without an associated DTD or XML Schema" a hundred times on a whiteboard or self-administer some other hard punishment. Seriously, XMLSPY offers two ways to jump-start DTD- or XML-Schema–based content model development, both of which are described in the following sections.

INFERRING A DTD BY ANALYZING ONE OR MORE INSTANCE DOCUMENTS

XMLSPY can inspect one or more XML document fragments and generate the corresponding DTD automatically. In the Chapter 3 project folder, you will find three related files named usecase1.xml, usecase2.xml, and usecase3.xml. They are all XML document fragments with no associated content model. In this example, I show how XMLSPY can automatically generate as much as 80% of the book.dtd file that you manually created earlier in this chapter. The use case files are listed in the following code:

```
<!-- Code listing for usecase1.xml -->
<?xml version="1.0" encoding="UTF-8"?>
<book isbn="1-8745-3543-7" language="English">
    <title>The XMLSPY Game</title>
    <logo file="cover.gif"/>
    <author-list>
      <author>
          <firstname>James</firstname>
          <lastname>Choi</lastname>
      </author>
    </author-list>
    <copyright>1999</copyright>
</book>

<!-- Code listing for usecase2.xml -->
<?xml version="1.0" encoding="UTF-8"?>
<book isbn="4-3241-4900-1" language="German">
    <title>XML the Hard way</title>
    <logo file="xml.gif"/>
    <author-list>
      <author>
          <firstname>Dilip</firstname>
          <lastname>Ogale</lastname>
```

```
      </author>
      <author>
         <firstname>Christopher</firstname>
         <lastname>Williams</lastname>
      </author>
   </author-list>
   <copyright>2002</copyright>
</book>

<!-- Code listing for usecase3.xml -->
<?xml version="1.0" encoding="UTF-8"?>
<book isbn="5-3324-4678-2" language="Spanish">
   <title>Building XML portals</title>
   <author-list>
      <author>
         <firstname>Allyson</firstname>
         <lastname>Fluke</lastname>
      </author>
   </author-list>
   <copyright>2001</copyright>
</book>
```

The three use cases are all book-related instance documents with a few minor differences: usecase2.xml has two authors whereas the others have only one, and usecase3.xml has no logo element. There is sufficient information contained in these three use case documents for XMLSPY to autogenerate a near-complete DTD. To do so, select all the use cases in the Project menu clicking on each file icon while holding down the Shift key. With the three icons selected and highlighted in the Project menu, right-click anywhere on the highlighted region. Then choose Generate DTD/Schema from the submenu that appears (see Figure 3-13).

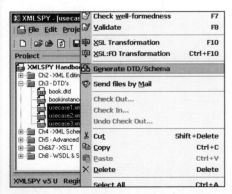

Figure 3-13: XMLSPY can autogenerate a
content model from an instance document.

Next, a generate DTD/Schema panel appears. Select DTD as the desired output language for the autogenerated DTD and click OK.

 Although this example highlights the autogeneration of a DTD, the auto-generated content models can be expressed in many different schema dialects, including DTD, XML Schema, DCD, XML Data (XDR), and Microsoft BizTalk Schema. You choose the desired output format in the Generate DTD/Schema configuration panel.

XMLSPY displays the autogenerated DTD as an external DTD file within the main editing window; the contents of the DTD are listed in the following code:

```
<?xml version="1.0" encoding="UTF-8"?>
<!ELEMENT author (firstname, lastname)>
<!ELEMENT author-list (author+)>
<!ELEMENT book (title, logo?, author-list, copyright)>
<!ATTLIST book
     isbn (1-8745-3543-7 | 4-3241-4900-1 | 5-3324-4678-2) #REQUIRED
     language (English | German | Spanish) #REQUIRED
>
<!ELEMENT copyright (#PCDATA)>
<!ELEMENT firstname (#PCDATA)>
<!ELEMENT lastname (#PCDATA)>
<!ELEMENT logo EMPTY>
<!ATTLIST logo
     file (cover.gif | xml.gif) #REQUIRED
>
<!ELEMENT title (#PCDATA)>
```

This autogenerated DTD is not an exact duplicate of the book.dtd file that you manually created earlier. But XMLSPY has inspected the three use case documents and has properly inferred some important aspects of your book content model, including the following:

◆ An author-list consists of at least one or more authors.

◆ Logo is an optional, empty element.

◆ isbn and language are required elements.

◆ The language attribute is an enumeration of possible values: English, German, Spanish.

Therefore, the autogenerated DTD is a reasonable content model approximation. You can manually refine the content model later by using your understanding of DTD syntax, as well as XMLSPY's Text view or Grid view.

The autogenerated content model could have resulted in an even closer approximation had there been more than three use case documents for XMLSPY to use as sample data.

CONVERTING CONTENT MODELS EXPRESSED IN ONE LANGUAGE TO ANOTHER

XMLSPY includes translation utilities to convert from a content model expressed in one schema dialect to another. XMLSPY supports content-model conversion from any combination of two schema dialects taken from the following group: DTD, DCD, XML-Data (XDR), Microsoft BizTalk Schema, and W3C XML Schema — for a total of 10 possible distinct conversions. In this section, I show you how to convert a content model expressed in one language to another. First, open the content model that you wish to convert from. Then, choose Convert → Convert DTD/Schema. The convert DTD/Schema window appears (see Figure 3-14).

Next, select the desired target language for the content-model conversion and click OK. The new file appears as a new pane within the XMLSPY editing environment.

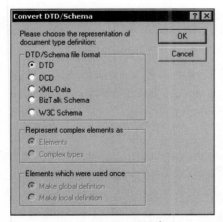

Figure 3-14: The Convert DTD/Schema window.

Conversion of an XML Schema to a DTD will be *lossy*. In other words, a considerable amount of information stored in the XML Schema–based content model is lost when converting to a DTD due to limitations of the DTD specification.

Limitations of DTDs

Clearly the biggest strength of the use of DTDs is their simplicity and concise syntax. Regrettably, this conciseness comes at the price of a few potential deficiencies, which are appropriate for motivating the upcoming two chapters dedicated to covering XML Schemas.

NOT XML

Document Type Definitions are specified using a separate, non-XML-based metalanguage which has very little to do with XML; they can't even be parsed by an XML parser.

NO NAMESPACE SUPPORT

All declarations in a DTD are global. This means that the name of a valid element inside an XML instance document must have the same element name as defined by its respective DTD. The unfortunate side effect of global declarations is that you end up with a *naming collision* if you define two different elements with the same name, even if they appear in separate contexts. This makes the use of DTDs potentially dangerous in B2B applications that are required to use content models of various companies. The XML Schema introduces support for namespaces, which enables a content author to overcome these naming limitations.

NO DATA TYPES

The absence of a mechanism for using existing predefined data types, as well as a mechanism for defining custom data types, makes it challenging to use DTD-based content models in conjunction with other strongly typed environments. These environments include relational databases, which contain an abundance of predefined SQL data types, as well as strongly typed programming languages such as Java and C++.

NOT OBJECT-ORIENTED

DTDs were created before the widespread usage of object-oriented programming methodologies. Object-oriented programming languages have helped to advance modern software development practices, particularly through the use of encapsulation, inheritance, and polymorphism. It can be challenging to use DTDs in conjunction with modern object-oriented programming languages such as C++, Java, or C# because DTDs have no notion of object-oriented features.

Summary

This chapter stressed the importance of creating content models for constraining and validating XML documents, which can be expressed using various schema dialects, most commonly DTDs and the XML Schema. This chapter covered these topics:

- Document Type Definition syntax, including defining elements, attributes, and entities, and how to reference a DTD from an XML document

- Editing and validating documents in XMLSPY

- Generation of content models through analyzing one or more related instance documents and outputting the resulting content models in a variety of different schema languages

- Conversion of content models expressed from one schema language to another

In the next chapter, I cover building content models expressed in an XML Schema using XMLSPY.

Chapter 4

Editing XML Schemas with XMLSPY

IN THIS CHAPTER

- ◆ Viewing XML Schemas using the XMLSPY Schema Editor
- ◆ Designing and building your first XML Schema
- ◆ Understanding XML Schema syntax and language constructs

THE XML SCHEMA SPECIFICATION, with all its power and flexibility, is considerably more complicated in syntax than DTDs. The XML Schema specification takes up about 200 pages of documentation, and entire books have been written about the XML Schema. DTDs, on the other hand, don't even have a dedicated specification. They are documented by a small section within the XML 1.0 specification. So although it may have been quite easy to write a DTD in Text view, in practice it is considerably more difficult to create any non-trivial XML Schema without the help of an XML Schema Editor. In this chapter, I walk you through using XMLSPY's built-in XML Schema Editor. The Editor supports viewing and editing XML Schemas based on the W3C's final recommendation of May 2, 2001.

This chapter begins by having you view an XML Schema in XMLSPY's Schema Design view. You become familiar with navigating the user interface and also learn about the various controls and options. Then, you use the XML Schema Editor to create a sample XML Schema, which you can use to edit and validate XML documents. Finally, you turn your attention to the technical syntax of XML Schemas as I review the important XML Schema constructs and how to edit them by hand. (The discussion on XML Schema syntax continues in the next chapter on advanced XML Schema development.) By the end of this chapter, you should have a solid understanding of XML Schemas so that you can effectively create and work with ones that are fairly sophisticated and complex.

Viewing an XML Schema in Schema Design View

As an XML-based metalanguage for structuring XML documents, the XML Schema describes constraints that govern the order and sequence of elements and specifies permissible value spaces for all data used inside the content model. XML Schema is a full recommendation from the World Wide Web Consortium (W3C) and has massive industry support — clearly, it is meant to be the successor of the DTD because no future versions of DTDs are planned. I believe that the majority of future content-model development will be done using XML Schema. Therefore, this chapter is a critical topic for XML developers.

XML Schema 1.0 is the result of more than two years of work by the W3C group working on XML Schema. If you have worked with an earlier beta version of XML Schema, XMLSPY can convert XML Schemas based on the April 7th 2000 Working Draft or on the Oct. 24th Candidate Recommendation that concerns XML Schemas conforming to the XML Schema 1.0 final recommendation.

To help you become familiar with navigating XMLSPY's Schema/WSDL Design view (Schema Design view for short), take a look at the prebuilt Purchase Order Schema shown in Figure 4-1. To access this schema, double-click order.xsd in the ch4 folder.

All example files used in this chapter are available in the XMLSPY Handbook Project, which installs itself as the default project if you are using the exclusive version of XMLSPY included with this book. If you are not using the version of XMLSPY from the CD (perhaps you downloaded a version from the Web), you can still access the example files. Simply locate the XMLSPYHandbook.spp file on the CD and copy it, along with all subdirectories, to your local file system. Then open the file by choosing Project → Open Project. The files used in this chapter are located in the ch4 folder.

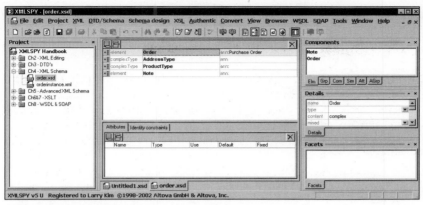

Figure 4–1: The XMLSPY Schema Overview page.

 Schema Design view is the default view when you open an XML Schema (.xsd is the file extension for XML Schemas). Just like any other XML document, however, you can also view XML Schemas in both Text view and Enhanced Grid view. Edits made in one view are synchronized with all other views. To change the default view associated with a particular file type, choose Tools → Options → File Types.

It is important to point out that only XML Schemas (and WSDL files that use some XML Schema syntax) can be viewed in Schema Design view. Attempting to view any other type of XML document in Schema view results in the error message Unable to show schema. In the Purchase Order Schema displayed in Figure 4-1, the Entry Helper windows on the right side are still there. They are usually used to display information about elements, attributes, and entities; in this case, however, they display more XML Schema–specific information, including information about components, details, and facets, as shown in Figure 4-2. All these properties will be discussed in the next few sections.

In the main editing area (the center region of Figure 4-1), XMLSPY displays a tabular listing of all schema components, such as globally defined elements and attributes that are defined in the schema — in this case Order, AddressType, ProductType, and Note. The schema components section of the Schema Overview page is shown in Figure 4-3.

Figure 4-2: XML Schema–specific Entry Helper windows in the Schema Overview page.

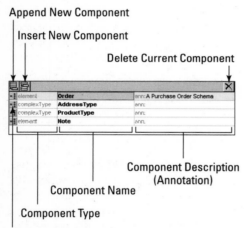

Figure 4-3: XMLSPY's Schema Overview page displays a tabular listing of all the XML Schema components defined in the current XML Schema file.

To view or graphically edit a particular XML Schema component, click the tree button that appears immediately to the left of each schema component name (labeled as View Graphical Representation of Schema Component in Figure 4-3). For example, if you click the tree button adjacent to the ProductType schema component, you see the ProductType component in a graphical editing view.

Throughout this book, whenever I want you to view or edit an XML Schema component in a graphical tree view, I simply ask you to *expand* the schema element. When you stumble across this instruction, click the tree button next to the indicated component to view it graphically. I refer to the editable, graphical view of an XML Schema simply as Schema Editing view.

Viewing schema components

In the Schema Editing view (available after you expand a component listed on the Schema Overview page), an XML Schema component is displayed as one or more colored boxes and connecting lines. Elements are displayed as rectangles, and attributes for a selected element are listed in the Attributes window located immediately below the schema diagram (see Figure 4-4). Entity declarations, per se, are not supported in the XML Schema. However, some other XML Schema language constructs discussed later in this chapter can be used in a similar way to entity declarations. An XML Schema component resembles a tree whose branches can be expanded or collapsed in Schema Editing view. Within the Schema Editing view, nodes can be expanded or collapsed by clicking on the plus (+) or minus (–) signs that appear on each side of each compositor. The *compositor* is the connector that specifies a relationship between parent and child elements.

Figure 4-4 shows the `ProductType` global complex element. It is a sequence of five elements — `Description`, `Price`, `Quantity`, `Ship-Date`, and `Note`. Both `Ship-Date`, and `Note` are drawn using broken (dotted) rectangular boarders and connecting lines, signifying that they are optional elements. Also, the `Note` element is a reference to a global element defined outside the `ProductType` definition; this is denoted by a little arrow button inside the `Note` element. By contrast, all other elements are defined locally within the `ProductType` definition. To navigate back to the Schema Overview page, click the Back button located at the top-left corner of Figure 4-4.

In Figure 4-4, I have configured Schema Editing view to display additional data type information for each element; this is displayed inside their respective element box diagrams. I talk more about changing the Schema Editing view's configuration later in the chapter. Briefly, you customize the configuration by choosing Schema Design → View Config. The Schema Display Configuration panel appears. There are two possible ways to configure an XML Schema diagram to display additional information:

◆ Click the Predefined button, which will load some default schema display settings (this is what I usually do).

◆ If you want to manually specify exactly what details to show on an XML Schema diagram, click the Add New Entry button (toward the top-left of the panel) and a new row appears. Click the drop-down arrow and choose the kind of information you want to display (`type`, `default`, `length`, and so on). Repeat this until you have added the number of additional details you want to display on the schema diagram; then click OK.

Back Button
(Return to Schema Overview page)

Compositor—click on + or - on
either side to expand or collapse
schema diagram

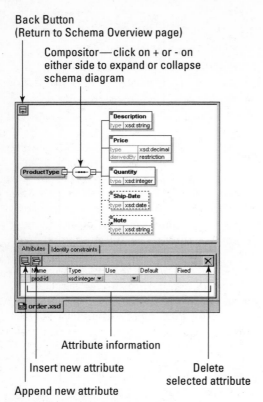

Attribute information

Insert new attribute

Delete
selected attribute

Append new attribute

**Figure 4–4: Viewing the ProductType schema
component in the Schema Editing view.**

Information about the currently selected element's attributes (including the
attribute's type and default value) is displayed in the Attribute Overview pane at the
bottom of Figure 4-4. The Attribute Overview pane also has buttons for inserting,
appending, and deleting attributes for the currently selected element.

The Schema Design view consists of two pages: the Schema Overview page,
which is a tabular listing of schema components defined in the current XML
Schema, and the Schema Editing page, which is where you graphically edit a
schema. To navigate from an XML Schema component viewed in the
Schema Editing page back to the Schema Overview page, click the Back button located on the top-left side of the Schema Editing view. Throughout this
book, when I ask you to return from the Schema Editing page to the Schema
Overview page, simply click the Back button to do so.

Editing XML Schemas in XMLSPY

You have had a chance to learn how to navigate through Schema Design view by reviewing a prebuilt schema. Next, you build the Purchase Order Schema of the previous section starting from scratch with the XMLSPY Schema Editor. This will be a relatively light technical process initially, but you will delve into the technical details of XML Schema syntax later on in the chapter in the section "XML Schema Syntax."

A major use of XML Schema is for describing business objects. The business objects are typically data elements (price, quantity, date, and so on) as well as prose-oriented, document-like elements (product descriptions, customer remarks, and so on). It is common for an XML Schema to contain both data and document-like elements. In the next example, you build a sample Purchase Order Schema. This is a very common example, as it could potentially be used in conjunction with other XML technologies in various business-to-business (B2B) application scenarios.

Choose File → New, and select XML Schema (.xsd). Save the file to your local hard drive as myorder.xsd. In the file, you should see an empty Schema Overview table. Double-click the text ENTER_NAME_OF_ROOT_ELEMENT_HERE and type **Order** because the principle element you are trying to build is the Purchase Order Schema. Then, double-click the Ann (annotation) column and type **A purchase order schema**. Your file should look like Figure 4-5.

Figure 4–5: Creating the Order element.

Any edits that you make in Schema Editing view are automatically reflected in the underlying source document. To verify this, switch back to Text view periodically so that you can see the code that XMLSPY is inserting for you as you are editing in Schema Design view. Here is the code listing for your sample XML Schema, thus far:

```
<?xml version="1.0" encoding="UTF-8"?>
<xsd:schema xmlns:xsd="http://www.w3.org/2001/XMLSchema"
elementFormDefault="qualified" attributeFormDefault="unqualified">
   <xsd:element name="Order">
      <xsd:annotation>
         <xsd:documentation>A purchase order schema</xsd:documentation>
      </xsd:annotation>
   </xsd:element>
</xsd:schema>
```

Using namespaces

In the partial XML Schema code listing shown in the preceding section, notice that the element names are all prefixed with the label `xsd:`, and the `xsd:schema` element declares an attribute called `xmlns:xsd` with the value `http://www.w3.org/2001/XMLSchema`. XML Schema makes extensive use of XML namespaces, a built-in mechanism for preventing naming *collisions*. A collision occurs when two symbols in an XML document (for example, names of elements, attributes, or entities) are defined using the same name, resulting in an error.

In our collaborative world today, it is likely that an XML application needs to process documents from different parties — a B2B exchange frequently processes Purchase Order Schemas from many companies, each representing its data elements in a different way. If used within the same document, the XML processing application requires a way to differentiate between the various data definitions. Consider the differences between the two hypothetical `Order` elements shown in the following code:

```
<Order>
   <ShippingAddress>
      <Street1>234 Anystreet</Street1>
      ...
<Order>
```

The preceding uses the `Order` element in a completely different way than it's used to describe orders from the company president in the next code block:

```
<Order>
   <from>Company President</from>
   <to>IT Department</to>
   <instructions>Convert website to XML-driven application
Immediately</instructions>
   ...
</Order>
```

Clearly, confusing the two `Order` elements would likely result in unpredictable program behavior. XML namespaces help prevent naming collisions and require only minimal work in both the XML Schemas and the XML instance document itself. If you assume that the two different `Order` elements are defined in two different XML Schemas, the first step is to assign a distinct name to each XML Schema. The name that you assign to an XML Schema in order to uniquely identify and differentiate it from other schemas is known as a *target namespace*. Assume that the boss's orders are described in an XML Schema with a target namespace of `http://www.company.com/management`, whereas the Purchase Order XML Schema is defined in the namespace `http://www.company.com/sales`. Specifying a target namespace in XML Schema ensures that your custom XML vocabulary is not confused with any other XML vocabulary, provided that the target namespace you choose is indeed unique.

 In Chapter 5, I show you an example of how you can build an XML Schema that imports type definitions from an externally defined XML Schema, using XML namespaces.

The second step in using namespaces is associating the namespace with a prefix in the XML instance document. In the previous example with the two conflicting Order elements (the boss's order and the purchase order), you could define two short prefixes: mgmt for the order coming from the company management and sales for the order coming from the sales department. Then, you could associate the prefixes with their respective target namespaces. The two different Order elements are then *qualified* (that is, differentiated from each other) by prepending their respective prefixes to the element name, as in mgmt:Order and sales:Order.

There is nothing special about the prefixes mgmt and sales. They are just a nonpermanent, abbreviated form of the full XML Schema target namespace – they are required to be unique in that specific instance document, but do not need to be unique across space and time. Therefore, using namespaces requires a two-step process: first, creating a globally unique namespace name (a target namespace) for your own XML vocabulary, and second, associating the namespace name with a short prefix. Listing 4-1 provides an example XML instance document that uses Order elements defined in two different XML Schemas.

Listing 4-1: An Instance Document That Uses Multiple Namespaces

```
<?xml version="1.0" encoding="UTF-8"?>
<mgmt:Order xmlns:mgmt="http://www.altova.com/management"
xmlns:sales="http://www.altova.com/sales"
xmlns:xsd="http://www.w3.org/2001/XMLSchema-instance"
xsd:schemaLocation="http://www.altova.com/management management.xsd
http://www.altova.com/sales sales.xsd" ... >
        <mgmt:to>XML programmer</mgmt:to>
        <mgmt:from>The Boss</mgmt:from>
        ...
        <sales:Order>
    <sales:ProductName>XMLSPY 5 Enterprise Ed.</sales:ProductName>
                </sales:Order>
</mgmt:Order>
```

UNDERSTANDING NAMESPACE MAPPINGS AND PREFIXES

Although some parts of Listing 4-1 have been omitted for the sake of brevity, two different `Order` elements are used that are presumably defined in different XML Schemas (not shown here). What you do know is that the two XML Schemas are uniquely identified by their respective target namespaces `http://www.altova.com/management/` and `http://www.altova.com/sales`. Figure 4-6 illustrates how you can associate the target namespaces of the two XML Schemas with the prefixes `mgmt` and `sales`.

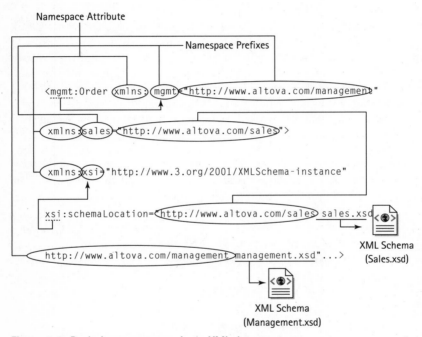

Figure 4–6: Declaring namespaces in an XML document.

You associate a target namespace with a namespace prefix by using a special attribute: `xmlns:` (XML namespace). The characters immediately following the `xmlns:` attribute indicate the prefix name, and the attribute's value is the target namespace. You may introduce multiple namespaces anywhere within an XML document, although the scope of the namespace is implicitly determined by where you introduce it. If you want to use an element belonging to a particular namespace, the namespace must be introduced as an attribute in either the current element or in one of its ancestor elements. In the instance document example of Figure 4-6, I introduced three namespaces inside the `mgmt:Order` element: `http://www.altova.com/sales` (`sales`), `http://www.altova.com/management`

(mgmt), and `http://www.w3c.org/2001/XML-Schema-instance` (xsi). The xsi namespace is used by the XML Schema processor to locate a physical location of the XML Schema file that corresponds to each namespace (in the form of a URI to a file on the network or local file system).

Two commonly used namespaces—`http://www.w3.org/2001/XMLSchema` and `http://www.w3.org/2001/XML-Schema-instance`—do not require that you specify the path to a corresponding physical XML Schema file. These two namespaces are frequently used by XML Schema–aware processors. Consequently, the processor already has its own internal copy of these well-known schemas and knows where to locate them. In this book, I use either xsd or xs as the namespace prefix to refer to the `http://www.w3.org/2001/XMLSchema` namespace. It doesn't matter what prefix you choose, provided that you are consistent within a single file.

Although the concept of namespaces is relatively new to XML, namespaces are certainly not a new technological feature and are used extensively throughout most modern programming languages including Java Packages and C++ Namespaces.

DECLARING A TARGET NAMESPACE

Namespaces are guaranteed to prevent naming collisions only if the target namespace that you are using to name your XML Schema is globally unique across all XML Schemas. An XML Schema processor would fail if it happened to encounter two different schemas with the same target namespace. Because the whole point of a namespace name is to differentiate your XML vocabulary from other potentially similar XML vocabularies, you should pick a name that is unique, descriptive, and permanent. Figure 4-7 shows a possible namespace name for a schema example from this book.

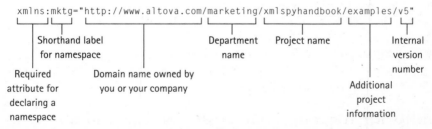

Figure 4-7: Declaring a target XML namespace name that is unique, descriptive, and permanent.

Because Internet domain names are, by definition, guaranteed to be unique, I recommend beginning your namespace with a domain name that you own or is registered to your company. When selecting your namespace, do not use a domain name that you do not own or is not affiliated with your company; this helps ensure that your chosen namespace is indeed unique. Next, include information such as your department name because, within a large organization, people in different departments could be building different XML Schemas. Append some information about the project for which you are using the XML Schema, followed by some kind of internal version number. Separate all this information by forward slashes. It is important to note that although a namespace's structure resembles a URL, it does not necessarily correspond to any physical resource on the Web (although some-times XML Schema authors do put a file at that location, but only because people confuse a namespace name with a Web resource and expect to find something there). Rather, your namespace is simply a string that is unlikely to be used by someone else and that provides some descriptive information about the schema author and the purpose of the XML Schema. Although the W3C does not provide any official guidance on how to name a namespace, I highly recommend this com-mon sense approach to naming namespaces to avoid naming collisions.

To declare a target namespace for the Purchase Order Schema, choose Schema Design → Schema Settings, click the Target Namespace button, and type **http://www.company.com/example/purchaseorder**. If you type nothing at all in the prefix column, you are setting your target namespace as the default namespace. As a result, any unqualified (that is, unprefixed) elements and attributes that you define in the current XML Schema will belong to the `http://www.company.com/example/purchase` namespace. XMLSPY automatically assigns `xmlns:="http://www.company.com/examples/purchaseorder"` as the target namespace for the current XML Schema file. Therefore, if you leave the prefix empty, there will be no prefix name after the `xmlns:` attribute, signifying the default namespace. By con-trast, if you explicitly enter a prefix, such as `myco`, to be used in conjunction with the target namespace, XMLSPY generates `xmlns:myco="http://www.company.com/examples/purchaseorder"` (substituting `company.com` to a domain name that you own or are affiliated with) as the target namespace assignment. In the event that you have explicitly specified a namespace prefix (that is, if the target name-space is not assigned to the default namespace), there are several other options in the Schema Settings panel, including the default element and attribute form. If you choose qualified, XMLSPY properly prefixes all user-defined elements and attrib-utes with the specified namespace prefix.

Building up the Purchase Order XML Schema

Now that you know something about namespaces, I want you to return to building the Purchase Order Schema. Expand the `Order` element in Schema Design view so that it can be visually edited. The example purchase order should be a sequence of elements such as an address (billing and/or shipping), product type, and a note to convey any special instructions. Each element is graphically depicted as a node (a rectangular box) in a diagram. Because the Order element contains child elements, it is said to be a *complex* type.

 Elements are classified in two categories: simple types and complex types. *Complex* types refer to elements that have either attributes or child elements or both. An element that contains only body content is considered a *simple* type. All attribute values are simple types because attributes cannot contain nested attributes or elements.

To add child elements to the Order element, first select the Order element so that it is highlighted. Next, right-click anywhere on the screen and a pop-up menu appears. Choose Add Child → Sequence. A compositor appears immediately to the right of the Order element. A sequence compositor enables you to add other elements. Be mindful of the order, however, because by default, the order in which you define the elements in your XML Schema is the same order in which they must appear within an XML instance document in order to be valid. First, build an address component that can be used for both billing and shipping addresses. Right-click the sequence compositor and choose Add Child → Element. A new (empty) element node appears. Double-click the New Element node and type **Address** as the name of the element.

The new Address is a complex element because it contains other child elements such as street name and apartment number (abbreviated as Street1 and Street2), as well as City, State, and Zip. Add a sequence compositor to the Address element, select the compositor, and then add five child elements to the compositor under the Address element. Name the elements Address1, Address2, City, State, and Zip. The partial diagram is shown in Figure 4-8. Make sure that yours looks similar, but don't worry if your diagram doesn't already display the type information. You add that next.

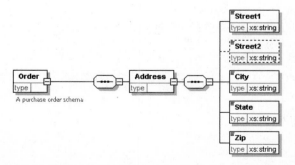

Figure 4–8: Building the Purchase Order Schema in Schema Design view.

Building Content Models with the XML Schema Editor

When you are building XML Schemas, the three most commonly used menu options are Add Child, Insert, and Append. These create new elements or compositors (sequence, choice, all, and so on). All three operations are performed relative to the currently selected node in the XML Schema Editing view, which is highlighted (typically in blue). The operations are accessible through a right-click menu.

The main difference between the three menu options is that the Add Child option creates the desired element or compositor at a lower depth than the currently selected node — in other words, farther to the right of the schema diagram. Insert and Append create the desired element or compositor at the same depth as the currently selected node, making the element or compositor a sibling of the currently selected node. In the case of Insert, the new node is placed on top of the currently selected node. In the case of Append, the new element or compositor is placed as the bottom-most element at the current level. Of course, there are many invalid menu options. For example, if you select the root element of a particular schema component as the current node, you cannot Insert or Append sibling elements or compositors because there can be only one root element per schema component. To make this clear, invalid menu selections are grayed out.

Take a moment to play around with the XML Schema Editor, trying out when it is possible to use the Add Child, Insert, or Append elements or compositors. Remember that if you make a mistake, you can always select the element or compositor and do one of the following: press the Delete key, drag it over to the correct location, or press Ctrl+Z (Undo).

So far, both Order and Address elements have been complex types because they both contain child elements. By contrast, the elements Street1, Street2, City, State, and Zip are known as *simple types* because they contain no attributes and no child elements — they contain only text content. Elements that are simple types must be assigned a corresponding data type that restricts the value space (that is, places constraints on what kind of textual information is considered to be valid). If a type declaration is omitted, the default value of anyType (an unconstrained value) is assumed. To assign a data type to an element, select the node, such as the Street1 element, on the Schema Editing page and choose from one of the many built-in XML Schema simple types. In the Details Entry Helper window, choose the xs:string type (see Figure 4-9).

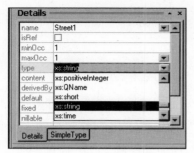

Figure 4–9: Assigning one of the XML Schema built-in data types to the Street1 simple type.

Figure 4-9 shows a partial listing of some of the many built-in XML Schema data types. In this screen shot, the XML Schema language constructs have all been prefixed with the `xs` prefix, which is the prefix associated with the `http://www.w3.org/2001/XMLSchema` namespace in this particular document. The `xs:` prefix has no meaning outside the context of this particular XML Schema, and `xsd` works just as well.

Assign a string data type to both `Street2` and `City`. Addresses often require two lines, with the second line used for apartment numbers and so on. You can specify the second line as an optional element by selecting the `Street2` element, right-clicking, and checking Optional. Alternatively, you can make this choice optional by setting the `minOcc` (minimum occurrence) equal to `0` in the Details Entry Helper window. Notice that the default for new elements is a `minOcc` equal to `1`, which means that the element is required. The contents of the `State` element is also set to a string; but you can further restrict the value space of the string by specifying an enumeration of string tokens containing valid two-character U.S. state abbreviations:

1. Select the `State` element on the Schema Editing page.

2. From the Facets window, choose the Enumerations tab.

3. Enter valid enumeration tokens by clicking the Add New Enumeration button and typing a token value, such as `CA`, `MA`, `NY`, `TX`, or `FL`.

The Facets → Enumerations window contains three buttons and is shown in Figure 4-10. From left to right, the buttons are for appending, inserting, and deleting tokens from the enumeration.

Figure 4–10: Inserting, appending, and deleting
possible enumeration values for the State element.

Finally, the Zip (U.S. postal code) element is set to be a string. However, you must further restrict the range of valid string values to exactly five characters, each being a number between zero and nine, with all leading zeros preserved. This requires the use of a regular expression, which is a string pattern-matching language discussed in Appendix C. Regular expressions are used for data validation, manipulation, conversion, and text extraction. Regular expressions in XML Schema are the same as regular expressions in the Perl programming language. Select the Zip element and in the Facets → Patterns Entry Helper window, insert a new pattern with the value [0-9]{5}. The numerical range of zero to nine is specified in square brackets, and the curly braces indicate that the pattern is to be repeated exactly five times. To remember this syntax, XMLSPY includes a built-in regular-expression builder in the Facets → Patterns Entry Helper window. Access the window by adding a pattern facet and then clicking the drop-down arrow. Some of the most common regular-expression–pattern syntaxes are displayed.

You have just completed one address structure, currently nested within the Order element (known as an *anonymous complex element*). However, you need two identical Address elements to represent the billing and shipping addresses, respectively. Rather than duplicate the effort of creating a similar address structure; you can simply convert the address structure into a global schema construct so that it can be reused. Select the Address element, right-click, and choose Make Global → Complex Type from the menu. XMLSPY automatically converts the anonymous sequence of elements into a global complex type called AddressType. This is graphically depicted by an orange box around the sequence of address elements. Switch back to the Schema Overview page, and you can see that there are now two schema components listed: AddressType and Order. Change back to the Schema Editing page and rename the element from Address to ShippingAddress, as shown in Figure 4-11.

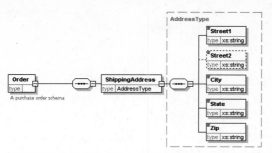

Figure 4-11: Modularizing the Purchase Order Schema.

Now that you have defined AddressType as a global complex type, you can add a BillingAddress element to the Order element by selecting the compositor to the right of the Order element, right-clicking (anywhere on the main editing screen), and choosing Add Child → Element. Type **BillingAddress** as the name of the element, and specify the type as AddressType from the Details Entry Helper window. The result should resemble the diagram shown in Figure 4-12.

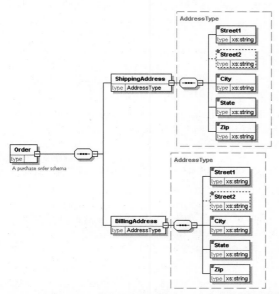

Figure 4-12: Declaring BillingAddress and ShippingAddress to be elements of type AddressType.

Next, create the Line-Items element, which is a sequence of one or more Product elements. Follow these steps to create the Line-Items element:

1. Select the compositor adjacent to the Order element, right-click, and choose Add Child → Element. Name the new element **Line-Items**.

2. Add a sequence compositor underneath Line-Items by selecting the Line-Items node, right-clicking, and choosing Add Child → Sequence.

3. Add an element to the newly added sequence compositor and choose Add Child → Element. Name the new element **Product**.

4. Click the Product element and add another sequence compositor.

5. Click the newly added sequence compositor (underneath Product). Then add the following elements and set their respective data type values: Description (xsd:string), Price (xsd:string), Quantity (xsd:positiveInteger), Ship-Date (xsd:date), Note (xsd:string).

You've completed the basic steps for creating a Line-Items element (an anonymous local element defined within the Order element). Follow these steps to place a few additional restrictions on the value spaces of the newly created elements to help ensure correct program behavior:

1. Restrict the Price element by specifying the following regular expression:

   [0-9]{1,}\.[0-9]{2}

   This represents a pattern of one to an unspecified number of numerical digits, followed by a period, followed by two more numerical digits. For example, 0.34, 4790.90, and 14.50 would all satisfy this regular expression.

2. Make Ship-Date and Note into optional elements by right-clicking and choosing Optional.

As with a DTD, an XML Schema has an easy way for you to specify the cardinality of a parent-child relationship. In the case of the Line-Items element, follow these steps to enforce the notion that the element must contain one to an unspecified number of products:

1. Expand the Order component on the Schema Editing page.

2. Click the compositor that joins Line-Items with Product, right-click, and select Unbounded from the pop-up menu.

You can add attributes to the Product element by following these steps:

1. Add an id attribute to the Product element by selecting Product on the Schema Editing page and clicking the Add New Attribute button located in the bottom frame (beneath the editing region). A new row appears.

2. Type **id** as the attribute name, specify the type as xsd:integer, and specify the use as required.

3. Add a department attribute, specify the type as xsd:string, and specify the use as optional.

Finally, you can modularize the XML Schema so that the Product complex type is defined as a global complex type and the Note element is a global element. By making these elements into either global types or global elements, they can subsequently be reused as building blocks for developing additional schema components. Although these two components are only declared once within the Order schema component, it is still a good idea to modularize your XML Schema to facilitate future development efforts. Follow these steps to perform the required modularization:

1. Right-click the anonymous Product element on the Schema Editing page and choose Make Global → Complex Type. This automatically creates a global complex element called ProductType. Now, instead of having a local anonymous element definition for Product located inside the Order element, change the Product element to declare itself to be of type ProductType. You can do this by selecting the Product element, and then, from the Details window, specify that the type is ProductType.

2. Right-click the Note element on the Schema Editing page and choose Make Global → Element.

Congratulations! You just built your first XML Schema with XMLSPY. You should now have something that looks like Figure 4-13. Make sure that you have four schema components on the Schema Overview page: Order, AddressType, ProductType, and Note.

In this example, you took a *top-down* approach to building the XML Schema. In other words, you created the Order element (the document element) and then created all other XML Schema components used within the Order element. You could just as easily have taken a *bottom-up* approach by independently creating the smaller schema components (AddressType, ProductType, and Note), creating the Order element, and then simply referencing or declaring the smaller schema components from within the Order element's definition. Both top-down and bottom-up XML Schema design concepts have their roots in proven object-oriented design techniques. Both are widely practiced and accepted as good programming practice throughout the software industry. In practice, I find that XMLSPY's capability to convert any section of a complicated XML Schema component into a separate global schema component (converting an anonymous element to either a global element or a global complex type) makes the XML Schema Editor ideal for a top-down development style. Ultimately, however, XML Schema design strategy is left up to the developer.

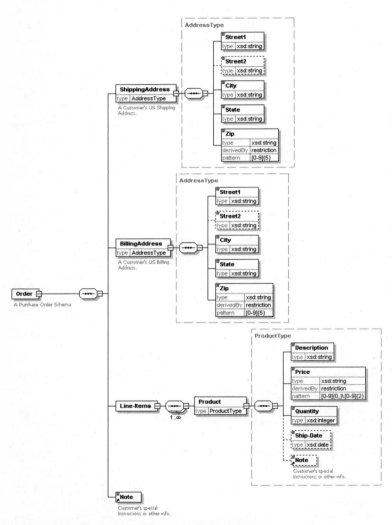

Figure 4–13: The completed Purchase Order Schema.

Configuring XML Schema Design view

When you expand an XML Schema component on the Schema Editing page, XML-SPY graphically displays a component's name in the element's box representation (also known as a node). The view can be configured to display as few or as many facets (details) about each schema component as you want. For relatively small schemas like the Purchase Order Schema, I recommend configuring XML Schema Design view to automatically display the data type of each component as well as other additional information. You do this by choosing Schema Design → View Config. In the configuration panel, click the Add New Entry button (near the top-left of the panel), and a new row appears. Click the drop-down arrow box and select Type. Add additional details to display as required and then click OK. A schema component diagram that shows an element's name, type, derivedBy, and pattern is shown in Figure 4-14.

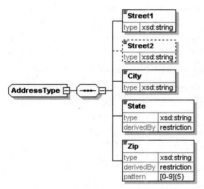

Figure 4-14: A schema diagram that shows additional component information such as type, derivedBy, and pattern.

The View Config panel also enables you to load or save different user-defined schema viewing configurations, as well as specify the distances and widths between components, the drawing direction (schemas can be viewed top to bottom instead of left to right), and several other Schema Design view settings. You can also zoom in or out of a schema diagram by choosing Schema Design → Zoom. Finally, you can generate graphic files of individual schema components as I have done in this chapter by viewing a selected schema component in Schema Design view and choosing Schema Design → Save Diagram. The output is a PNG (Portable Network Graphics) file, which you can use to help document and publish your XML Schema to others, including developers on your team or business partners wanting to integrate with your systems. The generated schema component diagrams contain a small `Generated by XMLSPY` message on the bottom-right side. If you would like a cleaner graphic, this message can be removed by choosing Tools → Options → File → Save File and unchecking Include XMLSPY Logo in Schema Diagram. If you embed XML-SPY-generated schema diagrams into you program's documentation, I guarantee that people reading the documentation will be impressed by the quality of the graphics.

Editing and validating XML documents using the XML Schema

XMLSPY can edit and validate XML documents using an XML Schema, just as you edited and validated XML documents in the previous chapter in conjunction with a DTD. All the editing support such as code completion, Entry Helper windows, error messages, and so on (which were discussed in the last chapter) also apply to XML Schemas.

Try creating a new XML document, assigning the Purchase Order XML Schema, and editing and validating the instance document. Choose File → New → XML Document and specify that the new XML document is to be based on an XML Schema. XMLSPY inspects the XML Schema file and attempts to figure out which element is the document element to be used as the root (document) element of the new XML document. If your XML Schema contains multiple global elements and it is ambiguous as to which element is intended to be the document element, XMLSPY will prompt you to pick a root element from a list of possible candidates. After this has been determined, XMLSPY autoinserts all the mandatory child elements into the file. XMLSPY also properly inserts the schemaLocation and imports the namespace that corresponds to the specified XML Schema. A sample valid XML instance document is shown in the following code:

```
<?xml version="1.0" encoding="UTF-8"?>
<Order xmlns="http://www.company.com/examples/purchaseorder"
xmlns:xsi="http://www.w3.org/2001/XMLSchema-instance"
xsi:schemaLocation="http://www.company.com/examples/purchaseorder
C:\Program Files\Altova\XMLSPY\examples\xmlspyhandbook\ch4\order.xsd">
    <ShippingAddress>
        <Street1>123 First St.</Street1>
        <City>Boston</City>
        <State>MA</State>
        <Zip>02115</Zip>
    </ShippingAddress>
    <BillingAddress>
        <Street1>22 Green St</Street1>
        <City>Cambridge</City>
        <State>MA</State>
        <Zip>02139</Zip>
    </BillingAddress>
```

```
<Line-Items>
   <Product>
      <Description>Kitchen Utensils</Description>
      <Price>4.99</Price>
      <Quantity>2</Quantity>
   </Product>
</Line-Items>
<Note>Please use expedited shipping</Note>
</Order>
```

XML Schema Syntax

Up to this point, with the exception of the discussion on XML namespaces, I have not delved into the syntax of XML Schema. However, I believe the forthcoming XML Schema language discussion will be far simpler for you because you have already created an XML Schema and validated an instance document against it. It is important to understand the underlying XML Schema syntax, and you can always view the XML Schema code in Text view. The source code for the Purchase Order Schema that you developed is shown in Listing 4-2:

Listing 4-2: The Purchase Order Schema

```
<?xml version="1.0" encoding="UTF-8"?>
<xsd:schema targetNamespace="http://www.company.com/examples/purchaseorder"
xmlns="http://www.company.com/examples/purchaseorder"
xmlns:xsd="http://www.w3.org/2001/XMLSchema" elementFormDefault="qualified"
attributeFormDefault="unqualified">
   <xsd:element name="Order">
      <xsd:complexType>
         <xsd:sequence>
            <xsd:element name="ShippingAddress" type="AddressType"/>
            <xsd:element name="BillingAddress" type="AddressType"/>
            <xsd:element name="Line-Items">
               <xsd:complexType>
                  <xsd:sequence maxOccurs="unbounded">
                     <xsd:element name="Product" type="ProductType"/>
                  </xsd:sequence>
               </xsd:complexType>
            </xsd:element>
            <xsd:element ref="Note"/>
         </xsd:sequence>
```

Continued

Listing 4–2 *(Continued)*

```
        </xsd:complexType>
    </xsd:element>

    <xsd:complexType name="AddressType">
        <xsd:sequence>
            <xsd:element name="Street1" type="xsd:string"/>
            <xsd:element name="Street2" type="xsd:string" minOccurs="0"/>
            <xsd:element name="City" type="xsd:string"/>
            <xsd:element name="State" type="xsd:string"/>
            <xsd:element name="Zip">
                <xsd:simpleType>
                    <xsd:restriction base="xsd:string">
                        <xsd:pattern value="[0-9]{5}"/>
                    </xsd:restriction>
                </xsd:simpleType>
            </xsd:element>
        </xsd:sequence>
    </xsd:complexType>

    <xsd:complexType name="ProductType">
        <xsd:sequence>
            <xsd:element name="Description" type="xsd:string"/>
            <xsd:element name="Price">
                <xsd:simpleType>
                    <xsd:restriction base="xsd:string">
                        <xsd:pattern value="[0-9]{0,}\.[0-9]{2}"/>
                    </xsd:restriction>
                </xsd:simpleType>
            </xsd:element>
            <xsd:element name="Quantity" type="xsd:positiveInteger"/>
            <xsd:element name="Ship-Date" type="xsd:date"
                         nillable="true" minOccurs="0"/>
            <xsd:element ref="Note" minOccurs="0"/>
        </xsd:sequence>
        <xsd:attribute name="prod-id" type="xsd:integer"/>
    </xsd:complexType>

    <xsd:element name="Note" type="xsd:string"/>
</xsd:schema>
```

In this section, I explain the semantics and language constructs of the XML Schema language. I make references to the sample Purchase Order Schema shown in Listing 4-2.

Simple types

Simple types are the most basic XML Schema data construct. You use them to define all attributes, as well as elements that contain only text and do not have any attributes associated with them. In the example Purchase Order, you defined many simple types, such as

```
<xsd:element name="Quantity" type="xsd:integer"/>
<xsd:element name="Ship-Date" type="xsd:date" nillable="true" minOccurs="0"/>
<xsd:element name="Street1" type="xsd:string"/>
```

To declare an element as a simple type, type **<xsd:element** to start the declaration, followed by **name=**"*elementname*" (where *elementname* should be substituted for whatever name you have chosen for the element), followed by **type=**"*element-type*" (where *elementtype* is one of the built-in XML Schema data types, such as xsd:integer, xsd:date, or xsd:string or any of the built-in types described in detail in Part 2 of the XML Schema section, located at www.w3.org/TR/xmlschema-2/). Finish the element declaration by closing the xsd:element tag. The data types begin with xsd:, which indicates that they belong to a namespace. In fact, they are defined in the same namespace used in the previous section: www.w3.org/2001/XMLSchema. Elements that are simple types can be declared globally as a child element of the schema element or locally within some other complexType.

The AddressType element (a global complex type) includes several elements that are of simple type: Street1, Street2, City, State, and Zip (see Listing 4-3).

Listing 4–3: The AddressType Global Complex Type Definition

```
<xsd:complexType name="AddressType">
   <xsd:sequence>
      <xsd:element name="Street1" type="xsd:string"/>
      <xsd:element name="Street2" type="xsd:string" minOccurs="0"/>
      <xsd:element name="City" type="xsd:string"/>
      <xsd:element name="State">
         <xsd:simpleType>
            <xsd:restriction base="xsd:string">
               <xsd:enumeration value="AL"/>
               <xsd:enumeration value="AK"/>
               <xsd:enumeration value="AZ"/>
               <!-- ... (lines omitted) ...-->
               <xsd:enumeration value="WV"/>
               <xsd:enumeration value="WY"/>
            </xsd:restriction>
         </xsd:simpleType>
```

Continued

Listing 4-3 *(Continued)*

```
      </xsd:element>
      <xsd:element name="Zip">
         <xsd:simpleType>
            <xsd:restriction base="xsd:string">
               <xsd:pattern value="[0-9]{5}"/>
            </xsd:restriction>
         </xsd:simpleType>
      </xsd:element>
   </xsd:sequence>
</xsd:complexType>
```

Deriving simple types

Simple types are defined using one of the 44 built-in data types such as string, integer, date, and Boolean. The built-in data types closely resemble the built-in data types of SQL or other popular programming languages. Using the built-in data types is the easiest option to define simple type elements, however you can just as well create your own custom simple types by selecting one (or possibly more than one) of the built-in data types to serve as a base. Customize the data type through the application of various restrictions to suit the particular needs of your application. Common restrictions might include restricting a string to be equal to a token in an enumeration of strings, specifying a range of valid minimum and maximum integer values, or specifying a sequence or pattern of characters. In fact, the built-in XML Schema data types are themselves derived from each other, with anySimpleType as the root of the simple type inheritance tree. anySimpleType, as its name suggests, can be any simple type (that is, it has no restrictions on its value space). The 44 built-in data types are, therefore, divided into two categories: primitive built-in types, which are not defined in terms of any other data types, and built-in derived data types, which are derived from the primitive built-in data types. The inheritance tree for the built-in data types (all simple types) is shown in Figure 4-15.

A complete listing of all the built-in XML Schema data types is also available in the Details Entry Helper window, accessed by clicking on the drop-down box that appears adjacent to the type property. This window also lists the names of any global elements or global complex types defined in the current XML Schema. There are three ways to create new simple types — by restriction, list, or union. The following sections explain these three methods.

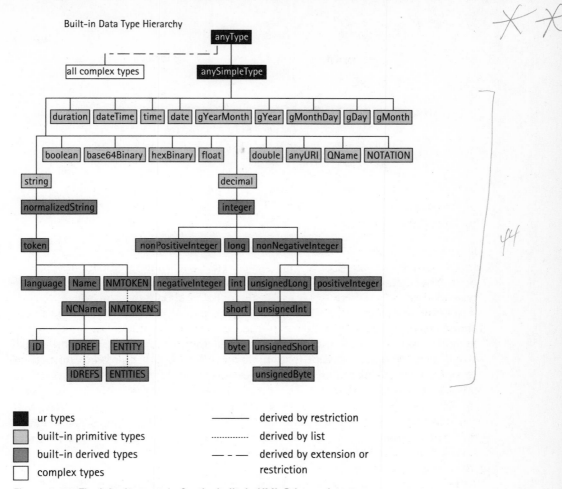

Figure 4-15: The inheritance tree for the built-in XML Schema data types.

RESTRICTION

Simple types can be derived by placing restrictions on their value. In Listing 4-3, you restricted the values for the Zip and Price elements, which were both simple types. Their definitions are listed in the following code:

```
...
<xsd:element name="Price">
   <xsd:simpleType>
      <xsd:restriction base="xsd:string">
         <xsd:pattern value="[0-9]{0,}\.[0-9]{2}"/>
```

```
          </xsd:restriction>
        </xsd:simpleType>
    </xsd:element>
    ...
    <xsd:element name="State">
      <xsd:simpleType>
        <xsd:restriction base="xsd:string">
          <xsd:enumeration value="AL"/>
          <xsd:enumeration value="AK"/>
          <!-- ... (lines omitted) ...-->
          <xsd:enumeration value="WV"/>
          <xsd:enumeration value="WY"/>
        </xsd:restriction>
      </xsd:simpleType>
    </xsd:element>
```

To restrict the values of a simple type, start by typing **<xsd:simpleType>** to begin the definition of the custom simple type, followed by **<xsd:restriction base="***basetype***">**, where *basetype* is the existing simple type on which you are basing the new simple type. This implies that the resulting data type will be a subset of the base type's value space. In the Purchase Order examples, the child element of the xsd:restriction element was the xsd:pattern element, which specifies a regular expression pattern to be fulfilled. Other possible restrictions include placing constraints on minExclusive, minInclusive, maxExclusive, maxInclusive, totalDigits, fractionDigits, length, minLength, maxLength, enumeration, and whitespace. These constraints are self-explanatory except, perhaps, for whitespace, which defines how to handle whitespace (preserve, collapse, and replace are the options available). All restrictions are listed in the Facets Entry Helper window in Schema Design view.

LIST TYPES

The list element creates a data type whose contents consist of a whitespace-delimited list of values. The data type of the tokens in the list is determined by the itemType attribute, which defines the base type that is to be used for the list. As an example, you could create a data type consisting of a whitespace-delimited list of integers as follows:

```
<xsd:simpleType name="points" type="xsd:integer">
...
<xsd:simpleType name="list-of-points">
 <xsd:list itemType="points"/>
</xsd:simpleType>
```

UNION TYPES

The union type is something of a multiple inheritance for simple types. I am not a great fan of this technique. A union type's value space is equal to the union of the value spaces of two or more base data types. The `memberTypes` attribute contains a whitespace-delimited list of base types participating in the union. For example:

```
<xsd:simpleType name="date-or-integer">
<xsd:union memberTypes="xsd:date xsd:integer">
</xsd:simpleType>
```

Global definitions

In the Purchase Order example, I talked a little about global types when you converted sequences of elements into reusable schema components. The two most common globally defined schema components are a global elements or global type definitions (either simple or complex types). Other global constructs do exist and are discussed in Chapter 5. You can easily identify a globally defined schema construct because they are defined as children of the `schema` element. Using global declarations can greatly increase the modularity of your XML Schema.

Complex types

A complex type is any element that contains either attributes or child elements. There are four cases to consider:

- ◆ Complex elements that contain child elements and possibly attributes (no textual content)

- ◆ Elements that contain both text content and attributes

- ◆ Empty elements (placeholders) with one or more attributes but no child elements or textual content

- ◆ Mixed-content elements that contain a mixture of both child elements and textual content

COMPLEX ELEMENTS CONTAINING
CHILD ELEMENTS AND ATTRIBUTES

The `AddressType` element of the Purchase Order Schema was an example of a complex element definition that contained only child elements, as shown in the following code:

```
<xsd:complexType name="AddressType">
   <xsd:sequence>
      <xsd:element name="Street1" type="xsd:string"/>
```

```
        <xsd:element name="Street2" type="xsd:string" minOccurs="0"/>
        <xsd:element name="City" type="xsd:string"/>
        <xsd:element name="State" type="xsd:string"/>
        <xsd:element name="Zip">
            <xsd:simpleType>
                <xsd:restriction base="xsd:string">
                    <xsd:pattern value="[0-9]{5}"/>
                </xsd:restriction>
            </xsd:simpleType>
        </xsd:element>
    </xsd:sequence>
</xsd:complexType>
```

The structure is very simple: Start with the `xsd:complexType` element to mark the beginning of the complex type definition, assign a value to the name attribute, open the `xsd:sequence` tag, and list the elements in the order that you would like them to appear. Then close off the `xsd:sequence` and `xsd:complexType` tags.

ELEMENTS THAT CONTAIN BOTH
TEXT CONTENT AND ATTRIBUTES

To add attributes to any element (no matter what kind) immediately before the closing `complexType` element, type **<xsd:attribute** from within a complex type definition, followed by **name="*attname*"**, where `attname` is replaced by the attribute's name, or **ref="*simpletype*"**, where `simpletype` is the name of a referenced, globally declared simple type or attribute definition. Because attributes themselves are simple types, all the rules governing the use of built-in data types, as well as those restricting and constraining their value spaces also apply to attributes. Complete the definition with a closing `/>` tag.

An attribute declaration must be defined at the very end of the complex type to which it belongs. If an element contains two or more attributes, the ordering of the attribute declarations within a complex element are irrelevant in so far as the XML processor is concerned. Attributes are inherently unordered, and there is no way to specify a particular sequence of attributes. The `ProductType` global complex type defined a required attribute, `id`, of type `xsd:integer`, and an optional attribute, `department`, of type `xsd:string`, shown in the following code after the closing `sequence` tag but before the closing `complexType` tag:

```
<xsd:complexType name="ProductType">
<xsd:sequence>
    <xsd:element name="Description" type="xsd:string"/>
    <xsd:element name="Price">
        <xsd:simpleType>
            <xsd:restriction base="xsd:string">
                <xsd:length value="1000"/>
                <xsd:whiteSpace value="preserve"/>
```

```
            <xsd:pattern value="[0-9]{0,}\.[0-9]{2}"/>
          </xsd:restriction>
       </xsd:simpleType>
  </xsd:element>
  <xsd:element name="Quantity" type="xsd:positiveInteger"/>
  <xsd:element name="Ship-Date" type="xsd:date"
                            nillable="true" minOccurs="0"/>
    <xsd:element ref="Note" minOccurs="0"/>
</xsd:sequence>
<xsd:attribute name="id" type="xsd:integer" use="required"/>
<xsd:attribute name="department" type="xsd:string" use="optional"/>
</xsd:complexType>
```

In the absence of the use="required" attribute within the xsd:attribute dec-laration, the attribute is assumed to be optional. You may explicitly dictate the value of an attribute by specifying use="fixed" and value="fixedvalue" where fixedvalue is the only valid value that the attribute can take on. For example:

```
...
<xsd:attribute name="maxItems" type="xsd:integer" use="fixed" value="100"/>
...
```

This specifies that the maxItems attribute, if present, must have a value of 100. I am not convinced that this is very useful. More likely, you would want to specify a default value for an attribute in the event that it is not present. For example:

```
...
<xsd:attribute name="language" type="xsd:string" use="default" value="English"/>
...
```

This code line specifies that if the language attribute is not present, the default language of English is assumed. In summary, you may add, delete, or modify any element by clicking on an element in Schema Editing view and using the Attribute Overview panel at the bottom middle of the screen.

EMPTY ELEMENTS

To define an empty element, such as the br element that represents a line break in HTML, simply use an empty complexType element, as shown here:

```
<xsd:element name="br">
        <xsd:complexType/>
</xsd:element>
```

If the empty element is meant to contain attributes, add attributes as described in the previous section and as shown here:

```
<xsd:element name="br">
   <xsd:complexType>
      <xsd:attribute name="length" type="xsd:int" use="optional"/>
      <xsd:attribute name="align" type="xsd:string" use="optional"/>
   </xsd:complexType>
</xsd:element>
```

ELEMENTS WITH MIXED CONTENT

Prose-oriented content (Web sites, books, manuals, and so on), if expressed in XML, is usually mixed content. Consider the following paragraph fragment:

```
...
<para>The <Emphasis>quick</Emphasis> brown fox jumped over the
<Underline>lazy</Underline> dog</para>
...
```

The paragraph tag contains a mixture of both text and child elements (the Emphasis and Underline tags) in any order. Mixed-content elements are an advanced topic because they require you to have some background on the various compositor types. Thus far, I have discussed only the sequence compositor, which defines a strict ordering of child elements.

 See Chapter 5 for more about compositor models and defining mixed element types.

GLOBAL ELEMENTS

In DTDs, all element definitions are said to be global by definition. Consider the following DTD fragment:

```
<!ELEMENT book (title)>
<!ELEMENT title (#PCDATA)>
```

This DTD fragment defines two global elements, book and title. The book element has one child element, which is an element *reference* to the title element. One consequence of using global types is that both the book and title elements are required to appear in an instance document having the same name as defined in the DTD, for example:

```
<book>
<title>The XMLSPY Handbook</title>
</book>
```

Using global elements is a simple, but inflexible, way to design XML content models.

GLOBAL TYPES

The XML Schema supports global elements (mostly for backward compatibility with DTDs), and introduces support for global complex type definitions (also referred to as *global complex types*, *global types*, or simply *types*), which are element definitions that have been assigned a unique name. After a global *type* has been defined, you can *declare* an element's type to be that of a known, existing type. Consider the following XML Schema code fragment that defines a similar book structure, as a global complex type:

```
<xs:schema>
  ...
    <xs:complexType name="book">
      <xs:sequence>
        <xs:element name="title" type="xs:string"/>
      </xs:sequence>
    </xs:complexType>
  ...
</xs:schema>
```

The preceding code listing defined the book element as a sequence of one element, title. The book global type definition can be used as a building block for developing more advanced XML structures in the form of types or elements. The book type definition becomes the content model of the element that declares it; however, the type definition does *not*, by itself, have a content model that can be expressed in an instance document. If you defined an XML Schema that had only type definitions and no global elements, the XML Schema would have no content model at all. That is, there would be no document element, and the XML Schema processor would produce an error message saying that the XML Schema had no content model. Typically, in schema design, you define several global types and then define one or more global elements that declare themselves to be of a specified type. For example, in the following code fragment I declare a product element to be of type book:

```
<xs:element name="product" type="book"/>
```

Here is how the product element might look like in an instance document:

```
<product>
<title>The XMLSPY Handbook</title>
</product>
```

Here you see that the product element (assume it is globally defined) is of type book (a global type). The ability to define, name, and subsequently declare elements is unique to XML Schema and greatly improves the flexibility by which a schema author can express a content model.

DECLARING AN ELEMENT

As discussed in the last section, after you have *defined* your types (that is, developed a type definition for any of the different complex types that I have discussed), you must *declare* elements to be of an existing type. For example, in the Purchase Order Schema, both the ShippingAddress and BillingAddress elements are *declared* to be of type AddressType.

```
<xsd:element name="Order">
              <xsd:complexType>
                    <xsd:sequence>
                            <xsd:element name="ShippingAddress"
type="AddressType"/>
                            <xsd:element name="BillingAddress"
type="AddressType"/>

                                    . . .

                    . . .
                    </xsd:sequence>
              </xsd:complexType>
</xsd:element>
```

REFERENCING A GLOBAL ELEMENT

Global element definitions can be reused. With a globally declared element, such as the Note element (a global element), create an element and *reference* a global element, for example:

```
<xsd:element name="Order">
   <xsd:complexType>
      <xsd:sequence>
         <xsd:element name="ShippingAddress" type="AddressType"/>
         <xsd:element name="BillingAddress" type="AddressType"/>
         <xsd:element ref="Note"/>
      </xsd:sequence>
   </xsd:complexType>
</xsd:element>
```

The principal difference between *declaring* a global type and *referencing* a global element is that the latter does not require name and type attributes because they are not applicable options for global elements. Global elements do not have an associated type.

GLOBAL TYPES VERSUS GLOBAL ELEMENTS

I don't believe there is much technical benefit in using a global element over a global complex type as the model for your XML Schema components; the reverse, however, is not true. There are huge benefits to using a global complex type over a global element. For example, in addition to giving you the ability to declare any element's type to that of a global complex type, you can use global types as bases to derive new type definitions. You can also use them to employ polymorphic design strategies through the use of substitution groups. (Both these benefits are discussed in the next chapter.)

So why did the W3C even bother with global elements in the first place? I believe it is primarily for reasons of providing backward compatibility with DTDs because in DTDs, everything is a global element. Global elements are conceptually easier to understand than global types. Consequently, support for global types in XML Schema also serves to lower the learning curve for XML Schema. Perhaps the W3C wanted to provide XML Schema with enough similarities to DTDs in order to facilitate XML Schema adoption.

Anonymous type definitions

Not all complex types are required to be reusable; it is often the case that an element is a complex type simply because it contains child elements or attributes, however it is only meant to be used in one place and nowhere else. Defining an *anonymous* complex type is the same as defining a global complex type with two differences:

◆ An anonymous type definition occurs nested *locally* within another global type or global element (that is, it is not defined *globally* as a child of the root schema element).

◆ The anonymous type declaration has no associated type attribute, hence the meaning of the term *anonymous*.

The Line-Items element definition, nested within the Order element is an example of an anonymous complex type definition as it meets the two criteria specified previously. It is shown here:

```
<xsd:element name="Order">
   <xsd:complexType>
     <xsd:sequence>
        <xsd:element name="ShippingAddress" type="AddressType"/>
        <xsd:element name="BillingAddress" type="AddressType"/>
        <xsd:element name="Line-Items">
           <xsd:complexType>
              <xsd:sequence>
```

```
        <xsd:element name="Product"
                type="ProductType" maxOccurs="unbounded"/>
        </xsd:sequence>
      </xsd:complexType>
    </xsd:element>
    <xsd:element ref="Note"/>
  </xsd:sequence>
 </xsd:complexType>
</xsd:element>
```

Two disadvantages of using anonymous complex elements (as opposed to global complex elements) are that you cannot use an anonymous complex element as a base for extension and substitution (covered in the next chapter), and, as previously stated, you cannot reuse anonymous complex elements anywhere else.

Publishing and Documenting Your XML Schema

The final and critical step in developing an XML Schema is to eventually publish the schema to your business partners or even to the general public, depending on the intended audience. This is a critical part because the purpose of building XML Schemas is to make it possible for other developers and computer applications to interoperate with your application.

Although XML Schema files contain all the necessary information to describe your application's content model, they are quite verbose and often difficult to grasp when they are complex. Annotations are a helpful XML Schema construct that provide documentation or human-readable commentary from the schema designer to someone else using the XML Schema. Annotations may be defined at the top level, immediately after the schema element, or at the top of any schema component defined within your XML Schema. The annotation element contains the documentation element, which has the author's remarks within its body content. In XML Schema Design view, you can add annotations to any node in an XML Schema by double-clicking the node (typically either an element or a compositor). A cursor appears, and you can type documentation comments directly beneath the node. If you take a look at the XML Schema in Text view, you can see that XMLSPY has generated the required XML code at the correct location, as in the following example:

```
<xsd:annotation>
    <xsd:documentation>A Purchase Order Schema</xsd:documentation>
</xsd:annotation>
```

You may also edit annotations from the Schema Overview page. XMLSPY provides a schema documentation generation utility that autogenerates either HTML or Microsoft Word files documenting your XML Schema. To run the documentation generator, choose Schema Design → Generate Documentation. Next, choose the desired output format and configure how you would like the documentation to appear. Click OK and specify the filename and path where you want to save the generated file. The generated documentation file includes the element name, a graphical representation, its data type, children, source definition, and any annotations (see Figure 4-16). In the case of HTML output, the file includes a hyperlinked navigation structure so that if you click on one of the children, the child element appears.

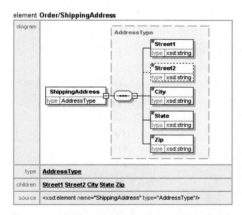

Figure 4–16: Generated documentation for the Purchase Order XML Schema example.

The documentation generation utility is a great way to keep your documentation in synch with the most recent XML Schema revision. The generated schema documentation files are ideally suited for conveying information about a complete and published XML Schema.

Summary

In this chapter, I introduced XML Schema as the preferred language for describing the content model of XML documents. This chapter covered these topics:

◆ A detailed overview of the XMLSPY Schema Design view, including navigating an XML Schema, understanding of the different windows, and configuring all the different user options

◆ Building a modular XML Schema using XMLSPY consisting using a top-down design methodology and then using that XML Schema to edit and validate XML Schema files

◆ Constraining the value space of simple types through the use of facets and other restrictions

◆ An introduction to namespaces, the problems that they solve, and how to declare and reference namespaces inside your XML Schema and related XML instance document

◆ A detailed technical overview of XML Schema syntax including a discussion on simple types, complex types, global elements, global types

◆ Publishing a completed XML Schema to the Web using the XMLSPY documentation generator

In the next chapter, I cover some more advanced XML Schema design topics including a more in-depth discussion on using multiple namespaces, deriving complex types, and the use of XML Schema in conjunction with relational databases and hybrid relational native XML databases.

Chapter 5

Advanced XML Schema Development

IN THIS CHAPTER

◆ Examining XML namespaces in detail

◆ Modularizing your XML Schema

◆ Working with object-oriented XML Schema design

◆ Using XML Schema with relational databases

THE OBJECTIVE OF THE XML SCHEMA SPECIFICATION was to address modern-day software development challenges. These challenges include maximizing a software application's flexibility in order to handle large-scale applications and providing the capability for new software applications to thrive along side modern software-development practices currently dominated by the object-oriented programming methodologies and the use of relational databases as a primary storage facility. In this chapter, I show you how to make the most of your XML Schemas through the presentation of various advanced topics and XML Schema constructs that were designed to enable your XML Schema to take on the above-mentioned challenges. Having spent time in Chapter 4 covering the basics of XML Schema design and the use of XML Schemas for document validation, you are ready to start tackling these issues head-on.

In Chapter 4, I introduced all the basic XML Schema constructs. I walked you through building an XML Schema using the XMLSPY Schema Editor, and then I showed you how to use the Schema for editing and validating instance documents. This chapter builds substantially on those earlier concepts, beginning with a more detailed discussion of XML namespaces and including several advanced examples. I cover the more advanced Schema constructs that serve to provide additional design flexibility and modularity in XML Schema development. These include the ability to name and reuse fragments of XML Schema code, as well as mechanisms for deriving types from existing types and much more.

In this chapter, I also help you examine options for implementing data constructs expressed in XML Schema using a programming language such as C++ or Java. In addition, I show you how to use an XML Schema in conjunction with relational databases. Specifically, you find out how XML Schema is being applied by vendors such as Oracle and Microsoft to bridge the gap between relational databases and XML technologies. Get ready to push your XML Schema development skills to the limits with XMLSPY!

Using Namespaces

You use namespaces in both XML Schemas and instance documents to tackle issues such as defining XML Schemas in multiple files and properly referencing XML Schema constructs within your instance documents. An XML Schema–validating XML processor such as XMLSPY makes extensive use of namespaces to control document validation.

Your XML Schema is a custom vocabulary of XML components that belong to and are uniquely identified by a target namespace. An XML Schema can have only one target namespace. All the schema components that you define in the XML Schema belong to your chosen target namespace. It is the target namespace that enables an XML processor to distinguish between various schema vocabularies and that, in turn, controls how an instance document is validated. As the schema author, you have several options in specifying XML component definitions within an XML Schema. These definitions affect how the components (such as elements and attributes) are represented in an XML instance document. The following sections show several examples of namespace settings and their implications for authoring XML instance documents.

The sample XML Schemas in this chapter are based on the Purchase Order XML Schema that you developed in Chapter 4. The file is contained within the XMLSPY Handbook Project, which installs itself as the default project when you use the exclusive version of XMLSPY included on the CD-ROM that accompanies this book. Look for the `Order_5-01.xsd file` in the `ch5` folder. You can also find all subsequent example files referenced in this chapter in the `ch5` folder.

If you are not using the version of XMLSPY from the CD, you can still access the example files. Simply locate the `XMLSPYHandbook.spp` file on the CD and copy it, along with all subdirectories, over to your local file system. Then open the file by choosing Project → Open Project.

Throughout the chapter, I make various modifications to the `Order_5-01.xsd` file to illustrate a particular XML Schema concept. In general, each individual example uses the schema of `Order_5-01.xsd` as the starting point and then adds some additional concepts. This straightforward approach enables you to look at any one topic independently of the rest of the chapter. That should help you avoid confusing the many different schema concepts examined in this chapter. I suggest that you always keep an unmodified copy of the `Order_5-01.xsd` file somewhere on your local file system so that you can follow along with all the examples in this chapter.

Default namespace example

Elements and attributes must be *qualified,* which means that you must somehow inform the XML processor what namespace they belong to, both in the XML Schema in which they are defined, and in any instance document that is meant to conform with a particular XML Schema. You can qualify an element or attribute in one of two ways: explicitly or implicitly. *Explicit* qualification of an element or attribute requires that you include a namespace prefix, followed by a colon and then the element or attribute name (`<xsd:complexElement>`). *Implicit* qualification of an element or attribute happens when you map a namespace to the default namespace, and then, any unqualified element or attribute appearing within the document is implied to belong to the default namespace.

To clarify the difference between explicit and implicit qualification of elements and attributes, consider the Purchase Order XML Schema example, provided in `Order_5-01.xsd`, which uses elements and attributes from two different namespaces. The assignment of namespaces to prefixes has been specified through the use of `xmlns` attributes placed in the root element of the XML Schema (that is, in the `schema` element) as shown below:

```
<xsd:schema targetNamespace="http://www.company.com/examples/
purchaseorder" xmlns:xsd="http://www.w3.org/2001/XMLSchema" xmlns=
"http://www.company.com/examples/purchaseorder" elementFormDefault=
"qualified" attributeFormDefault="unqualified">
```

For now, don't worry about the two attributes included (and set equal to `qualified` and `unqualified`) in the preceding code. I included `elementFormDefault` and `attributeFormDefault` for completeness here; I discuss them in greater detail at the end of this section. For now, I want to focus on the namespace declarations.

The `http://www.w3c.org/2001/XMLSchema` namespace is mapped to the `xsd` prefix, and the `http://www.company.com/examples/purchaseorder` namespace is both specified to be the schema's target namespace and is mapped to the document's default namespace. This namespace and namespace prefix assignment configuration imply that any XML constructs (such as elements or attributes) whose definitions are found within the Purchase Order XML Schema file belong to the `http://www.company.com/examples/purchaseorder` namespace. Any XML Schema constructs defined in the `http://www.w3c.org/2001/XMLSchema` namespace, such as `complexElement` or `sequence`, must be explicitly qualified using the `xsd` prefix.

There is nothing special about this namespace configuration. In fact, I could just as easily have chosen to assign the `http://www.w3c.org/2001/XMLSchema` namespace to be the default namespace and required explicit qualification of XML constructs belonging to the `http://www.company.com/examples/purchaseorder` namespace by using a namespace prefix such as `po`. Listing 5-1 shows what the XML Schema Purchase Order example file would look like if I did just that.

The complete listing for this code excerpt is located in the XMLSPY Handbook Project on this book's companion CD. Go to the `ch5` folder and look for the file `Order_5-02.xsd`.

Listing 5-1: Changing Namespace Prefix Mappings – Order_5-02.xsd

```
<-- Order_5-02.xsd, located in XMLSPY Handbook project file, chapter 5 folder -->
<schema targetNamespace="http://www.company.com/examples/purchaseorder"
xmlns:po="http://www.company.com/examples/purchaseorder" xmlns="http://www.
w3.org/2001/XMLSchema" elementFormDefault="qualified"
attributeFormDefault="unqualified">
    <element name="Order">
      <complexType>
        <sequence>
          <element name="ShippingAddress" type="po:AddressType"/>
          <element name="BillingAddress" type="po:AddressType"/>
          <element name="Line-Items">
            <complexType>
              <sequence>
                <element name="Product" type="po:ProductType"
                                     maxOccurs="unbounded"/>
              </sequence>
            </complexType>
          </element>
          <element ref="po:Note"/>
        </sequence>
      </complexType>
    </element>

    <complexType name="AddressType">
```

```
    <sequence>
        <element name="Street1" type="string"/>
        <element name="Street2" type="string" minOccurs="0"/>
        <!-- omitted for brevity -->
    </sequence>
</complexType>

<complexType name="ProductType">
    <sequence>
        <element name="Description" type="string"/>
        <!-- omitted for brevity -->
    </sequence>
</complexType>

<element name="Note">
    <!-- omitted for brevity -->
</element>
</schema>
```

I want to make several important points about the `Order_5-02.xsd` file show in Listing 5-1:

◆ All the component definitions (globally defined types `ProductType` and `AddressType` and global elements `Note` and `Order`) still belong to the `http://www.company.com/examples/purchaseorder` target namespace because I have not made any change in the `targetNamespace` attribute.

◆ XML Schema vocabulary, such as `complexType`, `element`, and `sequence`, as well as XML Schema–specific attributes such as `string` and `integer` belonging to the `http://www.w3c.org/2001/XMLSchema` namespace (the schema for XML Schemas), no longer need the `xsd` prefix. They are implicitly prefixed by means of the default namespace.

◆ In the `Order` element, `BillingAddress` and `ShippingAddress` are declared to be of type `po:AddressType`; the prefix is required.

The key difference between `Order_5-02.xsd` and `Order_5-01.xsd` is in how I *declare* elements as being of a particular complex type defined within the current XML Schema. The `Order` element declares two elements `ShippingAddress` and `BillingAddress` to be of type `po:AddressType`. In `Order_5-02.xsd`, the namespace prefix `po` is absolutely necessary to tell the XML validator where to find the definition of the `AddressType` component; omitting the prefix in this case will result in the XML validator reporting an error, to the effect of Undefined Value for Type. This explicit namespace association was not necessary in the Purchase Order Schema of `Order_5-01.xsd` because the unprefixed element type `AddressType` was prefixed implicitly by means of the default namespace being set to `http://www.company.com/examples/purchaseorder`.

In a similar fashion, the `Order` element defined in `Order_5-02.xsd` declares an element named `Note`, which is a reference to the global element `po:Note`, defined elsewhere in the `Order_5-02.xsd`, belonging to the `http://www.company.com/examples/purchaseorder` target namespace. Again in this case, omitting the namespace prefix `po` would result in the validator not being able to reference the specified element type definition required to perform validation. This example illustrates how namespaces convey critical information to the XML validator and controls how a validator locates the XML schema component definitions used in validating both XML Schemas and instance documents.

The easiest way to properly change namespace prefixes for all components referenced or declared within your XML Schema, including the XML Schema vocabulary belonging to the schema for XML Schemas, is to use the Schema Settings window. You can access the Schema Settings window from Schema Design view by choosing Schema Design → Schema Settings. Try editing the Purchase Order XML Schema of `Order_5-02.xsd`. Set the `http://www.company.com/examples/purchaseorder` namespace to be associated with a `mypo` (my purchase order) prefix and the `http://www.w3.org/2001/XMLSchema` namespace to be associated with the `schema` prefix, as shown in Figure 5-1.

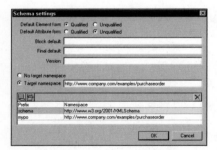

Figure 5–1: Assigning or changing namespace prefixes in XMLSPY.

In the Schema Settings dialog box, click OK and switch back to Text view. You can see that all element and attributes have been properly re-prefixed (both component declarations and references). The resulting XML Schema with modified namespaces is included in the `Order_5-03.xsd` file.

Two settings at the top of Figure 5-1 let you specify the default element form and the default attribute form. Currently, the settings are both set to `qualified` and `unqualified`, respectively, corresponding to the values for the `elementFormDefault` and `attributeFormDefault` attributes located in the `schema` element. Your choice of either `qualified` or `unqualified` locals determines how local elements and attributes should be qualified (that is, how they are to be prefixed) within an instance document meant to conform to your XML Schema. The next two sections help you determine what changes are necessary should you modify these default form settings.

UNQUALIFIED LOCALS

All of the varying Purchase Order Schemas used so far in this chapter define two global elements (Order and Note) and two global complex types (AddressType and ProductType). Within these global definitions are numerous locally declared elements and attributes, such as Street1, City, State, Zip, Quantity, and Price. Setting both the element form default and attribute form default to unqualified implies that it is not necessary to explicitly qualify local elements and attributes as they appear in an instance document. Listing 5-2 shows what an instance document conforming to the Order_5-01.xsd Purchase Order Schema would look like if you set both the elementFormDefault and attributeFormDefault attributes to unqualified:

Listing 5-2: Instance Document Using Unqualified Locals

```xml
<?xml version="1.0" encoding="UTF-8"?>
<po:Order xmlns:po="http://www.company.com/examples/purchaseorder" ... >
   <ShippingAddress>
      <Street1>200 Massachusetts Ave</Street1>
      <!-- Omitted for brevity -->
   </ShippingAddress>
   <BillingAddress>
      <Street1>250 Columbus Ave.</Street1>
      <!-- Omitted for brevity -->
   </BillingAddress>
   <Line-Items>
      <Product prod-id="820445">
         <Description>Dishes</Description>
         <!-- Omitted for brevity -->
      </Product>
   </Line-Items>
   <po:Note><Emphasis>Please</Emphasis> handle items with care.</po:Note>
</po:Order>
```

Notice that only the globally defined constructs, Order and Note, require explicit prefixing; by definition, all global elements must be qualified. Elements such as ShippingAddress, BillingAddress, Line-Items, and Description are all local elements of the Order element and are, therefore, not qualified explicitly. More specifically, their qualification can be inferred because they are local elements of the explicitly qualified Order element that envelops them. Similarly, the Note element must be explicitly qualified because it references a globally defined construct inside the Purchase Order XML Schema (Note is a globally defined element). However, local elements defined underneath Note, such as Emphasis, are local elements and do not require explicit qualification.

It is important to point out that this example works only because I am using a po namespace as opposed to the default namespace. Unqualified locals may not be used in conjunction with the default namespace because the default namespace implicitly qualifies un-prefixed elements!

QUALIFIED LOCALS

If an XML Schema specifies that the attributes elementFormDefault and attributeFormDefault are qualified, all elements and attributes (global or local) must be explicitly qualified. Listing 5-3 shows a sample instance document that conforms to a Purchase Order Schema that uses qualified locals. The main difference between this code and the code shown in Listing 5-2 is that all elements and attributes are explicitly qualified in Listing 5-3.

Listing 5-3: Instance Document Using Qualified Locals

```
<po:Order xmlns:po="http://www.company.com/examples/purchaseorder" ...>
   <po:ShippingAddress>
      <po:Street1>300 Newbury St.</po:Street1>
      <!--Omitted for brevity -->
   </po:ShippingAddress>
   <po:BillingAddress>
      <po:Street1>325 Tremont Ave.</po:Street1>
      <!--Omitted for brevity -->
   </po:BillingAddress>
   <po:Line-Items>
      <po:Product po:prod-id="12345">
         <po:Description>Cat Food</po:Description>
         <!--Omitted for brevity -->
      </po:Product>
   </po:Line-Items>
   <po:Note>Postal carrier: <po:Underline>Beware of Cat</po:Underline></po:Note>
</po:Order>
```

In Listing 5-3, all elements and attributes defined in the XML Schema (either global or local) must be explicitly qualified in an instance document. Failure to do so results in a document validation error. You may specify a mixture of qualified and unqualified element and attribute default forms by specifying elementFormDefault equal to qualified and attributeFormDefault equal to unqualified, or the reverse. This would require explicit qualification of either elements or attributes, but not both.

The XML Schema examples I use in this chapter have `elementFormDefault` set to `qualified` and `attributeFormDefault` set as `unqualified`. Although the choice of what default form to choose is ultimately made by you, the schema author, I believe that this mixed form is intuitive and easily understood. When looking at XML documents containing multiple namespaces, you will immediately know where an element definition is located. This mixed element and attribute default form configuration is also the built-in configuration whenever you create a new XML Schema in XMLSPY.

You can force a particular element or attribute to always appear either `qualified` or `unqualified` in an instance document by using the form attribute within the element or attribute definition. For example:

```
<xsd:element name="MyElement" form="qualified"/>
```

This defines an element named `MyElement` that must be explicitly qualified in any instance document that references it.

EDITING NAMESPACE PREFIXES

In the event that you find yourself manually searching and replacing namespace prefixes in an instance document, recall from the discussion of Grid view in Chapter 2 how Grid view enables you to edit XML documents as a whole. You can use Grid view to quickly change namespace prefixes in a document. To change a namespace prefix in Grid view, follow these steps:

1. Open an instance document in Grid view and expand the document so that you can select the regions of the document to which you want to apply namespace prefix replacements.

2. Choose XML → Namespace Prefix and type (or modify) the desired namespace.

3. Click to check the appropriate box to which you want to apply this namespace change — Elements, Attributes, or both.

4. Click OK, and XMLSPY carries out the namespace replacement operation for you (see Figure 5-2).

Figure 5-2: Changing the namespace prefix
of a selected region in Grid view.

Schemas in multiple files

All the XML Schema examples that I have shown you so far have been contained
in a single file that defined all the schema's respective components (such as element
and attribute definitions). This works fine for simple examples. However, to deal
with the complexities of real-world scenarios, you soon realize that it is impossible
to build advanced XML Schemas entirely in a single file, just as it would be impossible to build an entire software application in a single file. Therefore, XML
Schemas can be defined and assembled from components residing in multiple
documents. There are two possible scenarios when working with schemas that are
constructed from multiple files:

◆ When two (or more) separate XML Schema files define XML Schema constructs that belong to the same target namespace (or belong to no namespace
   at all), an XML Schema may *include* an external component definition.

◆ When an XML Schema belonging to a particular namespace imports one
   or more schema components defined in different file(s) *and* belongs to a
   different namespace, an XML Schema may *import* an external component
   definition.

In the following sections, I modify the Purchase Order example to show you how
to deal with both situations using XMLSPY.

INCLUDING SCHEMA FILES

It is dangerous for two people to be editing the same file at the same time because
of the potential for versioning problems. Yet, complex applications are generally
developed by teams of programmers, not by individuals working in isolation. So a
balance must be found that allows all programmers to continue working without
working on the same file, minimizing the risk of versioning problems. Generally,
the most practical solution is to separate complex schema files into several files. If
the externally defined XML Schema components belong to the same target namespace or do not declare a target namespace, you only have to include the separate
files in a master schema. For example, I split up the Purchase Order Schema,
defined in `Order_5-01.xsd`, into two separate schemas under the same namespace:
`Order_5-05a.xsd`, which contains the definitions for `Order`, `ProductType`, and

Note, and `Order_5-05b.xsd`, which contains the `AddressType` complex type definition. The abbreviated code for `Order_5-05a.xsd` is shown in Listing 5-4. You can find the full listing in the XMLSPY Handbook Project in the `ch5` folder.

Listing 5-4: Including an Externally Defined Schema Component — Order_5-05a.xsd

```
<xsd:schema
targetNamespace="http://www.company.com/examples/purchaseorder"
xmlns="http://www.company.com/examples/purchaseorder"
xmlns:xsd="http://www.w3.org/2001/XMLSchema"
elementFormDefault="qualified" attributeFormDefault="unqualified">
    <!-- include Address construct From Order_5-05b.xdf -->
    <xsd:include schemaLocation="Order_5-05b.xsd"/>


    <xsd:element name="Order">
       <-- Abbreviated for Brevity -->
    </xsd:element>

    <xsd:complexType name="ProductType">
       <xsd:sequence>
          <xsd:element name="Description" type="xsd:string"/>
          <-- Abbreviated for Brevity -->
       </xsd:sequence>
       <xsd:attribute name="prod-id" type="xsd:integer"
use="required"/>
    </xsd:complexType>

<xsd:element name="Note">
       <xsd:complexType mixed="true">
          <-- Abbreviated for Brevity -->
       </xsd:complexType>
    </xsd:element>
</xsd:schema>
```

The listing for `Order5_5a.xsd` is nearly identical to the original `Order5_1.xsd` file — the difference is that the `AddressType` complex type definition has been deleted and replaced with an `xsd:include` statement, which specifies a path to an external XML Schema:

```
<xsd:include schemaLocation="Order_5-05b.xsd"/>
```

In turn, the `Order_5-05b.xsd` file contains the definition for the external `AddressType` complex type definition that is needed to properly validate Purchase Order instance documents:

```
<!-- Order_5-05b.xsd -->
<xsd:schema
targetNamespace="http://www.company.com/examples/purchaseorder"
xmlns:xsd="http://www.w3.org/2001/XMLSchema" xmlns="http://www.
company.com/examples/purchaseorder" elementFormDefault="qualified"
attributeFormDefault="unqualified">
   <xsd:complexType name="AddressType">
      <xsd:sequence>
         <xsd:element name="Street1" type="xsd:string"/>
         <-- Abbreviated for Brevity -->
      </xsd:sequence>
   </xsd:complexType>
</xsd:schema>
```

Note that all schema components defined in both `Order_5-05a.xsd` and `Order5_5b.xsd` belong to the same target namespace: `http://www.company.com/examples/purchaseorder`. `xsd:include` will not work if the included component definition(s) belong to a different namespace. If no namespace is declared in the external XML Schema, it is treated as though it belongs to the same namespace as the master XML Schema. The `Order_5-05a.xsd` schema file works identically to the schema defined in `Order_5-01.xsd`.

To include an XML Schema into another XML Schema using XMLSPY, follow these steps:

1. Open the XML Schema (the one that includes the external XML Schema) and display it in the Schema Overview page.

2. Click the Add Global Schema Component button (the left-most button in the top-left corner) and choose Include (see Figure 5-3).

Figure 5-3: Including external XML Schema
components belonging to the same namespace.

3. From the File Picker dialog box, find the XML Schema file that you want to include from your local file system or type the URI that points to where the external schema is located.

IMPORTING SCHEMA COMPONENTS

As a schema designer, you often need to use schema components, defined in another file, that belong to a separate namespace. This happens often enough that XML Schemas can become very complex, and it is unreasonable to assume that all XML Schema development will start from scratch. It is more likely that as you are designing an advanced XML Schema, you will borrow schema components from other XML Schemas, perhaps from some of the many publicly available industry-standard XML Schemas. This sensible approach enables you to reduce work duplication in schema design. As an example, I present a slightly different Purchase Order Schema that has been divided into two separate schemas under different namespaces: `Order_5-06a.xsd` and `Order_5-06b.xsd`. `Order_5-06a.xsd` contains the definitions for `Order`, `ProductType`, and `Note`, which all belong to the `http://www.company.com/examples/purchaseorder` target namespace, and `Order_5-06b.xsd` contains the `AddressType` complex type definition, which belongs to a new `http://www.company.com/examples/address` namespace. I highlight the important aspects of the XML Schemas, as shown in Listings 5-5 and 5-6.

Listing 5-5: Importing External XML Schema Components — Order_5-06a.xsd

```
<xsd:schema targetNamespace="http://www.company.com/examples/purchaseorder"
xmlns:xsd="http://www.w3.org/2001/XMLSchema" xmlns="http://www.company.
com/examples/purchaseorder"
xmlns:add="http://www.company.com/examples/address"
 elementFormDefault="qualified" attributeFormDefault="unqualified">

  <!-- Import Address Components From order_5-6b.xdf -->
  <xsd:import namespace="http://www.company.com/examples/address"
schemaLocation="Order_5-06b.xsd"/>

    <xsd:element name="Order">
      <xsd:complexType>
        <xsd:sequence>
          <xsd:element name="ShippingAddress" type="add:AddressType"/>
          <xsd:element name="BillingAddress" type="add:AddressType"/>
          <-- Omitted for brevity -->
        </xsd:sequence>
      </xsd:complexType>
    </xsd:element>
    <xsd:complexType name="ProductType">
      <xsd:sequence>
        <xsd:element name="Description" type="xsd:string"/>
        <-- Omitted for brevity -->
      </xsd:sequence>
      <xsd:attribute name="prod-id" type="xsd:integer" use="required"/>
    </xsd:complexType>

    <xsd:element name="Note">
      <-- Omitted for brevity -->
    </xsd:element>
</xsd:schema>
```

The `Order_5-06a.xsd` schema contains three important modifications that are required to properly import a schema component defined in a different file under a separate namespace. First, the namespace of the imported component is introduced inside of the root `schema` element; in `Order_5-06a.xsd`, I have associated it with the `add` prefix (shorthand for Address). Secondly, I have introduced a new element, `xsd:import`, which has two attributes, `namespace` and `schemaLocation`, with values `http://www.company.com/examples/address` and `Order_5-06b.xsd`, respectively.

Because both `Order_5-06a.xsd` and `Order_5-06b.xsd` are located in the same directory, I simply specify the external filename with no additional path information in the `schemaLocation` attribute. If the external schema was located elsewhere on the network, you would need to specify the location to the external schema in the form of either a path on the local file system or a URI. Next take a look at the changes in `Order_5-06b.xsd`, shown in Listing 5-6.

Listing 5-6: Imported XML Schema Components—Order_5-06b.xsd

```
<xsd:schema targetNamespace="http://www.company.com/examples/purchaseorder"
xmlns:xsd="http://www.w3.org/2001/XMLSchema" xmlns="http://www.company.com/
examples/address" elementFormDefault="qualified" attributeFormDefault="unqualified">
    <xsd:complexType name="AddressType">
        <xsd:sequence>
            <xsd:element name="Street1" type="xsd:string"/>
            <xsd:element name="Street2" type="xsd:string" minOccurs="0"/>
            <xsd:element name="City" type="xsd:string"/>
            <-- Omitted for brevity -->
        </xsd:sequence>
    </xsd:complexType>
</xsd:schema>
```

There are no major surprises here. Notice that the `AddressType` definition belongs to the `http://www.company.com/examples/address` target namespace. Also, only Global Schema components (such as global elements or named global complex types) may be imported. Here is what an instance document corresponding to the `Order_5-06a.xsd` schema looks like. I have deliberately not used the default namespace so that you can see where the validator is getting the type definitions:

```
    <po:Order xmlns:po="http://www.company.com/examples/purchaseorder"
xmlns:add="http://www.company.com/examples/address" xmlns:xsi="http://www.w3.
org/2001/XMLSchema-instance" xsi:schemaLocation="http://www.company.com/
examples/purchaseorder
C:\Program Files\altova\XMLSPY\Examples\xmlspyhandbook\Order_5-06a.xsd">
    <po:ShippingAddress>
```

```
        <add:Street1>100 Huntington Ave.</add:Street1>
        <!-- Abbreviated -->
    </po:ShippingAddress>
    <po:BillingAddress>
        <add:Street1>300 Dartmouth St.</</add:Street1>
        <!-- Abbreviated -->
    </po:BillingAddress>
    <po:Line-Items>
        <po:Product prod-id="12345">
            <!-- Abbreviated -->
        </po:Product>
    </po:Line-Items>
    <po:Note> Next day air express delivery.</po:Note>
</po:Order>
```

The preceding instance document declares both `http://www.company.com/examples/address` **and** `http://www.company.com/examples/purchaseorder` namespaces. The imported components are properly prefixed as specified by the schema definitions. To import an external XML Schema into your XML Schema using XMLSPY, open the XML Schema (the one that is importing the external XML Schema) and view it in the Schema Overview page. Click the Add Global Schema Component button and choose Import. A File Picker dialog box appears and prompts you to find the XML Schema file you wish to include. Locate the file on your local file system, or type in the URI corresponding to the XML Schema's location.

GENERATING XML INSTANCE DOCUMENTS

By now you have created several variations on the Purchase Order XML Schemas and have created several instance documents that correspond to the various XML Schemas. XMLSPY can automate the manual instance document generation process by autogenerating instance documents and populating them with random (but valid) data. To autogenerate an XML instance document, open the XML Schema or DTD for which you want to generate an instance document in the XMLSPY editing environment so that it is the active document; next, select DTD/Schema → Generate Sample XML File; the window shown in Figure 5-4 appears.

Figure 5-4: Autogenerating an instance document from an XML Schema.

The contents of an autogenerated instance document is completely configurable; you can specify if optional elements and attributes should be generated, how many times repeatable elements should be repeated, and so on. After checking or unchecking the appropriate options, click OK. You can now use the generated instance document as a starting point to test and verify your XML Schema. Of course, you'll probably want to manually add additional sample data to the auto-generated instance document to adequately test the boundaries of the value spaces of your XML Schema data types; still, the autogenerated instance files can certainly serve as a testing starting point.

XML Schema Modeling

In Chapter 4, I showed you how to create global elements and global complex type definitions that could be either referenced or declared repeatedly throughout an XML Schema. These global constructs, in turn, served to greatly improve the reusability and modularity of an XML Schema over a Document Type Definition. XML Schema provides facilities to further improve the development, testing, and maintainability of your XML Schema through the use of *compositors* and *groups*. A compositor enables you to define sequences, choices, or any ordering of elements. A *group* is a clustering of elements (that is, a section of an XML Schema's content model) that is given a distinct name. You'll see that compositors and groups can provide greater flexibility and modularity in terms of content model design, in comparison to parameter entities in Document Type Definitions.

Compositor models

An XML Schema can be thought of as functional groupings of XML elements and other XML components whose relationships are expressed through the use of compositors. Up until now, I have used only the sequence compositor. The Order element, for example, uses a sequence compositor to express the fact that an Order element was defined as a sequence of ShippingAddress, BillingAddress, Line-Items, and Note complex elements, as shown in Figure 5-5.

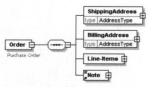

Figure 5-5: A sequence compositor is used to define the Order element.

The `sequence` compositor defines a strict structural hierarchy that specifies the order in which child elements must occur in an instance document — it is the most commonly used compositor because it defines a straightforward relationship that is easy for both processors and content authors to understand. As the XML Schema designer, you have three distinct compositor models to choose from when specifying the relationships between schema components: `sequence`, `choice`, and `all`. The following sections talk about the two types we haven't discussed yet: `choice` and `all`.

CHOICE COMPOSITORS

The `choice` compositor allows an instance document author to make a choice of any one option from an enumeration or listing of several allowable options. Take, for example, the following XML Schema code fragment that defines a complex type called `Dinner`, which may contain either `Hamburger` or `Pizza`, but not both.

```
<xsd:complexType name="Dinner">
   <xsd:choice>
      <xsd:element name="Hamburger" type="xsd:string"/>
      <xsd:element name="Pizza" type="xsd:string"/>
   </xsd:choice>
</xsd:complexType>
```

The `xsd:choice` element can include values for `minOccurs` and `maxOccurs` as attributes that enable you to build more flexible constructs. Take, for example, the `Note` element of the Purchase Order Schema that was meant to convey any additional customer remarks. `Note` defined three child elements `Emphasis`, `Underline`, and `br` (an empty element representing a line break). It was meant to allow simple text content such as

```
<Note>Please use the cheapest ground shipping method available</Note>
```

but also to be able to handle more complex mixed content such as

```
<Note>Dear Customer Service,<br/> the Last order arrived <Emphasis>
two weeks late</Emphasis> and was <Emphasis>on Fire</Emphasis>!<br/>
Please <Underline>expedite</Underline> this order.<br/>Thank You.<br/></Note>
```

The content just shown contains mixed element and textual content, with child elements appearing anywhere and any number of times. To achieve this result, the `Note` element was specified using a `choice` compositor. The `Note` element definition is shown in the following code:

```
<xsd:element name="Note">
   <xsd:complexType mixed="true">
      <xsd:choice minOccurs="0" maxOccurs="unbounded">
```

```
        <xsd:element name="Underline" type="xsd:string"/>
        <xsd:element name="Emphasis" type="xsd:string"/>
        <xsd:element name="br">
           <xsd:complexType/>
        </xsd:element>
     </xsd:choice>
  </xsd:complexType>
</xsd:element>
```

First, the Note element is specified to have a mixed content model that allows it to contain plain text content along side the previously mentioned child elements. A choice compositor is required to allow any one of the listed child elements to appear in any order. Next, by setting the minimum occurrence (minOccurs) of the choice compositor equal to zero, I allow for the possibility of having no child elements and possibly only having text content (because the Note element has mixed content). By setting the maximum occurrence (maxOccurs) of the choice compositor to be unbounded, I allow for the possibility of using multiple child elements, appearing in any order, which is the desired result. Figure 5-6 shows the Note element as it is graphically represented in Schema Design view.

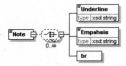

Figure 5–6: A choice compositor.

Inserting a choice compositor into your XML Schema is done the same way that you would insert a sequence compositor:

1. In Schema Design view, select a schema component to edit.

2. Expand it so that it is displayed graphically in the Schema Editing page.

3. Select the element or component to which you want to add the choice compositor (such as the Note element). Right-click and select Add Child → Choice.

   The choice compositor is visually represented as a switch, implying that only one of several possible choices can be selected. The choice compositor's minimum and maximum occurrence constraints are indicated graphically beneath the compositor. A broken line indicates an optional component, and an infinity symbol indicates that the maximum occurrence is unbounded. If you don't explicitly specify values for minOccurs and maxOccurs on the choice compositor construct, the Note element will consist of plain text content along with one of three possible child elements: Underline, Emphasis, and br.

ALL COMPOSITORS

A compositor of type `all` is a loosely defined construct that requires all of its child elements to appear in an instance document, in any order. By explicitly specifying a `minOccurs` value equal to zero for any of the choices, you can make them optional, relaxing the default requirement that all choices must appear. For example, the Purchase Order Schema could include an `EmergencyContact` complex element, which might consist of preferred methods of reaching the customer, ranked in descending order of precedence. Possible options could include `HomePhone`, `WorkPhone`, `MobilePhone`, or `Email` — of course, it is unreasonable to expect that every customer possesses home, work, and mobile numbers, as well as an e-mail address. Therefore, I modify the `all` compositor to allow the customer to include whatever contact methods they want, omitting others. Here is the XML Schema source listing for the `EmergencyContact` element:

```
<xsd:element name="EmergencyContact">
   <xsd:complexType>
      <xsd:all>
         <xsd:element name="HomePhone" type="xsd:string" minOccurs="0"/>
         <xsd:element name="WorkPhone" type="xsd:string" minOccurs="0"/>
         <xsd:element name="MobilePhone" type="xsd:string" minOccurs="0"/>
         <xsd:element name="Email" type="xsd:string" minOccurs="0"/>
      </xsd:all>
   </xsd:complexType>
</xsd:element>
```

By specifying in each child element a minimum occurrence of zero (`minOccurs` = 0), a valid XML instance document may contain any or all the listed elements, in any order, a maximum of once per element. The model for an `EmergencyContact` complex element is shown in Figure 5-7.

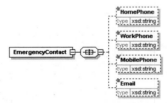

Figure 5-7: An all compositor graphically represented in Schema Design view.

An `all` compositor is graphically represented in Figure 5-7 as a connection with an equal number of lines going in as there are going out. This graphical representation suggests a relationship in which all nodes are participating, and indeed all elements listed in the `all` compositor must appear in an instance document because that is the default behavior. In the case of Figure 5-7, however, the child elements of the all compositor are depicted using broken lines because I explicitly specified them to be optional elements. The complete code listing for this all component example is listed in Order_5-07.xsd. Please note that an all compositor must appear as the sole child at the top of a content model; in other words, the following is illegal because the *illegalExtraElement*'s presence makes the all compositor not the sole child:

```
<xsd:element name="EmergencyContact">
   <xsd:complexType>
      <xsd:all>
         <xsd:element name="HomePhone" type="xsd:string" minOccurs="0"/>
         <xsd:element name="WorkPhone" type="xsd:string" minOccurs="0"/>
         <xsd:element name="MobilePhone" type="xsd:string" minOccurs="0"/>
         <xsd:element name="Email" type="xsd:string" minOccurs="0"/>
      </xsd:all>
      <xsd:element name="illegalExtraElement" type="xsd:string"/>
   </xsd:complexType>
</xsd:element>
```

CHANGING COMPOSITOR MODELS

To change a compositor model in Schema Design view, click on any compositor displayed in a Schema Editing page and choose Change Model. The underlying XML Schema syntax will be changed according to your selection, as shown in Figure 5-8.

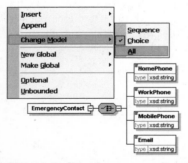

Figure 5-8: Changing a compositor model in XMLSPY.

Groups

Groups are a construct within XML Schema. By using groups, you can create smaller, more granular assemblages of elements (or attributes, as discussed in the next section) that are subsequently meant to be used when constructing complex elements. Any section of XML Schema code defined inside the Order, AddressType, Note, or ProductType complex types are possible candidates for replacement by a group construct. Take for example the AddressType complex type definition in the Purchase Order example, which defines a required element Street1 and an optional element Street2, both of type xsd:string. These two elements always appear together as a group and could potentially appear together in other complex type definitions such as a new credit card account or a driver's license registration, or anything else for that matter. I could, therefore, combine Address1 and Address2 into a single group called Address and then reference that group construct from within the AddressType complex type definition. The schema of Order_5-08.xsd shows how the original purchase order would appear after I make this modification; as usual, I have included the important code fragments in the following listing. You can find the complete source code listing for Order_5-08.xsd on the companion CD.

```
<!-- Order_5-07.xsd - Using Groups to construct complex types -->
<xsd:schema targetNamespace="http://www.company.com/examples/
purchaseorder" xmlns:xsd="http://www.w3.org/2001/XMLSchema"
xmlns="http://www.company.com/examples/purchaseorder"
elementFormDefault="qualified" attributeFormDefault="unqualified">

    <xsd:element name="Order">
        <xsd:complexType>
            <!-- Omitted for Brevity -->
        </xsd:complexType>
    </xsd:element>

    <xsd:complexType name="AddressType">
        <xsd:sequence>
            <xsd:group ref="Street"/>
            <xsd:element name="City" type="xsd:string"/>
            <xsd:element name="State">
            <!-- Omitted for Brevity -->
        </xsd:sequence>
    </xsd:complexType>

    <xsd:complexType name="ProductType">
        <!-- Omitted for Brevity -->
    </xsd:complexType>

    <xsd:element name="Note">
        <!-- Omitted for Brevity -->
    </xsd:element>

    <xsd:group name="Street">
```

```
    <xsd:sequence>
        <xsd:element name="Street1" type="xsd:string"/>
        <xsd:element name="Street2" type="xsd:string" minOccurs="0"/>
    </xsd:sequence>
</xsd:group>

</xsd:schema>
```

In the Purchase Order Schema of Order_5-08.xsd just shown, I introduced a named xsd:group construct having name equal to Street; this named group definition is located at the root level (that is, a child of the xsd:schema element) and is, therefore, a global schema component. The named Street group consists of a sequence of two elements, Street1 (required) and Street2 (Optional) both of type xsd:string — these two elements must occur in an instance document in the same order as defined in the in the xsd:group construct. The AddressType definition, in turn, declares an unnamed reference to the group construct also using the same xsd:group syntax. Therefore, the XML Schema xsd:group element is used both for the definition of a group construct and for subsequent referencing of any named group. An xsd:group element, which defines a group structure, is called a *named group*; whereas an xsd:group, which references an existing named group, is called an *unnamed group*. The consequence of this is that a group element cannot contain both a name and a reference. You can use a model group to define a set of elements that can be repeated through the document. The Purchase Order Schema of Order_5-08.xsd is functionally equivalent to the Purchase Order Schema of Order_5-01.xsd and will validate instance documents in the same fashion.

Creating a group using Schema Design view is very similar to creating a global element or global complex type definition. From the Schema Overview page, you click the Add New Schema Component button (the second button from the left in the top-left corner) and select Group as shown in Figure 5-9.

		ann:Purchase Order
Import	ype	ann:
Include	pe	ann:
Redefine		ann:
		ann:
Element		
Group		

Figure 5-9: Adding a group component to an XML Schema.

All top-level or global schema components such as globally defined elements, complex types, simple types, and groups (including attribute groups discussed in the next section) can be added to an XML Schema from the Schema Overview page.

After you have added the new group to the Schema Overview page, type in Street as the name of the component; then expand the component (by clicking on the tree-button adjacent to the component name) and continue editing the component in the Schema Editing page. Groups are represented in the XML Schema Editing page as an octagon-like shape with the name of the group inside of the octagon. To finish defining the Street named group component, follow these steps:

1. Expand and select the Street named group component, right-click, and choose Add Child → Sequence.

2. Select the sequence compositor, right-click, and choose Add Child → Element.

3. Name the new element Street1 and assign it to be of type xsd:string from the Details window.

4. Repeat this for the Street2 element, but also make it an optional element by specifying minOccurs (minimum occurrence) equal to zero.

The completed Street named group component should resemble the diagram shown in Figure 5-10.

Figure 5–10: Editing a named group construct using the Schema Design view.

Next, you need to modify the AddressType definition so that it references the newly created named Street group instead of declaring the two simple types Street1 and Street2. To modify the definition, follow these steps:

1. Expand the AddressType complex type definition and delete the old Street1 and Street2 elements.

2. Right-click the sequence compositor directly beneath the AddressType node and choose Add Child → Group.

3. Double-click the group octagon and choose Street from the drop-down list box.

The modified AddressType definition, which references the newly defined Street named group, should appear as shown in Figure 5-11.

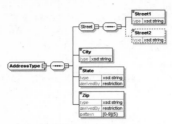

Figure 5–11: Developing complex type definitions using groups as building blocks.

To a certain extent, named groups mimic the functionality of parameter entities in DTDs. They allow for macro-like textual substitution in defining DTDs. In XML Schemas, however, groups go one step further. They allow you to specify cardinality constraints on the number of times elements belonging to a group may appear within an instance document. That means you may specify values for minimum and maximum occurrences by providing appropriate values for minOccurs and maxOccurs attributes. For example, consider the following unnamed group reference:

```
<xsd:group ref="mygroup" minOccurs="1" maxOccurs="5"/>
```

This code requires the hypothetical grouping of elements named *mygroup* to occur in an instance document at least once and up to a maximum of five times. Until now, you have seen how a named group can specify how a sequence of elements should appear within a complex type definition. Keep in mind that any group constructs may include any of the compositor models: sequence, choice, and all, covered earlier in this section. Thus, you can control or specify patterns of different element orderings and configurations. The next two sections present an example of how to use the choice and all compositors in a group.

CHOICE GROUP

A choice group is simply a named group that contains a choice compositor. The choice compositor, discussed earlier in this section, allows only one of its children to appear in an instance document. In the preceding discussion of compositors, I used a choice compositor in the definition of Note (Order_5-07.xsd). This choice compositor can be made into a named choice group so that other element constructs requiring the same structure could reference the group. The following listing shows the code for a named group called Paragraph that can contain a choice of child elements: Emphasis, Underline, and br. If you specify a minOccurs of zero and maxOccurs of unbounded, the model allows the listed child elements to appear any number of times and in any order:

```
<xsd:group name="Paragraph">
  <xsd:choice minOccurs="0" maxOccurs="unbounded">
    <xsd:element name="Emphasis" type="xsd:string"/>
```

```
        <xsd:element name="Underline" type="xsd:string"/>
        <xsd:element name="br">
           <xsd:complexType/>
        </xsd:element>
     </xsd:choice>
</xsd:group>
```

The complete XML Schema containing the previously listed code is located in Order_5-08.xsd. The Paragraph group can be subsequently referenced by the Note element as shown in the following code:

```
<xsd:element name="Note">
   <xsd:complexType mixed="true">
      <xsd:group ref="Paragraph"/>
   </xsd:complexType>
</xsd:element>
```

Figure 5-12 shows the global element Note, which is defined to be a complex type with mixed content. The Note definition contains a single child node (the octagon), which is a visual representation for an unnamed group that references the newly defined Paragraph group.

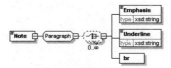

Figure 5-12: A Note element that references a choice group.

ALL GROUP

An all group is simply a group that uses an all compositor to constrain its respective contents. As previously explained, use of an all compositor requires by default that all the child elements defined in the group must appear once (unless you specify a minOccurs = 0), in any order. The all group must appear as a top-level element for the group, and the group's children must all be individual elements (no nested groups permitted). Here is the EmergencyContact global element expressed as a named group instead:

```
<xsd:group name="EmergencyContact">

   <xsd:all>
      <xsd:element name="HomePhone" type="xsd:string" minOccurs="0"/>
      <xsd:element name="MobilePhone" type="xsd:string" minOccurs="0"/>
      <!-- Omitted --/>
```

```
   </xsd:all>

</xsd:group>
```

The complete code listing for the `EmergencyContact` group can be found in the `Order_5-08.xsd` file. The `EmergencyContact` named `all` group is visually represented as a group octagon having an `all` compositor, as shown in Figure 5-13:

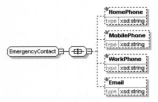

Figure 5-13: An all group, represented in XML Schema Design view.

Attribute groups

You can use an attribute group to cluster common attributes, which may potentially appear in numerous complex elements. Attribute groups in XML Schemas function in a similar manner to parameter entities in DTDs – they improve readability and maintainability. In the Purchase Order Schema, the `ProductType` definition contains two attributes: `id` and `department`. You can combine these as a named attribute group as shown in the following code:

```
<xsd:attributeGroup name="CommonAttributes">
   <xsd:attribute name="id" type="xsd:integer" use="required"/>
   <xsd:attribute name="department" type="xsd:string" use="optional"/>
</xsd:attributeGroup>
```

You can then reference an attribute from within any complex type as follows:

```
<xsd:complexType name="ProductType">
   <xsd:sequence>
      <xsd:element name="Description" type="xsd:string"/>
      <!-- Omitted for Brevity -->
   </xsd:sequence>
   <xsd:attributeGroup ref="CommonAttributes"/>
</xsd:complexType>
```

You can edit attribute groups from the Schema Overview page. Click the Add New Global Schema Component button located at the top-left of Figure 5-14 and choose Attribute Group. The definition of an attribute group is done from the Attribute window shown at the bottom of Figure 5-14.

Figure 5-14: Editing attribute groups
in the Schema Overview page.

Object-Oriented Schema Design

Thus far, the discussion of XML Schema design has included coverage of numerous globally defined constructs (schema components defined directly underneath the root schema element) such as global complex types and groups. These serve to help improve the overall reusability and modularity of your schema components. Globally defined complex elements allow you to define a schema component and explicitly assign the complex type a respective type name. You can then declare elements elsewhere throughout an XML Schema under a separate local name and specify the element type to be that of a named complex type defined elsewhere. Similarly, groups allow us to define and name smaller assemblages of elements, which can be subsequently referenced throughout an XML Schema, thereby constituting building blocks for constructing other complex types.

Global constructs, such as the various groups discussed in the last section, coupled with the capability to easily work with multiple XML Schema files and components defined under potentially different namespaces serve to greatly increase the flexibility of XML Schema design. They exceed the flexibility of DTDs, yet they fall short of providing true extensible object-oriented design capabilities, which are so deeply rooted in modern software development practices. In particular, these include the common practice of building component types through the use of inheritance and polymorphism. To support true extensible object-oriented design, the XML Schema defines a straightforward mechanism for deriving complex types and specifying equivalency between elements, thus emulating polymorphic XML behavior – this is the subject of the next several sections.

Deriving complex types by extension

Deriving a complex type enables you to build upon an existing complex type definition, adding to it whatever additional schema components or parts meet your application design requirements. The technique of developing a complex type through derivation is similar to the process discussed in Chapter 4 for deriving custom simple types. The main difference is that in Chapter 4, the base type was always a simple type; whereas in this chapter, the base type is a complex type.

Consider the `AddressType` complex type definition from the sample Purchase Order Schema. It is limited in its potential usage because it is specifically designed to deal with U.S. addresses — this is because U.S.-specific data elements such as `State` and `Zip` are included in the model. In contrast, a Canadian address requires elements for `Province` and `PostalCode`. An object-oriented approach to designing the `AddressType` complex type so that it could work with both U.S. and Canadian mailing addresses would be to first separate the common address components, `Street1`, `Street2`, and `City`, from the regionally specific address elements as shown in the following code listing:

```
<xsd:complexType name="AddressType">
   <xsd:sequence>
      <xsd:element name="Street1" type="xsd:string"/>
      <xsd:element name="Street2" type="xsd:string" minOccurs="0"/>
      <xsd:element name="City" type="xsd:string"/>
   </xsd:sequence>
</xsd:complexType>
```

The next step is to create the derived complex types `CanadianAddress` and `USAddress`, extending the `AddressType` listed above to include additional regionally specific data elements. The schema code listing for the `CanadianAddress` complex type is listed in the following code. The `USAddress` is not shown, although it is virtually identical. The complete schema listing for this example is located in the `Order_5-09.xsd` file on the companion CD. The important aspects appear in bold in the following listing.

```
<xsd:complexType name="CanadianAddress">
    <xsd:complexContent>
        <xsd:extension base="AddressType">
           <xsd:sequence>
               <xsd:element name="Province">
                  <xsd:simpleType>
                     <xsd:restriction base="xsd:string">
                        <xsd:enumeration value="AB"/>
                        <xsd:enumeration value="BC"/>
                        <!-- Canadian Province Abbreviations -->
                     </xsd:restriction>
                  </xsd:simpleType>
               </xsd:element>
```

```
                    <xsd:element name="PostalCode">
                        <xsd:simpleType>
                            <xsd:restriction base="xsd:string">
                                <xsd:pattern value="\p{L}\d\p{L}\d\p{L}\d"/>
                            </xsd:restriction>
                        </xsd:simpleType>
                    </xsd:element>
                </xsd:sequence>
            </xsd:extension>
        </xsd:complexContent>
    </xsd:complexType>
</xsd:schema>
```

The CanadianAddress complex type definition begins with the complexContent element, which allows you to derive new content. Next the extension element appears and specifies the base type as being AddressType. Finally, a sequence compositor is used and contains locally defined data elements, Province and PostalCode, which are themselves simple types that have been derived by restriction. The Province element has different enumerated values corresponding to Canadian province abbreviations, and the PostalCode element specifies a different pattern consisting of a letter (uppercase or lowercase) followed by number, repeated three times (for example, R3R3B6 would be valid).

The complete model of the CanadianAddress complex type is the model of the base type, plus the additional data elements that were locally defined inside the type definition. The content of the base plus additional data elements are treated as though they were both children of the same sequence compositor. Furthermore, only complex types may serve as base types through which extended types are defined (either through extension or restriction). This is a major additional reason to use global complex types instead of global element definitions.

To create a complex type based on an extension of an existing complex type, follow these steps:

1. Using the Schema Design view, create a new complex type, as you normally do, from the Schema Overview page.

2. Expand the new complex type so that it is graphically editable.

3. From the Details window, set derivedBy to extension and base to AddressType. The sequence compositor and the additional Province and PostalCode elements are shown in Figure 5-15. Note that the base type is visually represented inside a colored region, and the extended elements appear outside that region.

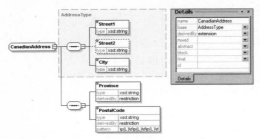

Figure 5-15: Extending complex types using XMLSPY.

Deriving complex types by restriction

In addition to deriving new complex types by extending content models, XML Schema supports the derivation of new types by restricting the models of existing complex types. In Chapter 4, I used restriction to place constraints on the value space of simple types; restriction in terms of complex types involves creating a subset of the schema component by eliminating unwanted parts of the model. These may include deleting an element defined in the base type or imposing additional cardinality constraints by means of specifying different values for minOccurs or maxOccurs. This has the net result of constricting the possible range of occurrences for a particular element or compositor with respect to what was originally permitted in the base type definition. Generally, I find that deriving complex types by restriction is less useful than extending complex types. In fact, it can be problematic due to numerous inconsistencies and other issues surrounding the use of a proper validation of complex types derived by restriction.

As an example, I will create a new complex type definition called BulkOrder that is identical to an OrderType element (a complex type representation of the Order global element) except that it requires a minimum of 10 line items so that it can qualify as a bulk order. The source code for this example is located in the Order_5-10.xsd file. The Order_5-10.xsd file has several changes with respect to the other Purchase Order Schemas. First, I had to convert the Order global element into a global complex type called OrderType. This was necessary because global elements cannot be derived — only complex types can. Here is the code listing for the derived BulkOrderType complex type that is derived by restriction based on the OrderType complex element:

```
<xsd:complexType name="BulkOrderType">
   <xsd:complexContent>
      <xsd:restriction base="OrderType">
         <xsd:sequence>
            <xsd:element name="ShippingAddress" type="AddressType"/>
            <xsd:element name="BillingAddress" type="AddressType"/>
```

```
        <xsd:element name="Line-Items">
            <xsd:complexType>
                <xsd:sequence minOccurs="10" maxOccurs="unbounded">
                    <xsd:element name="Product" type="ProductType"/>
                </xsd:sequence>
            </xsd:complexType>
        </xsd:element>
        <xsd:element ref="Note"/>
    </xsd:sequence>
  </xsd:restriction>
 </xsd:complexContent>
</xsd:complexType>
```

BulkOrderType, the restricted derived type, is enveloped by a complexContent element that allows you to derive a model by either restriction or extension. Next, the restriction element appears and specifies a base element of OrderType. The rest of the type definition corresponds to the OrderType definition with one modification; the minOccurs attribute for the Line-Items sequence compositor has been increased to 10. A type definition that is derived by restriction appears to be the opposite of the previous derivation by extension example, which did not need to include the actual definition of the base complex type. Types derived by restriction must explicitly repeat all the components of the base type definition that are to be included in the derived type. Furthermore, elements appearing in the restricted type must be a subset of the base type. That means you may delete elements or other components from the base complex element. You cannot, however, introduce any new elements or components into the model of the new type. Any changes that you make to the values of the minOccurs or maxOccurs must result in a more restricted range (a smaller range) of possible occurrences in the derived type.

As previously mentioned, there are several inconsistencies between the implementations of validating XML Schema parsers when dealing with validation of complex types derived by restriction. This is possibly due to some ambiguity in the schema specification. It results in undesirable program behavior when you switch between any of the well-known parser implementations. Therefore, I recommend against the use of restricted complex types for the time being. It is likely that future XML Schema specifications will clarify this subject and eventually resolve the matter. For these reasons XMLSPY has only limited support for editing and no support for validating complex types derived by restriction in Schema Design view. To create a new complex type by restriction in XMLSPY, follow these steps:

1. Add a new complex type to your schema from the Schema Overview page.

2. Expand the new component; in the Details window set the base complex type to the complex type definition you intend to use as a base type.

3. Set the `derivedBy` attribute to `restriction`, as shown in Figure 5-16.
   XMLSPY will automatically copy over the model of the base type; you, as
   the schema author, can then delete or make legal changes to the `minOccurs`
   or `maxOccurs` attributes. XMLSPY does not have a way of graphically displaying the elements that have been omitted in the restricted type, nor does
   it perform any validation or additional checking for illegal editing operations as you are editing.

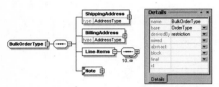

Figure 5-16: Deriving complex types by restriction.

Redefining complex types from external schemas

Now that you have learned how to derive complex types based on extension or
restriction, the question arises: How do you make changes to an externally defined
complex type definition? XML Schema provides a simple `redefine` mechanism for
doing exactly that. The following example builds on the example of
`Order_5-05a.xsd` and `Order_5-05b.xsd`. These imported an externally defined
`AddressType` definition from an external file that belonged to the same target
namespace. In this example, I redefine the imported `AddressType` definition to
include an additional field called `CustomerName` — the abbreviated code listing is
shown in the following code, and the complete source is located in the
`Order_5-11a.xsd` and `Order_5-12.xsd` files on the companion CD.

```
<xsd:schema targetNamespace="http://www.company.com/examples/purchaseorder"
xmlns:xsd="http://www.w3.org/2001/XMLSchema" xmlns="http://www.company.com/
examples/purchaseorder" elementFormDefault="unqualified"
attributeFormDefault="unqualified">
    <!-- Redefine Address construct From order_5-11b.xsd -->
    <xsd:redefine schemaLocation="order_5-11b.xsd">
        <xsd:complexType name="AddressType">
            <xsd:complexContent>
                <xsd:extension base="AddressType">
                    <xsd:sequence>
                        <xsd:element name="CustomerName" type="xsd:string"/>
                    </xsd:sequence>
                </xsd:extension>
            </xsd:complexContent>
        </xsd:complexType>
```

```
    </xsd:redefine>

    <xsd:element name="Order">
      <xsd:complexType>
        <xsd:sequence>
          <xsd:element name="ShippingAddress" type="AddressType"/>
          <xsd:element name="BillingAddress" type="AddressType"/>
          <-- Omitted for Brevity -->
      </xsd:complexType>
    </xsd:element>

    <-- Omitted for Brevity -->
</xsd:schema>
```

The redefinition syntax is straightforward. It is just like any type derivation syntax except that an enveloping redefine element is required to help locate the externally defined component. As a cautionary note, type redefinition only works when the externally defined schema component belongs to the same namespace or does not declare a target namespace. Furthermore, you should use redefine with caution. Type redefinitions can result in unknown and potentially dangerous side effects if the author of the externally defined schema component makes a change to the schema that conflicts with the component redefinition. A question arises: What if you, as the schema author, would like to impose a restriction prohibiting the redefinition of a particular schema component? This is indeed possible, as you see next.

Restricting the use of complex types

Although deriving types by either restriction or extension can have many positive aspects in terms of improving the overall design of your XML Schema, there are times that you might want to specify that a complex type definition should be final. You do not permit further derivation. An XML Schema can restrict type derivation either by restriction, extension, or both, specifying it to be final as shown in the following code:

```
<complexType name="Order" final="extension">
 <sequence>
  <!-- Omitted for Brevity -->
 </sequence>
</complexType>
```

The final attribute specifies that the complex type definition may not be further derived by extension; specifying a final attribute value of restriction will disallow derivation by restriction, and the value #all will completely disallow type derivation of any kind.

Substitution groups and abstract type definitions

Substitution groups in XML Schema enable you to specify a grouping of different element types as being equivalent, and thus allowing them to be used interchangeably — elements belonging to the same substitution group may be substituted for one another inside of an instance document. An abstract element type refers to an element definition that cannot be referenced within an instance document; rather a member of the abstract type's substitution group must appear in its place.

These two concepts — substitution groups and abstract element types — are used together to enable *polymorphism*, a widely used object-oriented programming concept, also known as *late-binding* in compiler-speak. Polymorphism (from the Greek meaning "having multiple forms") describes the characteristic of being able to assign a different meaning or use to something in different contexts. Polymorphism, as far as XML Schema is concerned, refers to the practice of defining a family of equivalent, or substitutable, components.

As an example, consider the schema of `Order_5-09.xsd`, which defined two complex types, `USAddress` and `CanadianAddress`, through derivation. One unfortunate side effect was that the `Order` element that declared the `BillingAddress` and `ShippingAddress` elements (which used to be of `AddressType`), had to be changed to include a `choice` compositor consisting of two elements. These are `CA`, declared to be of type `CanadianAddress`, or `UA`, declared to be of type `USAddress`, as shown Figure 5-17.

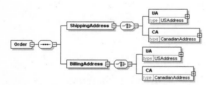

Figure 5-17: The modified order element of Order_5-09.xsd handles either Canadian or U.S. addresses.

Although the `Order` element of Figure 5-17 can properly handle either U.S. or Canadian shipping and billing addresses, this approach is unwieldy. Imagine if you added any other international address type meant to be substitutable. The `Order` element would greatly increase in complexity. It would be ideal, instead, to structure the XML Schema so that the `ShippingAddress` and `BillingAddress` types could accept U.S. and Canadian address elements, in addition to any other kind of address type — including ones that haven't yet been defined.

XML Schema substitution groups, in conjunction with abstract types, can be employed to make your XML Schema handle any kind of address element as follows: Define an abstract element type called `Address`. This will be designated as a *head element*, which is essentially a placeholder for an undetermined type (such as `USAddress`, `CanadianAddress`, or any other future address elements). The `Address` abstract type definition doesn't define a model because abstract element types by

definition cannot be used in an instance document. Next, create two global element
definitions: USAddress and CanadianAddress, each containing its respective complete element definition. Designate that they be substitutable elements with the
Address element.

In practice, the XML Schema code for this scenario requires numerous modifications to the Purchase Order examples that you have been using thus far. Using substitution groups can be considered the opposite of type derivation. In type
derivation, I made an existing type definition more specific by either adding or
deleting parts of the definition. In contrast, substitution groups have the effect of
making an element definition more general, allowing for the possibility of accept-
ing elements that have not yet been defined. Furthermore, whereas type derivation
was only applied to type definitions (globally declared complex types), substitution
groups may only be used in global element definitions.

The complete listing for a Purchase Order Schema that uses substitution groups
and an abstract type is located in the Order_5-11.xsd file. The important aspects
are shown in the following listing:

```
<xsd:schema targetNamespace="http://www.company.com/examples/purchaseorder" ... >

    <xsd:element name="Address" abstract="true"/>

    <xsd:element name="USAddress" substitutionGroup="Address">
        <xsd:complexType>
            <xsd:sequence>
                <xsd:element name="Street1" type="xsd:string"/>
                <!-- Omitted for Brevity -->
            </xsd:sequence>
            <xsd:attribute name="addressType" type="xsd:string" use="required"/>
        </xsd:complexType>
    </xsd:element>

    <xsd:element name="CanadianAddress" substitutionGroup="Address">
        <xsd:complexType>
            <xsd:sequence>
                <xsd:element name="Street1" type="xsd:string"/>
                <!-- Omitted for Brevity -->
            </xsd:sequence>
            <xsd:attribute name="addressType" type="xsd:string" use="required"/>
        </xsd:complexType>
    </xsd:element>

    <xsd:element name="Order">
        <xsd:complexType>
            <xsd:sequence>
```

```
            <xsd:element ref="Address"/>
            <xsd:element ref="Address"/>
            <!-- Omitted for Brevity -->>
         </xsd:sequence>
      </xsd:complexType>
   </xsd:element>


   <!-- Omitted for Brevity -->
</xsd:schema>
```

Starting from the top, the `Address` element is specified to be an abstract element through the presence of the `abstract` attribute being set to `true`. `Address` will be used as the head element for the substitution group you are developing. Next you define the `USAddress` and `CanadianAddress` and specify that they belong to the `Address` substitution group as specified by the `substitutionGroup` attribute. I had to add an additional attribute to both `USAddress` and `CanadianAddress` to specify the kind of address (for example, billing or shipping) because they are represented as global elements. Before, I had used global complex types. Next, the `Order` element appears, which references the `Address` abstract element twice. In an instance document, a `CanadianAddress` or `USAddress` or any other element belonging to the `Address` substitution group must appear in its place in order to be valid. The instance document fragment below is valid:

```
<Order xmlns="http://www.company.com/examples/purchaseorder" ...>
   <USAddress addressType="shipping">
      <Street1>123 Westland Ave</Street1>
      <City>Boston</City>
      <State>MA</State>
      <Zip>02115</Zip>
   </USAddress>
   <CanadianAddress addressType="billing">
      <Street1>100 Front St.</Street1>
      <City>Toronto</City>
      <Province>ON</Province>
      <PostalCode>T3G1L4</PostalCode>
   </CanadianAddress>
   <!-- Omitted for Brevity -->
</Order>
```

To create a substitution group in XMLSPY's Schema Design view, add global elements to your schema as you would normally do. Then, using the Details window, specify that a type is either abstract or belongs to a substitution group. The `Order` element that I just discussed is shown in Figure 5-18.

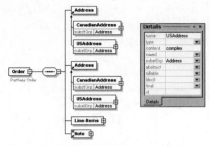

Figure 5-18: Visual representation of substitution groups in XMLSPY.

Using XML Schemas with DTDs

Because you can use any XML document in conjunction with a DTD and because an XML Schema is itself an XML document, it should be no surprise that you can use DTD constructs in defining an XML Schema. The most common reason why this is sometimes done is to define and use general entity definitions inside your XML Schema. There is no real equivalent of a general entity definition in XML Schema. General entities appearing in an XML Schema are all resolved before the XML Schema is used for validation. Therefore, to define a general entity in a DTD for use inside an XML Schema, simply follow the instructions for creating a DTD and a general entity, as discussed in Chapter 3, and use the entities as you would with any other XML document.

Generating class files from XML Schemas

As I near the end of this discussion on XML Schemas, I remind you of the fact that XML is not a full programming language because it cannot be compiled or executed as a standalone, binary executable file. Rather XML documents must be bound to an external software application or runtime environment. Therefore, XML development does not end after schema design or even after editing and validating instance documents based on an XML Schema. Rather you (or someone on your team) will ultimately need to implement the software code used for the processing of XML documents within the context of a software application. Creating a *program language binding* requires writing and implementing the necessary software class files so that object representations of your XML document can be replicated in-memory and operated on. Your class files ultimately need to implement methods (or functions) that provide programmatic access to the contents of your XML document, as well as to load, create, validate, process, transform, modify, and flush an XML document.

You can write an XML program code binding in any software programming language, such as Java or C++. Writing of the language binding is facilitated through the use of high-level XML processing Application Programming Interfaces (APIs) such as Microsoft MSXML and Apache Xerces, which are freely available and have implementations targeted at various programming languages. (See Appendix A for a complete listing of XML processors and where to obtain them.) An analogy to this is how, after completing a schema design for a relational database and populating the various tables with data, you still need to implement a database application using higher-level APIs. These might include Active Data Objects (ADO), Open Database Connectivity (ODBC), or Java Database Connectivity (JDBC), all of which could accomplish the desired business application functionality. XMLSPY is not a conventional Integrated Development Environment because it is not meant to compile and debug Java or C++ programs as you might be accustomed to doing using tools such as Borland JBuilder or Microsoft Visual Studio.NET. Still, XMLSPY includes code-generation capabilities meant to accelerate the transition from XML Schema design to the coding and implementation phase of an XML application. Program code generation in XMLSPY is driven by your XML Schema and an XMLSPY template file (.spl), which specifies how output code should look. You have the option of creating your own templates or using the predefined templates.

To generate program code for your Schema, follow these steps:

1. Open the XML Schema.

2. Choose DTD/Schema → Generate Program Code. The window shown in Figure 5-19 appears.

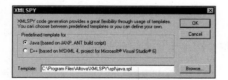

Figure 5-19: Generating class files based on your completed XML Schema.

3. Choose a predefined template or specify a path to your own template and click OK. An XMLSPY File Directory Picker asks you for the desired output directory. Specify a directory on your local file system and click OK. The generated program code will be output to the specified directory.

At the time of this writing, XMLSPY includes two built-in templates for generating Java and C++ code. It is expected that other templates for languages, such as C# and Visual Basic.NET, will be made available in the near future. The predefined templates generate one class file corresponding to each globally declared element or complex type in your XML Schema, preserving the inheritance tree as defined in your XML Schema. Additional code is implemented, such as functions that read XML files into a DOM in-memory representation, write XML files from a DOM representation back to a system file, as well as XML validation and transformation. The outputted program code is expressed in C++ or Java programming languages. The C++ generated output targets MSXML 4.0 and includes a Visual Studio 6.0 project file; the generated Java output is written against the industry-standard Java API for XML Parsing (JAXP) and includes a Sun Forte for Java project file. You can modify the appearance of generated code by editing the built-in templates or by creating new ones from scratch.

Output code is completely customizable via a simple yet powerful template language, which gives full control in mapping XML Schema built-in data-types to the primitive data types of a particular programming language. Additionally, you can build your own templates to automate the generation of code for such things as Enterprise JavaBeans, SQL scripts, and Active Server Pages.

Using XMLSPY's Schema Editor in conjunction with code generation templates makes XMLSPY well suited as a software modeling tool, allowing XML applications to be prototyped at a high level in XML Schema and then automatically generated. Changes to an application's XML Schema content model can be immediately reconciled with a software implementation simply by rerunning the code generator. Although the generated code does not produce a completed application, it does free you from having to write and test low-level infrastructure code, allowing you to focus on implementing business logic.

Additional information on program code generation is available in the online Help menu. Choose Help → Contents → Code Generator → The Way to SPL (Spy Programming Language).

XML Schema and Relational Databases

XML is clearly not meant as a replacement for relational databases both because relational databases are so pervasive throughout the software industry and because they are extremely efficient at storing and indexing large volumes of tabular data. Still, XML and native XML servers and repositories, such as Software AG's Tamino server and others listed in Appendix A, offer considerable benefits when it comes to storing, indexing, and retrieving prose-oriented content such as structured documents. So I view relational databases and XML technologies as being highly complementary going forward. It is most likely that future information storage systems will employ either both relational and native XML databases or simply use traditional relational databases, which have in the past year implemented considerable support for storing XML documents. To make XML documents work with relational databases, XMLSPY implements both relational database-to-XML Schema and XML Schema-to-database conversion utilities. These utilities are the focus of this section.

Converting relational databases into XML Schemas

Because your organization likely already has considerable infrastructure in the form of existing relational-database schemas, and considering the fact that an XML Schema will likely contain similar data elements, it makes sense to use the database schemas that someone has already created to jump-start the XML Schema design process. XMLSPY can convert relational databases into XML Schemas. Virtually all databases are supported, including Microsoft SQL Server 2000, Oracle 8i/9i, Microsoft Access — or any database that supports programmatic access via ODBC or ADO.

To perform a database-to-XML Schema conversion, follow these steps:

1. Choose Convert → Create Database Schema.

2. With the Microsoft Access button selected, click the Choose File button and select the `altova.mdb` file located in the `Program Files\Altova\ xmlspy\Import\Altova` directory. In this example, connect to a Microsoft Access database because it is part of the default Microsoft Office installation. However, you would use the same process for any other database, except that you would have to type the database connection string or build a connection string using the integrated ODBC and ADO connection builder.

3. Click OK and XMLSPY reads the database's schema, generates global elements corresponding to the different tables, maps SQL types to XML Schema built-in simple types, and preserves any predefined relationships. Your final XML Schema may look different because a generated XML Schema is only an approximation. You may wish to make further refinements. Still, it's not a bad idea to use the autogenerated XML Schema as a starting point for speeding up XML Schema design.

Converting XML Schemas into relational databases

XMLSPY can also convert an XML Schema into a relational database. Again, the database generation uses either ODBC or ADO, so most relational databases are supported. The conversion algorithm used by XMLSPY is quite simple. It converts any global elements defined in the XML Schema into relational database tables and maps XML Schema built-in simple types to corresponding SQL data types. As an example, try adding additional global elements to the XML Schema that was generated from the Microsoft Access Database in the previous section. To convert the modified XML Schema to a relational database, follow these steps:

1. Switch to Schema Design view and choose Convert → Create DB Structure Based on Schema.

2. There are several options and utilities for specifying or building a database connection string; but for this example, select Create a New Microsoft Access Database Structure

3. Click OK.

It is likely that you will need to perform some additional development work on the resulting relational database, although it is a great starting point for representing an XML Schema in a relational database.

Using XML Schema extensions

Both Oracle9iR2 and Microsoft SQL Server 2000 databases implement support for XML Schemas. Oracle has a complete native XML database implementation called Oracle XML DB, and SQL Server 2000 has SQLXML 3.0, which contains some additional add-on programming APIs for working with SQL Server and XML. Both Oracle XML DB and SQL Server 2000's XML features use a special mapping schema to instruct the database in how to persist an XML document in the database. A mapping schema is simply an XML Schema with additional elements and attributes, appearing under a separate namespace, which contain additional data type information needed in order to persist an XML document conforming to a particular XML Schema, to the underlying data store. Although the additional metadata includes a proprietary set of tags, these do not interfere with XML document validation and processing outside of a database-specific application. These tags belong to a separate namespace and can be ignored by an XML Schema validator if need be. To enable support for editing XML Schema extensions, in Schema Design view, choose Schema Design → Enable Oracle Schema Extensions, and/or Schema Design → Enable SQL Server Extensions. XMLSPY is currently the only schema editor to support mapping of an XML Schema to a database using mapping schemas. This will add two additional tabs to the Details window. These tabs have additional attribute inspectors used to specify type mappings, as shown in Figure 5-20.

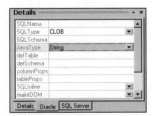

Figure 5-20: Annotating XML Schemas to work in conjunction with relational databases.

An annotated XML Schema would potentially look like the following code listing:

```
<xs:schema xmlns:xs="http://www.w3.org/2001/XMLSchema"
xmlns:xdb="http://xmlns.oracle.com/xdb">
   <xs:complexType name="PersonType">
     <xs:sequence>
       <xs:element name="First" type="xs:string"
           xdb:SQLName="FIRST" xdb:SQLType="VARCHAR2"/>
       <xs:element name="Middle" type="xs:string" minOccurs="0"
          xdb:SQLName="MIDDLE" xdb:SQLType="VARCHAR2"/>
       <xs:element name="Last" type="xs:string"
          xdb:SQLName="LAST" xdb:SQLType="VARCHAR2"/>
       <xs:element name="Age" type="xs:integer"
          xdb:SQLName="AGE" xdb:SQLType="NUMBER"/>
     </xs:sequence>
   </xs:complexType>
</xs:schema>
```

Notice the presence of an additional `http://xmlns.oracle.com/xdb` namespace and additional attributes, `SQLType` and `SQLName`.

 See Appendix A for a complete listing of add-on programming APIs.

Summary

In this chapter, I covered the most important advanced XML Schema concepts and showed you how to use them to build XML Schemas with XMLSPY. This chapter covered these topics:

◆ Using namespaces for uniquely identifying and validating XML Schema components

◆ Building composite XML Schemas consisting of externally defined XML Schema type definitions

◆ Using different compositor models to define advanced element structures and relationships

◆ Modularizing an XML Schema through the use of groups

◆ Extending existing XML Schema components through the use of object-oriented XML Schema design techniques

◆ Using XML in conjunction with relational databases and native XML repositories

This chapter wraps up the discussion of content models and validation carried through the past three chapters. It began with Document Type Validation and finished with the most advanced XML Schema concepts. In the next chapter, I begin a discussion on XML transformation, which includes a detailed discussion of the core XML technologies XSL and XSLT.

Chapter 6

Introduction to XSLT

IN THIS CHAPTER

- ◆ Introducing XSLT using XMLSPY
- ◆ Writing XSLT scripts
- ◆ Referencing XML elements

XSLT CAN SOMETIMES BE FRUSTRATING. I know that when I wrote my first XSLT script, I kept wondering where that extra information came from or why certain other information did not show up. I also wondered why certain elements could not be selected. In this chapter, I show you the essence of XSLT, how to reference XML elements, and how to transform XML documents.

Introducing XSLT by Debugging It

Trying to explain how XSLT works is often very complicated because those used to traditional programming languages (C++, Java, or Visual Basic) find that XSLT executes oddly. I think the best way to explain XSLT is to have you debug a simple Hello World example. Instead of trying to figure out some weird matching node process, you see XSLT in action.

In a nutshell, XSLT is the process of combining an XML document with an XSLT (Extensible Stylesheet Language Transformation) document to produce a new document. The XSLT document is a specially coded XML document that transforms XML content into other XML or text-based content. Listing 6-1 shows you the XSLT process in action.

Listing 6-1: Original XML Document

```
<?xml version="1.0" encoding="UTF-8"?>
<data>
    <elements>Hello</elements>
    <elements>World</elements>
</data>
```

This XML document includes two elements: `Hello` and `World`. The contents `Hello` and `World` form the basis of the generated output of the Hello World example. The following listing shows the XSLT code used to process the XML:

```
<?xml version="1.0" encoding="UTF-8"?>
<xsl:stylesheet version="1.0"
xmlns:xsl="http://www.w3.org/1999/XSL/Transform"
xmlns:fo="http://www.w3.org/1999/XSL/Format">
</xsl:stylesheet>
```

The preceding XSLT example contains no actions, just the base XML tag `stylesheet`. Notice, however, that the namespaces `xsl` and `fo` are defined. The `xsl` namespace references the XSLT specification created in 1999. The `fo` namespace references the XSL formatting objects specification. XSL formatting objects make it possible to lay out output exactly, similar to the PDF format from Adobe. XSL formatting objects, however, are beyond the scope of this book.

XMLSPY 5 includes a debugger. But before you begin the debugging process, here is something you need to understand. If you edited the preceding two documents in the order in which they are presented here, the last document that has the focus within the XMLSPY IDE is the XSL sheet. In this situation, if you start the debugger by choosing XSL → Start Debugger/Go, a dialog box asks for the sample XML file that you want to debug. If, from within the XMLSPY IDE, you edited the XML document last and then started the XMLSPY debugger, a dialog box asks for the sample XSL file that you want to debug. In either case, you can select the other document and click the OK button to begin debugging.

After the selected document has been loaded, XMLSPY switches into debug mode and reassembles to look like Figure 6-1.

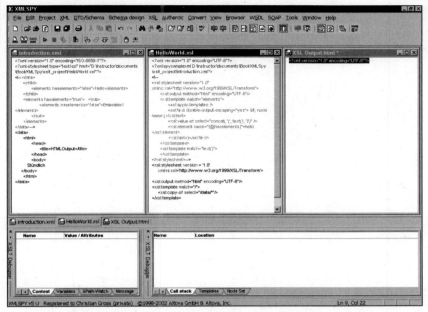

Figure 6-1: XMLSPY IDE layout after the XSLT debugger has been started.

Depending on the speed of your computer, you will likely see a few flashes and window activity. Your application has just been debugged and content generated. The output has been sent to the XSL Output.html window shown in Figure 6-1. Notice that in the window containing the output, the Hello World text is generated without any spaces between the words *Hello* and *World*.

What is interesting about this example is that output has been generated even though no action was specified in the XSLT stylesheet. The output is a default action from a default template that is invoked with every XSLT processor. In other XSLT processors and XSLT debuggers, the default template is not shown, just assumed. In XMLSPY, however, you can show the default template by stepping through the XSLT debugging process.

To invoke the XSLT debugging process, choose XSL → Step-Into. The XMLSPY IDE changes to resemble Figure 6-2.

 When repeatedly debugging or stepping into the XSLT sheet, you can skip the process of associating the XML or XSL document because the Find dialog box remembers the last debugging session. Consequently, you only have to click OK in the Find dialog box.

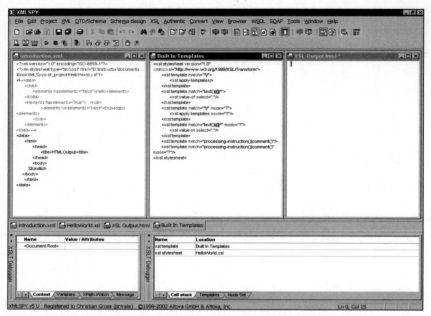

Figure 6-2: XMLSPY IDE layout after stepping into the XSLT sheet.

As you go through the debugging process, you should notice a window activation flicker and then see a new window, Built In Templates, in the center of the XMLSPY window. The file Built In Templates is an optional default XSLT file that handles any situation not handled in your XSLT document. In your live session, the XML `xsl:template` tag is highlighted, and the debugger is starting to debug the first node of the XML document. That first node is the highlighted node, and it has matched the specific XML node within the Built In Templates XML document. If you press F11 continuously, the highlighted sections change windows and skip between the XML nodes shown in the XML and XSL documents.

Please note that the term XML *node* and XML *tag* are used interchangeably at times. The difference is that an XML node can be any type of XML structure, whereas an XML tag is a type of XML node.

Analyzing the XSLT debugging process

When an XSLT document executes on an XML document and the XSLT does not select a specific node in the document, a default handler in the XSLT default template takes over. In the preceding debugging example, this was the file Built In Templates. The rules within the default template handler are just other XSLT statements. The default template within the XMLSPY IDE is shown in the following listing:

```
<xsl:stylesheet version="1.0" xmlns:xsl="http://www.w3.org/1999/XSL/Transform">
    <xsl:template match="*|/">
```

```
        <xsl:apply-templates/>
    </xsl:template>
    <xsl:template match="text()|@*">
        <xsl:value-of select="."/>
    </xsl:template>
    <xsl:template match="*|/" mode="?">
        <xsl:apply-templates mode="?"/>
    </xsl:template>
    <xsl:template match="text()|@*" mode="?">
        <xsl:value-of select="."/>
    </xsl:template>
    <xsl:template match="processing-instruction()|comment()"/>
    <xsl:template match="processing-instruction()|comment()" mode="?"/>
</xsl:stylesheet>
```

When the debugger started, the first element selected was the `xsl:template match="*|/"` XML node. This node is selected first because of the `match` attribute. The `match` attribute is a regular expression that specifies the rule to select the current XML node within the XML document.

The best way to understand the XSLT logic is to consider the XSLT processor as a running rule engine that, in a serial manner, selects each node in the XML document and attempts to match that node to an XSLT node.

In the original XML document shown in Listing 6-1, the first XML node selected is the `data` XML tag, which is kept as a selected reference in the XSLT processor. Going through the originally created XSLT document, there will be no match. But in the default template there is the match as defined in the regular expression of the backward slash, which is the root node match. After the XSLT processor has found a match in the XSLT document, the XSLT processor executes the contained XML nodes. In the case of the default template, this is the `xsl:apply-templates` XML node. The effect of `xsl:apply-templates` is that the XSL processor will process all the immediate children of the selected XML node in the XML document. What makes this selection special is the `mode` attribute. For the moment, you can ignore this. Notice that the selected XSLT node executes no specific subaction on its own.

As the XSLT processor iterates through the various XML nodes in the XML document, it attempts to match the XML node to the XSLT document. The text `Hello` and `World` are XML text nodes, and the XSLT XML node that is the associated match is `xsl:template match="text()|@*"`. The result of the matched XSLT node is to output the value of the XML text node using the `xsl:value-of` XML node.

Moving On with XSLT

As you found out by debugging, XSLT is a specially formatted XML document that operates on another document. The XSLT specification is defined by using `http://www.w3.org/1999/XSL/Transform` as a namespace identifier. Traditionally, an XSLT document uses the prefix xsl to define the XSLT namespace. However, XMLSPY and other XSLT processors can digest any other namespace. In your code examples, it is a good idea to use xsl as a prefix, especially when you are learning the XSLT techniques. Consistently using the same namespace prefix makes it easier to understand the code and to cut and paste already-created examples.

Within an XSLT document, various XML *nodes* represent XSLT instructions. It is as if an XML parser executed the value of each XML node, based on the identifier of the XML node. The XSLT processor can execute a condition, do loops, call functions, and create other generic programming constructs. Keep in mind, however, that XSLT is not a programming language in the classical sense, like Java, C++, and C#. XSLT is a programming language specifically geared toward the transformation of XML content into content that can be used for another purpose, such as presenting the text on a Web page.

Doing a simple node selection

In the debugging example shown in the preceding section, the debugging process requires the developer to constantly specify which XSLT document to debug or which XML document to associate with the XSLT document. To simplify debugging and XSLT execution, you can associate the XML file with the XSLT sheet by following these steps:

1. Within the XMLSPY IDE, select the XSLT document so that it is the window with the focus.

2. Choose XSL → Assign Sample XML. A message box appears asking if XMLSPY can reformat your XML code.

3. Click OK and the Find dialog box shown in the debugging process is displayed.

4. Select the XML file that you want to associate and click OK. At the top of the XSLT document, an additional XML instruction is added that looks similar to the following XML fragment:

```
<?xml version="1.0" encoding="UTF-8"?>
<?xmlspysamplexml D:\Instructor\BookXMLSpy\xslt_project\introduction.xml?>
<xsl:stylesheet version="1.0"
```

The XML instruction xmlspysamplexml is specific to the XMLSPY IDE and allows the debugger and XSLT processor to know which XML document should be processed by the XSLT document.

In the earlier debugging example, the XSLT processor output the XML content as default content. This form of content is not compatible with HTML because it does not contain any specific HTML tags. Most HTML browsers would read this content as simple text. To create content consumable by an HTML browser, consider the following XSLT document:

```
<?xml version="1.0" encoding="UTF-8"?>
<?xmlspysamplexml D:\Instructor\BookXMLSpy\xslt_project\introduction.xml?>
<xsl:stylesheet version="1.0" xmlns:xsl="http://www.w3.org/1999/XSL/Transform">
    <xsl:template match="*">
        <html>
            <body>
                <table>
                    <tr>
                        <td>
                            <xsl:value-of select="elements"/>
                        </td>
                    </tr>
                </table>
            </body>
        </html>
    </xsl:template>
</xsl:stylesheet>
```

The XSLT document just shown matches the node as defined by the XML node xsl:template. In this XSLT example, the match expression is *, which says "match any node." The template definition includes a series of HTML tags and also the xsl:value-of XML node. When the XSLT processor finds a match, it executes the content within the found XML node. The default execution of non-XSL tags outputs the non-XSL tags to the output stream. In this example, the default execution means the generation of HTML tags. When the xsl:value-of XML node is hit, the XSLT processor executes the instruction. In the case of xsl:value-of, the XSLT selects the node specified by the select attribute and outputs the text values of that content. The select attribute specifies to find all subchild elements where the XML node tag identifier is elements. If you refer back to Listing 6-1, you can see that it has two elements XML nodes. Executing the XSLT as is results in the following XML output:

```
<html>
    <body>
        <table>
            <tr><td>Hello</td></tr>
        </table>
    </body>
</html>
```

It would appear from the HTML output that the XSLT processor made an error because only the `Hello` content is output and the `World` content is missing. It is not an XSLT processor error, but an XSLT document-instruction error.

TRACING THE XSLT PROCESSING STEPS

As it goes through the XSLT processing steps, the XSLT matches the `xsl:template`. But this match only occurs once because when a match is found, that node and all subnodes are considered found. So, in the case of the XML document, the `data` XML node is found. Then the contents of the found node are executed, and the XSLT processor exits. The `data` XML node is the root node, and all subnodes are tagged for further processing. The result is that the XSLT does not have any other nodes to process.

When the `xsl:template` items are being executed, the `xsl:value-of` instruction outputs only the first matched element, which in this case is the first `elements` XML node. The later `elements` XML node is skipped. Because of this and because the XSLT processing marks all `elements` XML nodes as found, only one `elements` XML node is displayed.

When all the XML nodes within the `xsl:template` are executed, you can assume that the nodes are legal XML. This is an important consideration because HTML is not XML-compliant. Specifically, the HTML tag `<br>` does not require a closing `</br>` tag. When a sole `<br>` HTML tag is added to the XSLT document, the XSLT processor will cause an error indicating the incorrectness of the XSLT document. Therefore, when you generate HTML content from an XSLT document, the HTML content must be valid XML.

Iterating within an XSLT document

You can iterate through the XML content in two ways, as defined by the original XML document. The first way is to specifically select the element. The other is to specifically iterate a node set. These two methods are described in the following sections.

SPECIFICALLY SELECTING AN ELEMENT

Thus far, the template matches have been wildcard matches, which means that the root XML node is selected. To select a specific node, you can change the `match` attribute to a specific XML node identifier, as shown in the following XSLT document. Notice that the HTML content generation has been removed for simplicity.

```
<?xml version="1.0" encoding="UTF-8"?>
<?xmlspysamplexml
    D:\Instructor\BookXMLSpy\xslt_project\introduction.xml?>
<xsl:stylesheet version="1.0"
    xmlns:xsl="http://www.w3.org/1999/XSL/Transform">
    <xsl:template match="*">
        (<xsl:value-of select="."/>)
```

```
    </xsl:template>
    <xsl:template match="elements">
        (<xsl:value-of select="."/>)
    </xsl:template>
</xsl:stylesheet>
```

The second `xsl:template` has a `match` value of `elements`. Executing the XSLT document results in the following output:

```
<?xml version="1.0" encoding="UTF-8"?>
    (HelloWorld)
```

This result is not what you want. Instead, it is a result of the XSLT processing rule that says that when a node is selected, so are all the child nodes. To prove this, the `xsl:value-of` within the XSLT document is changed to the following:

```
(<xsl:value-of select="name()"/>)
```

Within the `select` attribute, as was shown previously, a node can be selected and called a regular expression. This new version is still a regular expression, but it is also an XPath expression. *XPath* is a specification that an XSLT processor uses to select individual XML nodes. But it is also possible with XPath to call specific functions that retrieve the values of an XML node. In the modified `xsl:value-of` node, the textual identifier of the currently selected XML node is output. Executing the modified XSLT document results in the following output:

```
<?xml version="1.0" encoding="UTF-8"?>
    (data)
```

This output shows that, indeed, the root XML element has been selected and the XSLT processor exits processing. There is a way out of this problem: reselecting all the child nodes. You do this by using the `xsl:apply-templates` XSLT instruction, which allows iteration of the child nodes. Here is the modified XSLT document:

```
<?xml version="1.0" encoding="UTF-8"?>
<?xmlspysamplexml
    D:\Instructor\BookXMLSpy\xslt_project\introduction.xml?>
<xsl:stylesheet version="1.0"
    xmlns:xsl="http://www.w3.org/1999/XSL/Transform">
    <xsl:template match="*">
        <xsl:apply-templates />
        (<xsl:value-of select="name()"/>)
    </xsl:template>
    <xsl:template match="elements">
        (<xsl:value-of select="name()"/>)
```

```
    </xsl:template>
</xsl:stylesheet>
```

To make the XML document more interesting, the first `elements` XML node is embedded within a `child` XML node. The modified XML document is as follows:

```
<?xml version="1.0" encoding="UTF-8"?>
<?xml-stylesheet type="text/xsl"
    href="D:\Instructor\BookXMLSpy\xslt_project\HelloWorld.xsl"?>
<data>
    <child>
        <elements>Hello</elements>
    </child>
    <elements>World</elements>
</data>
```

If the modified XSLT document is executed, the following results are generated:

```
<?xml version="1.0" encoding="UTF-8"?>
            (elements)

            (child)

            (elements)

            (data)
```

Looking at this output, you can see that the `elements` nodes have indeed been selected along with the individual `child` and `data` nodes. Simply put, instead of a single node selection, all nodes have been selected.

A compromise is to select only the `elements` XML nodes by commenting out the `xsl:template` with a wildcard `match` attribute, as shown by the following modified XSLT document fragment:

```
<xsl:stylesheet version="1.0"
    xmlns:xsl="http://www.w3.org/1999/XSL/Transform">
    <!--<xsl:template match="*">
        <xsl:apply-templates />
        (<xsl:value-of select="name()"/>)
        </xsl:template>-->
    <xsl:template match="elements">
```

Now instead of selecting every XML node in the document, only the `elements` XML nodes are selected. Executing the modified XSLT document results in the following output:

```
<?xml version="1.0" encoding="UTF-8"?>
    (elements)

    (elements)
```

The generated output gives you what you originally wanted.

After you see the various XSLT modifications, it should become apparent that selection is not such a simple thing. Another complication that can occur is when found elements are embedded within each other.

Consider the following modified XML document:

```
<?xml version="1.0" encoding="UTF-8"?>
<?xml-stylesheet type="text/xsl"
    href="D:\Instructor\BookXMLSpy\xslt_project\HelloWorld.xsl"?>
<data>
    <child>
        <elements>Hello</elements>
    </child>
    <elements>World<sub>
    <elements>Embedded</elements></sub></elements>
</data>
```

In this modified XML document, the elements XML node has an embedded elements XML node. Running the modified XSLT document on the modified XML document results in the following output:

```
<?xml version="1.0" encoding="UTF-8"?>
    (elements)

    (elements)

    (elements)
```

The modified XML document contains four references to elements XML nodes, but only three are output. This result is a problem because only the outer elements XML node has been selected; the inner elements XML node has been ignored. This means that information has been lost. To get around this, you have to apply the xsl:apply-templates rule within the found template, as shown in the following XSLT document fragment:

```
<xsl:template match="elements">
    <xsl:apply-templates />
    (<xsl:value-of select="name()"/>)
</xsl:template>
```

Running the modified XSLT document on the modified XML document results in the following output:

```
<?xml version="1.0" encoding="UTF-8"?>WorldEmbedded
    (elements)
    (elements)
    (elements)
    (elements)
```

Now the correct output has been generated because all elements XML nodes have been selected. The flipside of this may be that the developer intended for the embedded elements XML node to be ignored. But that is a decision that must be made when designing the XML data and XSLT document.

ITERATING A FOUND ELEMENT

The other way of iterating various XML nodes is to use the XSLT instruction xsl:for-each. This XSLT instruction builds a node set based on the matching criteria identical to the xsl:value-of select attribute. Consider the following XML document:

```
<data>
    <child>
        <elements>Hello</elements>
    </child>
    <elements>World<sub>
        <elements>Embedded</elements></sub>
    </elements>
</data>
```

The simplest iteration strategy is to select the data root XML node and then iterate through the various elements XML nodes. You can apply the following XSLT document:

```
<xsl:stylesheet version="1.0"
    xmlns:xsl="http://www.w3.org/1999/XSL/Transform">
    <xsl:template match="*">
        <xsl:for-each select="elements">
            (<xsl:value-of select="name()"/>)
        </xsl:for-each>
    </xsl:template>
</xsl:stylesheet>
```

The xsl:for-each instruction must be within the found xsl:template and is applied to the currently found node. In this case, the found node would be the data node because of the wildcard match. The xsl:for-each select attribute specifies the `elements` XML node XPath expression. Running the XSLT document on the XML document results in the following output:

```
<?xml version="1.0" encoding="UTF-8"?>
    (elements)
```

This result is only partially correct. Only one of the three possible `elements` has been found because the XPath expression was written incorrectly. In the XSLT document, the XPath only selects the `elements` XML nodes that are directly below the `data` XML node. This means that only the first-level `child` nodes are selected. With respect to this XML document, there is only a first-level child `elements` node. To select all the child `elements` XML nodes, you need to modify the XPath to the following:

```
<xsl:for-each select="//elements">
```

The added double slash is a special function in XPath that says, "Select all the XML nodes with the identifier `elements`, regardless of where they appear in the current selection." Running the modified XSLT document on the XML document results in the following output:

```
<?xml version="1.0" encoding="UTF-8"?>
    (elements)

    (elements)

    (elements)
```

This is the result that you want considering that there are three child `elements` XML nodes. But change your query to match all `elements` XML nodes within a specific `child` XML node. The XSLT query to execute against the XML document at the beginning of this section is as follows:

```
<xsl:stylesheet version="1.0"
    xmlns:xsl="http://www.w3.org/1999/XSL/Transform">
    <xsl:template match="child">
        <xsl:for-each select="//elements">
            (<xsl:value-of select="name()"/>)
        </xsl:for-each>
    </xsl:template>
</xsl:stylesheet>
```

The expected result of this document is for the XSLT processor to iterate all the XML nodes. When it finds a `child` XML node, all the descendant child `elements`

XML nodes are iterated and displayed. Running the modified XSLT document on the XML document results in the following output:

```
<?xml version="1.0" encoding="UTF-8"?>
    (elements)

    (elements)

    (elements)
    WorldEmbedded
```

This result is not the desired output because the XML document at the beginning of this section has one `child` XML node and only one contained `elements` XML node. All `elements` XML nodes in the document have been selected because the XPath query did not reference the current XML node location. Here is the correct XPath:

```
<xsl:for-each select=".//elements">
```

The difference in this selection is the period before the double slash. The period is an XPath instruction that says, "Start the search in the current context and not in the root document." Executing the new XSLT query results in the following output:

```
<?xml version="1.0" encoding="UTF-8"?>
    (elements)
    WorldEmbedded
```

This output is correct because only one `elements` XML node has been selected.

What is a bit bothersome is that the content `WorldEmbedded` is generated even though it has nothing to do with the XSLT document. The answer to this problem requires an additional inspection of the original XML document and the location of the generated content. Consider the original XML document again and look at the bold section:

```
<data>
    <child>
        <elements>Hello</elements>
    </child>
    <elements>World<sub>
        <elements>Embedded</elements></sub>
    </elements>
</data>
```

What should become apparent is that the bold XML elements are not selected by the XSLT document specified by the user. Instead, those XML elements are selected by the default template, as shown by the following XSLT default template fragment:

```
<xsl:template match="*|/" mode="?">
    <xsl:apply-templates mode="?"/>
</xsl:template>
<xsl:template match="text()|@*" mode="?">
    <xsl:value-of select="."/>
</xsl:template>
```

Notice the second xsl:template, which has a match of text(). This XSLT instruction is responsible for generating the extra output. This output informs the developer that some XML content has not been accounted for. To get rid of this unwanted side effect, you need to modify the XSLT document to the following:

```
<xsl:stylesheet version="1.0" xmlns:xsl="http://www.w3.org/1999/XSL/Transform">
    <xsl:template match="child">
        <xsl:for-each select=".//elements">
            (<xsl:value-of select="name()"/>)
        </xsl:for-each>
    </xsl:template>
    <xsl:template match="text()">
    </xsl:template>
</xsl:stylesheet>
```

The additional xsl:template with a match of text() overrides the default template handler without affecting the XSLT generation of the document. The function text() is another Xpath-specific function. In this case, the match XML attribute indicates that if there is a text node that has a value, true is returned for matching.

TIP

Because I am writing a book, when I am trying to diagnose an XSLT problem like the one just outlined, I have time to experiment and figure out why certain problems arise. But in a production-coding scenario, you do not have that luxury. The easiest way to diagnose any XSLT problem is to debug it using the XMLSPY XSLT debugger. Following any other course of action is a lesson in futility.

Finding the Intended Content

One thing you may have noticed is that it isn't always easy to find the intended content within an XML document by using XPath and regular expressions. Often in XSLT, a query is executed and the result contains extra bits that are either added to the result or are missing from the result. And to get those extra bits included in the result, other bits magically appear. XSLT selection can be a mind-boggling problem that generates strange side effects. The simplest way to understand XPath expressions is to consider an XPath expression as a directory location alteration.

When you type the following command, you expect to move up a level in the directory structure:

```
cd ..
```

When you type this next command, you expect to change directories to the subdirectory `documents`:

```
cd documents
```

XPath works in a similar way to these directory identifiers except that the path manipulations are much richer, more flexible, and do not require the `cd` command.

Using the XMLSPY Evaluate XPath functionality

To edit an XPath expression, a simple approach is to type the XPath in the XSLT document and run the XSLT document. If the XPath is correct, XML content is generated. But if you want an experiment that gives immediate gratification, the XMLSPY XPath Evaluator is better. To access the XPath Evaluator, select the XML document that you want to test and then choose XML → Evaluate XPath. This command sequence results in the dialog box shown in Figure 6-3.

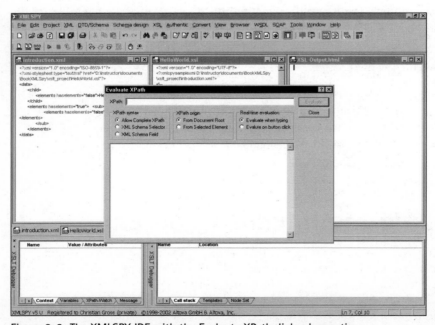

Figure 6-3: The XMLSPY IDE with the Evaluate XPath dialog box active.

The Evaluate XPath dialog box dynamically executes an XPath on the loaded XML document and shows the results in the dialog box text area. As a simple test, type the following into the XPath text box in the dialog box:

```
//elements
```

The results are similar to those shown in Figure 6-4.

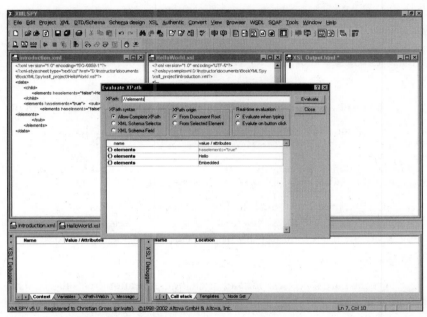

Figure 6-4: The XPath Evaluation output.

XPath basics

The examples shown thus far are all relatively simple and straightforward. The following XPath example is a bit more sophisticated:

```
child::elements[ attribute::embedded != "true"]
```

What this XPath example says is "Find all the child `elements` XML nodes in which the embedded XML attribute is not equal to the value of `true`." In this more sophisticated example, the concepts of axis, predicates, and so on have been used.

CHANGING POSITION IN XML

When you reference XML nodes in an XPath expression, a position change occurs. Usually in XPath, the way to reference a sub-element would be use one of the following notations:

```
*

/item

/*[ 1]

//item[ 1]
```

In all these examples, the sub-element is specified using special characters, which are defined as follows:

- ◆ *: Match all sub-elements specified at the current context (current location).

- ◆ /: Select the root document element as the current context (lack of / indicates selection starts at the current context).

- ◆ //: Make all nodes the current context (consider this as an XML document where all the nodes have the chance to be a root node).

- ◆ [ ]: Specify a predicate from which the nodes selected thus far are filtered according to the rules indicated inside the brackets (in the samples shown, the predicates are to find the first element of the selection).

- ◆ .: Select the current context (usually is not referenced).

- ◆ ..: Select the parent element instead of changing location to a sub-element.

- ◆ @: Select a specific attribute based on the current context (when used with the wildcard *, will select all attributes).

The XPath examples shown previously are called *abbreviated syntax XPath* because they use the special characters shown in the preceding list. As the following examples demonstrate, however, you can express the previous examples by using standard XPath with axis specifiers:

```
child::*

child::item

child::*[ 1]

descendant::item[ 1]
```

The *axis specifier* is the text before the double colon. Following the double colon is the same text as in the abbreviated XPath syntax. The wildcards and predicates are still applicable. The axis specifiers are defined as follows (note that all axis identifiers are relative to the current context):

- `child`: References all the children of the current context

- `descendant`: References all the children of the current context, which includes children of children

- `parent`: References the parent of the current context

- `ancestor`: References the parent of the current context, which includes the parent of the parent

- `ancestor-or-self`: References the current context or the parents of the current context, which includes the parent of the parent

- `following-sibling`: References all the following XML nodes from the current context

- `preceding-sibling`: References all the preceding XML nodes from the current context

- `following`: References all XML nodes after the current context

- `preceding`: References all the XML nodes before the current context

- `attribute`: References a specific attribute from the current context

- `namespace`: Contains the namespace nodes of the current context

- `self` : References the current context

- `descendant-or-self`: References the current context and all descendants

- `ancestor-or-self`: References the current context and all ancestors

DEMONSTRATING AXIS SPECIFIERS

The best way to illustrate what an axis specifier does is to illustrate it through various examples.

The axis specifier examples do not show that I used the Evaluate XPath dialog box; however, I want to reiterate that I did. You may be under the impression that I used the XSLT query expression. You should also use this dialog box when you're experimenting with XPath.

The XPath expressions that I execute in the following examples are all based on this XML document:

```
<data>
    <child>
        <elements>Hello</elements>
    </child>
    <elements>World<sub>
        <elements>Embedded</elements></sub>
    </elements>
</data>
```

In the following examples, an XPath expression is defined, executed on the XML document, and the result is highlighted in the XML document. Notice that I use bold in the XPath expression results to indicate the selected XML nodes.

Starting with a simple child selection, consider the following XPath:

```
child::*
```

The selected nodes are shown in bold, as follows:

```
<data>
    <child>
        <elements>Hello</elements>
    </child>
    <elements>World<sub>
        <elements>Embedded</elements></sub></elements>
</data>
```

Notice that selection results are the root node. This may seem a bit puzzling because you would expect that the child nodes are child and elements XML nodes. The selected nodes are still the same, even if you modify the XPath to the following:

```
/child::*
```

The reason for this is the XML specification. The root node is not the data XML node, but the XML document, which has a child XML node data. It is a small item to remember, but you need to keep it in mind because it can be confusing at times.

Now consider the following XPath that selects a specific XML node:

```
/child::*/child::child
```

The selected nodes are shown in bold in the following:

```
<data>
    <child>
        <elements>Hello</elements>
    </child>
        <elements>World<sub>
            <elements>Embedded</elements></sub></elements>
</data>
```

This selection is fairly obvious because it is an XML node drill down. To make this selection a bit more interesting, use the descendant axis specifier, as in the following expression:

```
/child::*/descendant::elements
```

The selected nodes are shown in bold:

```
<data>
    <child>
        <elements>Hello</elements>
    </child>
    <elements>World<sub>
        <elements>Embedded</elements></sub></elements>
</data>
```

The descendant axis specifier makes it possible to select a current context and then select each child XML node within it. This is useful when you want to select every XML node or a specific set of XML nodes beneath a specific context.

If, however, you want to find XML nodes after a found condition, use the following axis specifier, as shown by the following example:

```
/child::*/child::child/following::elements
```

The selected nodes are shown in bold:

```
<data>
    <child>
        <elements>Hello</elements>
    </child>
    <elements>World<sub>
        <elements>Embedded</elements></sub></elements>
</data>
```

The `following` axis specifier is like a `descendant` axis specifier in that all element nodes are selected including the embedded `elements` XML node. If only the first level of the following XML nodes are to be selected, the `following` axis specifier needs to be replaced with `following-sibling`, as in this example:

```
/child::*/child::child/following-sibling::elements
```

The selected nodes are shown in bold:

```
<data>
      <child>
              <elements>Hello</elements>
      </child>
      <elements>World<sub>
              <elements>Embedded</elements></sub></elements>
</data>
```

The `preceding` and `preceding-sibling` axis specifiers function identically to the `following` and `following-sibling` axis specifiers, except that the `preceding` and `preceding-sibling` axis specifiers search the XML nodes before the current context. Consider the following use of the `preceding` axis specifier:

```
/child::*/child::child/preceding::*
```

The selected nodes are shown in bold:

```
<data>
      <child>
              <elements>Hello</elements>
      </child>
      <elements>World<sub>
              <elements>Embedded</elements></sub></elements>
</data>
```

Notice that nothing is selected, even though the `data` XML node is before the `child` XML node. But the `data` XML node is a level higher, meaning that it is a parent and therefore is not part of the selection. To make this selection work, the `ancestor` axis specifier is used as shown in the following example:

```
/child::*/child::child/ancestor::*
```

The selected nodes are shown in bold:

```
<data>
      <child>
```

```
                <elements>Hello</elements>
        </child>
        <elements>World<sub>
                <elements>Embedded</elements></sub></elements>
</data>
```

The selected `data` XML node is a correct selection because it is the parent of the `child` XML node. Note that if there were a parent to the `data` XML node, it would be selected as well. A tweak to this selection is to include the current context in the XPath, as the following example shows:

```
/child::*/child::child/elements/ancestor-or-self::*
```

The selected nodes are shown in bold:

```
<data>
        <child>
                <elements>Hello</elements>
        </child>
        <elements>World<sub>
                <elements>Embedded</elements></sub></elements>
</data>
```

Notice in the XPath, the `elements` XML node is referenced directly without an axis specifier. This is legal and implies the `child` axis specifier. The node set is correct and includes the current context.

> **TIP** When using the `self` keyword within an axis specifier, be careful about looping because the current context is in the selection. This could lead to an infinite loop.

If only the parent is to be selected, you use the `parent` axis specifier, as shown in the following example:

```
/child::*/child::child/elements/parent::*
```

The selected nodes are shown in bold:

```
<data>
        <child>
                <elements>Hello</elements>
        </child>
        <elements>World<sub>
```

```
                <elements>Embedded</elements></sub></elements>
</data>
```

The result is as expected, but only because the `parent` axis specifier has a wild-card parent selection. If the wildcard were to be exchanged with a specific XML node identifier, such as `elements`, the XPath would return an empty parent node set. This type of selection is very useful when testing if the parent is a specific XML node type.

The `attribute` axis specifier is not useful when the default XML document is utilized. A modified XML document that includes an attribute looks like the following:

```
<data>
        <child haselements="true">
                <elements>Hello</elements>
        </child>
        <elements>World<sub>
                <elements>Embedded</elements></sub></elements>
</data>
```

Execute the following XPath expression:

```
/child::*/child::child/attribute::*
```

The selected node is shown in bold:

```
<data>
        <child haselements="true">
                <elements>Hello</elements>
        </child>
        <elements>World<sub>
                <elements>Embedded</elements></sub></elements>
</data>
```

The node set includes a number of attributes. In the XML document, there is only one. It is important to realize that when attributes are selected, axis specifiers such as `following` and `preceding` still apply.

DETERMINING WHEN TO USE AXIS SPECIFIERS AND ABBREVIATED SYNTAX

After you have gone through the axis specifier syntax and abbreviated syntax, it could be tempting to rewrite the preceding example using the `attribute` axis specifier to the following abbreviated syntax:

```
/child::*/child::child[@*]
```

But when the XPath is evaluated, the node set is not the same as the attribute axis specifier example. The square brackets are predicates that filter out XML nodes that contain attributes. The correct XPath that returns the same result set as if you used the attribute axis specifier is as follows:

```
/child::*/child::child/@*
```

Now the XPath returns the same selection of attributes. This leads us to an interesting finding. XPaths require some experience to fully understand how the selection occurs. In the simplest case, XPaths are used in XSLT to set a current context, and most likely the abbreviated syntax is used. But there are situations where fine-tuning or a more specific type of selection is required. In that scenario, the axis XPath specifiers are very useful because they allow exact definition of a node set. Axis XPath specifiers are not as cumbersome as the abbreviated syntax, but this does not mean that you should always use the axis specifier syntax. The reason for the creation of the abbreviated syntax is to allow a developer to quickly write a generic XPath expression without having to be too verbose.

USING XPATH EXPRESSIONS

Also possible in XPath is the capability to use functions to retrieve information about a given context. The axis specifiers and the abbreviated syntax allow a developer to select a specific context or node set. But that node set is useless when trying to transform content because the node set will be output without the control of the XSLT document. To get specific control of the output, XPath expressions are used. But XPath expressions can also be used to manage multiple conditions. For example, the XMLSPY Built In templates debugged at the start of this chapter had the following rule:

```
<xsl:template match="*|/" mode="?">
      <xsl:apply-templates mode="?"/>
</xsl:template>
```

The `xsl:template` match uses the vertical bar (|) to denote one condition or another. If you're a C, C++, C#, or Java programmer, you know that this bar is an `or` operator used in a conditional statement. The operators can combine with expressions, which were used in the `xsl:value-of` XSLT XML nodes.

Taking a Close Look at Other XSLT Statements

XSLT is like a functional programming language in that XSLT has loops, conditions, and selection statements. In this part of the chapter, you experiment with these XSLT constructs. To experiment with these constructs, a modified version of the XML document employed previously is used again. The modifications are added to make the results more interesting. For this section the modified XML document is as follows:

```
<data>
    <child>
        <elements haselements="false">Hello</elements>
    </child>
    <elements haselements="true">World<sub>
        <elements haselements="false">Embedded</elements></sub>
    </elements>
</data>
```

Repetition with xsl:for-each

The core instruction for iterating through a node set is the `xsl:for-each` statement. The `xsl:for-each` statement does not require an already-selected node set, but selects a node based on the `select` attribute. To iterate all the descendant nodes, the following XSLT can be executed:

```
<xsl:stylesheet version="1.0" xmlns:xsl="http://www.w3.org/1999/XSL/Transform">
    <xsl:template match="/">
        <xsl:for-each select="descendant::*">
            node name (<xsl:value-of select="name()" />)
            node value (<xsl:value-of select="text()"/>)
        </xsl:for-each>
    </xsl:template>
    <xsl:template match="text()">
    </xsl:template>
</xsl:stylesheet>
```

When this XSLT is executed on the XML document, the following content is generated:

```
<?xml version="1.0" encoding="UTF-8"?>
                    node name (data)
                    node value ()

                    node name (child)
                    node value ()

                    node name (elements)
                    node value (Hello)
```

```
node name (elements)
node value (World)

node name (sub)
node value ()

node name (elements)
node value (Embedded)
```

If you cross-reference the output with the XML document, the generated output iterates every XML node and outputs the associated XML text values. In the xsl:for-each statement, the select attribute is required and must result in a node set. For example, the following XPath in the select attribute causes an error:

```
<xsl:for-each select="descendant::*/attribute::haselements='true'">
    node name (<xsl:value-of select="name()" />)
    node value (<xsl:value-of select="text()"/>)
</xsl:for-each>
```

The preceding generates an error because the XPath, with the inclusion of the equal character, performs a conditional test that generates a true or false result. A true or false result is not a node set. The following shows a modified XPath with a conditional test that is legal and implements a filter in which the haselements XML attribute is true:

```
<xsl:for-each select="descendant::*[@haselements='true']">
    node name (<xsl:value-of select="name()" />)
    node value (<xsl:value-of select="text()"/>)
</xsl:for-each>
```

The conditional test is removed and added as a filter, which queries a node to see if a specific condition is true. This is the desired effect because the filter is defined by the square brackets, which should return either a true or false value. The filter does not need to only query attributes, but it could be used to test for any condition that can be defined using an XPath expression.

USING XSL:TEMPLATE AND XSL: FOR-EACH TOGETHER

In this next set of examples, you search for embedded elements XML nodes. The purpose of these examples is to show that an XSLT repetition and a template match can be used to accomplish the exact same thing as what you did when I initially explained the purpose of xsl:for-each. To find the various embedded element tags, the following XPATH can be used in the XSLT:

```
<xsl:template match="/">
    <xsl:for-each select="descendant::elements[ancestor::elements]">
```

```
        node name (<xsl:value-of select="name()" />)
        node value (<xsl:value-of select="text()"/>)
    </xsl:for-each>
</xsl:template>
```

When executed, this code results in the following output:

```
<?xml version="1.0" encoding="UTF-8"?>
    node name (elements)
    node value (Embedded)
```

Notice that the xsl:template match attribute is set to the root XML node. Then a selection in the xsl:for-each iterates through all the descendant nodes with an XML node identifier of elements. The filter ancestor::elements ensures that the found elements XML node is embedded in another elements XML node. The search strategy is not to find an elements XML node and then check for embedded elements XML nodes, but the inverse.

The same result can be achieved using the following modified xsl:template match:

```
<xsl:template match="elements">
    <xsl:for-each select="descendant::elements">
        node name (<xsl:value-of select="name()" />)
        node value (<xsl:value-of select="text()"/>)
    </xsl:for-each>
</xsl:template>
```

In this example XSLT, the xsl:template match is not the root element, but the individual elements XML nodes. And the xsl:for-each select attribute is set to find all embedded elements XML nodes. Notice the use of the descendant axis specifier so that all child elements XML nodes are iterated. In contrast to the previous selection, a specific element is found and then the various subchildren elements XML nodes are selected.

After you study both these examples, you might want to clarify which method of selecting nodes is better. The answer is that neither way is better. To a large degree, the method you use is a matter of personal preference. The only real difference between them is that the second approach (selecting an individual node) distinctly separates the various functionalities of the XSLT. For example, in the root node match example, there could be various xsl:for-each matches. By using function calls and references, you can compensate for the downside of this method. To repeat, in the end, it is really a matter of personal preference.

Conditional processing with an xsl:if

Another approach to solving the embedded `elements` XML node problem is to use a condition. As in the second approach where the various `elements` nodes are iterated, a test is made if there is a parent `elements` XML node. The XSLT would be as follows:

```
<xsl:template match="elements">
    <xsl:apply-templates />
    <xsl:if test="ancestor::elements">
            node name (<xsl:value-of select="name()" />)
            node value (<xsl:value-of select="text()"/>)
    </xsl:if>
</xsl:template>
```

When executed, this code results in the following output:

```
<?xml version="1.0" encoding="UTF-8"?>
    node name (elements)
    node value (Embedded)
```

This is desired output, but it is only possible if the `xsl:apply-templates` XSL instruction is added. Remember from previous discussions that without this instruction, the embedded `elements` XML nodes are not iterated because those elements are marked as read. This effect did not occur in the previous example because the various `elements` nodes were manually iterated.

The `xsl:if` XSL instruction uses a Boolean result to know whether or not to execute the contained instructions. If the XPath contained within the test attribute is a non-zero result, the test is considered `true`. Otherwise, the test is considered `false`. The way that results are converted to `true` or `false` is by using the same rules applied when a value is converted to an XSLT Boolean type. After a `true` result, the XML nodes within the `xsl:if` statement are executed. The test attribute does not change the location of the current context, even though tests of other XML nodes can be executed.

TIP

Late at night, I was writing this conditional processing code and forgot the `xsl:apply-templates` XSL instruction. The XSLT processor initially did not return the correct result. As an experiment, I used the XPath `not(ancestor::elements)`, which returned all elements that I expected. This puzzled me, and I quickly decided to use the XMLSPY XSLT debugger. Within a few seconds the problem was solved. The moral of the story? Use the XMLSPY XSLT debugger to figure out why your code is not working and your life will be simpler.

In the example, the `xsl:if` the test was simple: Does a node set exist or not? The `not` function can be used to invert the result. A `not` converts a `false` value into a `true`, and a `true` value into a `false`. The following is a list of available operators (note that not all can be used in the context of an XSL condition):

◆ `not`: Converts the contained result value to the inverse value. The function `not` returns either a Boolean `true` or `false` and not a node set. If a populated node set is inverted, a `false` is returned. If an empty node set is inverted, a `true` is returned.

◆ `=`: Equality comparison. Typically used to compare two different values to see if they are identical. The equality operator does not modify the original data types, but converts each to a similar type, which when compared returns either a `true` for a match or `false` for no match.

◆ `!=`: Inequality comparison. Typically used to compare two different values to see if they are not identical. The equality operator does not modify the original data types, but converts each to a similar type, which when compared returns either a `true` for a mismatch or `false` for a match.

◆ `<`, `<=`: Less-than and less-than-or-equal-to operator. This tests to see if a value is less than another. For example, 1 is less than 2. Typically this operator is used on numeric values because strings or node sets return odd results that are not entirely useful.

◆ `>`, `>=`: Greater-than and greater-than-or-equal-to operator. This tests to see if a value is greater than another. For example, 2 is greater than 1. Typically, this operator is used on numeric values because strings or node sets return odd results that are not entirely useful.

◆ `and`: The `and` operator is a bit type operator that combines two values and returns a value. When used in a condition, that value is converted into a Boolean value.

◆ `or`: The `or` operator is a bit type operator that combines two values and returns a value. When used in a condition, that value is converted into a Boolean value.

◆ `|`: The vertical bar operator is also an `or` operator. But it is not an abbreviated `or` because the result is different. When using a vertical bar and the results are two node sets, the two node sets are concatenated into one node set. When using the formal `or` operator a Boolean result is returned. If either `or` is used in a condition, the same result is returned because both results are converted to Booleans.

Conditional processing with an xsl:choose

The `xsl:if` statement is a single condition test. Typically, in other programming languages, you have the capability to test a condition and, if that condition does not work, to test another condition. In XSLT that same approach is possible, but the xsl:choose instruction must be used as in the following example:

```
<xsl:template match="elements">
    <xsl:apply-templates />
    <xsl:choose>
        <xsl:when test="@haselements = 'true'">
            node value (<xsl:value-of select="text()" />)
            true value
        </xsl:when>
        <xsl:when test="@haselements = 'false'">
            node value (<xsl:value-of select="text()" />)
            false value
        </xsl:when>
    </xsl:choose>
</xsl:template>
```

The xsl:choose instruction is the start of a block of contained xsl:when instructions. Each xsl:when instruction has a test attribute, which performs a test identical to the xsl:if instruction. When the first xsl:when test returns a value of true, the XML nodes within the xsl:when instruction are executed. At the end of the executed xsl:when block, the XSLT processor jumps out of the xsl:choose block and continues executing other XSLT instructions.

You can write the same conditions using the xsl:if instruction as follows:

```
<xsl:template match="elements">
    <xsl:apply-templates />
    <xsl:if test="@haselements = 'true'">
        node value (<xsl:value-of select="text()" />)
        true value
    </xsl:if>
    <xsl:if test="@haselements = 'false'">
        node value (<xsl:value-of select="text()" />)
        false value
    </xsl:if>
</xsl:template>
```

In contrast to the xsl:choose instruction, if the first xsl:if results in a true value, the second xsl:if may be executed as well. Of course in the example shown, that cannot be the case because the attribute haselements cannot have the value true and false at the same time. What is more likely to happen if a test is executed is that a different test may execute as well. Therefore, knowing which condition to choose in an XSLT is simple. In a single condition test, use xsl:if; in a multicondition test, use xsl:choose.

The other additional option with `xsl:choose` is the `xsl:otherwise` instruction. The `xsl:otherwise` option is executed when no `xsl:when` condition matches true. For example, you could write the following XSLT:

```
<xsl:template match="*">
     <xsl:apply-templates />
     <xsl:choose>
          <xsl:when test="@haselements = 'true'">
              node value (<xsl:value-of select="text()" />)
              true value
          </xsl:when>
          <xsl:when test="@haselements = 'false'">
              node value (<xsl:value-of select="text()" />)
              false value
          </xsl:when>
          <xsl:otherwise>
              node name (<xsl:value-of select="name()" />)
              node value (<xsl:value-of select="text()" />)
          </xsl:otherwise>
     </xsl:choose>
</xsl:template>
```

In this example of `xsl:choose`, there are two tests and a default execution. This multicondition `xsl:choose` executes the logic that if the found XML node has a true or false value, do something. Otherwise, perform the default of printing out the XML node identifier and value. In a real business application, this logic could be an error generation to indicate a condition that should not have occurred.

In the case of either `xsl:if` or `xsl:choose`, it is possible to embed one condition within another. For example, if an `xsl:if` results in a true, there could be an `xsl:choose` instruction within the `xsl:if`. This is also true for an `xsl:choose`, except that the embedded `xsl:if` must be embedded within an `xsl:when`.

The sort feature

By default, when executing a repetition or a templates application, the order of the nodes is dependent on their position in the XML document. There are situations in which a node set should be sorted according to specific criteria. The `xsl:sort` instruction is responsible for sorting the data. A simple example of sorting all the elements XML nodes is as follows:

```
<xsl:template match="/">
    <xsl:for-each select="descendant::elements">
        <xsl:sort select="text()" data-type="text"
            order="ascending" />
            node name (<xsl:value-of select="name()" />)
```

```
            node value (<xsl:value-of select="text()"/>)
    </xsl:for-each>
</xsl:template>
```

The `xsl:sort` instruction is a child of the `xsl:for-each` or `xsl:apply-templates` instruction. Although the specification indicates that only the `xsl:sort` instruction must be a child, placing the `xsl:sort` instruction as a child of position index > 1 causes the sort to be ignored. If you check the XSLT specification, it is not clear if this is a correct interpretation of the XMLSPY XSLT processor. Therefore, the XMLSPY interpretation is assumed to be correct.

Each `xsl:sort` instruction represents a sort order to the node set that has been selected. Multiple `xsl:sort` instructions can be present, but each additional `xsl:sort` instruction represents an additional sort order. If, in the previous sort example, another `xsl:sort` instruction were added, the sorting would be first to the `text()` value and then to the added `xsl:sort` critieria.

In most cases, every `xsl:sort` should have three individual attributes that specify how the sort should occur. The full specification is as follows:

- ◆ `select`: Expression used as a key for sorting purposes. Typically, the expression should not be another node set. The select should return a string or something that can be converted to a string and be used as a unique key. Usable commands are those that return positions, `true`/`false` values, or string buffers.

- ◆ `lang`: Specifies the language of the keys. This is useful when manipulating XML documents not written in English.

- ◆ `data-type`: Sorting of the data according to the data type, which can be text, number, and XML QNames. The default sort data type is `text`. If the sort data type is `number`, the string is converted into a numeric value.

- ◆ `order`: Specifies how the nodes in the node set will be sorted. They can be in either ascending or descending order.

- ◆ `case-order`: The case-order is a small but important consideration. When text is sorted, a sorting will happen according to the case. Therefore, if there is a `hello` and `Hello`, the locations in the node set may not necessarily be the same as just illustrated. The order of the words according to case depends on the language.

In the explanation of the `xsl:sort select` attribute in the preceding list, I explain that all keys used for the sorting must be string based. The XPath must, therefore, generate a string and not a node set. Consider the following XPath that generates a node set:

```
ancestor::*
```

When this XPath is used in the context of an xsl:sort, the node set is converted into a string. Consider the following XSLT, which demonstrates how this happens:

```
<xsl:template match="/">
    <xsl:for-each select="descendant::elements">
        <xsl:sort select="ancestor::*" data-type="text"
            order="ascending" />
        (<xsl:value-of select="ancestor::*" />)
        node name (<xsl:value-of select="name()" />)
        node value (<xsl:value-of select="text()"/>)
    </xsl:for-each>
</xsl:template>
```

When the XSLT is executed the following result is output:

```
<?xml version="1.0" encoding="UTF-8"?>
    (Embedded)
    node name (elements)
    node value (Embedded)

    (Hello)
    node name (elements)
    node value (Hello)

    (HelloWorldEmbedded)
    node name (elements)
    node value (World)
```

Notice that the node set that is selected as a key, when converted into a string, uses the default template generation of individual nodes. Is this a useful feature? Probably not, but it does show the automatic conversion of a node set into a string buffer.

 Sorting is a powerful feature. But sorting has its issues, mainly with respect to multiple languages. I speak English, German, and French, all of which have funny characters that have special sorting rules. If you speak languages only expressible in Unicode, you are probably familiar with the ignorance of many developers regarding Unicode languages. XMLSPY is a tool that understands Unicode and, hence, uses sorting rules according to the Unicode specification. If you are a developer who speaks solely a non-Unicode language, check out the Unicode specification to fully understand Unicode sorting.

Text, variables, and data

Thus far, all the XSLT I have discussed relates to writing programs that process XML content. I have not discussed how to generate output from an XSLT process. The output generation has basic identifiers and text values. But output generation such as XSL:FOP is an entire subject on its own and beyond the scope of this book. As an example, notice how the various XSLT outputs shown in this chapter are neatly formatted with carriage returns and how they start on the next line in the correct column. This feature is both desirable and undesirable.

UNDERSTANDING AND USING WHITESPACE

To understand whitespace, consider the following XSLT:

```
<xsl:template match="*">
    <xsl:apply-templates />
    node name (<xsl:value-of select="name()" />)
</xsl:template>
```

Executing this XSLT document on the original XML document generates the following output:

```
<?xml version="1.0" encoding="UTF-8"?>
    node name (elements)

    node name (child)

    node name (elements)

    node name (sub)

    node name (elements)

    node name (data)
```

Notice the use of whitespace, which includes spaces, carriage returns, and line feeds. The indent of individual node name texts occurs because of the indent of the text in the XSLT. What is not clear is where the line feeds are coming from. The lines result from the line feeds in the XSLT. To get rid of the empty lines, you need to rewrite the XSLT like this:

```
<xsl:template match="*">
    <xsl:apply-templates />
    node name (<xsl:value-of select="name()" />)</xsl:template>
```

Executing this XSLT document on the original XML document generates the following output:

```
<?xml version="1.0" encoding="UTF-8"?>
    node name (elements)
    node name (child)
    node name (elements)
    node name (sub)
    node name (elements)
    node name (data)
```

Now all the output is generated in a nice, neat, table formation. The cost of doing this operation is mucking up of the formatting of the XSLT document. The current positioning of the closing `xsl:template` XML node is not aligned for easy reading of the code.

This is where the problem of whitespace and XML exists. When XSLT code is nicely aligned for easy code reading comprehension, it adds whitespace that the parser cannot simply ignore. Consider the following XML:

```
<data>
    <embedded>
        <pre> embedded
            text
        </pre>
    </embedded>
</data>
```

The pre-XML node in XML terms means nothing; but when presented to an HTML parser, the line feed present in the embedded text means a line feed when rendering the document. Hence, the XML parser cannot willy-nilly get rid of the whitespace. The objective is to create XSLT code that encapsulates the XML tags to remove unwanted line feeds but is still easy to read. One rather unorthodox solution for the XSLT is as follows:

```
<xsl:template match="*">
    <xsl:apply-templates />
    node name (<xsl:value-of select="name()" />)</xsl:template
>
```

In this solution, there is no space between the individual characters; but where whitespace is disregarded, a line feed is introduced. In XML terms, whitespace is ignored within the declaration of an XML node. Many programmers have proposed this solution, and yet people have not flocked to it. My guess is that it has to do with the formatting look that, although it is better, takes getting used to.

Another solution, used more often, is to use the xsl:text instruction as in the following example:

```
<xsl:template match="*">
    <xsl:apply-templates />
    <xsl:text>node name (</xsl:text>
    <xsl:value-of select="name()" />
    <xsl:text>)</xsl:text>
</xsl:template>
```

Executing this XSLT document on the original XML document generates the following output:

```
<?xml version="1.0" encoding="UTF-8"?>node name (elements)node name
(child)node name (elements)node name (sub)node name (elements)node
name (data)
```

So instead of having the text formatted neatly in a table format, all the text is output as single stream. It would appear from first glance that the XSLT processor sometimes ignores whitespace and line feeds and other times does not. But that's not the case. The result has to do with significant whitespace versus insignificant whitespace. Significant whitespace is whitespace that contains something other than line feeds, carriage returns, spaces, and tabs. In the modified XSLT, there is no significant whitespace.

ESCAPING CHARACTERS

The xsl:text instruction is a special instruction that tells the XSLT processor to output the embedded text as formatted text. The single attribute that can be applied to an xsl:text is disable-output-escaping. To understand what this attribute does, consider the following XSLT:

```
<xsl:template match="/">
    <xsl:text disable-output-escaping="yes"> &lt; hello &gt;
</xsl:text>
</xsl:template>
```

Executing this XSLT document on the original XML document generates the following output:

```
<?xml version="1.0" encoding="UTF-8"?><hello>
```

Using this attribute, it is possible to dynamically create XML content. Within the XML specification, it is possible to create reserved characters using an escaped character buffer. In the case of the example XSLT, the characters < represent the less-than character and the characters > represent the greater-than character. It is not possible to do this in a generic XSLT stream as the following XSLT shows:

```
<xsl:template match="/">
    &lt;<xsl:value-of select="name()" />&gt;
</xsl:template>
```

Executing this XSLT document on the original XML document generates the following output:

```
<?xml version="1.0" encoding="UTF-8"?>
        &lt;data;&gt;
```

In the xsl:text instruction, the default value for the disable-output-escaping attribute is No. A reason for escaping XML tags is because you might want to build up XML incrementally, but doing that would violate the rules of XML. Consider the following XSLT:

```
<xsl:template match="elements">
    <xsl:apply-templates />
    <xsl:if test="@title = 'true'">
        <title>
    </xsl:if>
    <!-- some instructions -->
    <xsl:if test="@title = 'true'">
        </title>
    </xsl:if>
</xsl:template>
```

This XSLT is very common in that you do a test to determine whether or not to generate a block header start. If you must generate a block header, generate the title XML tag. After the condition, the other elements are created and output. To make the generated XML legal, the closing title XML tag is generated. But the problem is that the title tag violates the rules for the XML parser because the title tag starts in one XML block and ends in another XML block. To get around this problem, set the xsl:text with the disable-output-escaping to true. The modified XSLT is as follows:

```
<xsl:template match="elements">
    <xsl:apply-templates />
    <xsl:if test="@title = 'true'">
    <xsl:text
        disable-output-escaping="yes"> &lt; title &gt; </xsl:text>
    </xsl:if>
    <!-- some instructions -->
    <xsl:if test="@title = 'true'">
        <xsl:text
          disable-output-escaping="yes"> &lt; /title &gt; </xsl:text>
```

```
    </xsl:if>
</xsl:template>
```

The `disable-output-escaping` attribute can also be applied to the `xsl:value-of` instruction, with the same effects.

Another way of generating simple XML elements is to use the `xsl:element` instruction, as shown in the following example:

```
<xsl:template match="elements">
    <xsl:apply-templates />
    <xsl:element name="{@haselements}">hello</xsl:element>
</xsl:template>
<xsl:template match="text()">
</xsl:template>
```

Executing this XSLT document on the original XML document generates the following output:

```
<?xml version="1.0"?><false>hello</false><false>hello</false><true>hello</true>
```

The XML nodes `false` and `true` mean very little, but what was shown in the previous code is that an attribute can serve as an identifier for an XML element. The advantage of the using the `xsl:element` instruction is that it is simpler and cleaner. Within the `xsl:element` instruction there is an attribute name, which identifies the name of the element.

CHILD ELEMENTS

It is not possible to add any `xsl` instructions as `child` XML nodes of the `xsl:text` instruction. The XSLT processor generates an error if `xsl` instructions do exist. For example, it may be tempting to write the following incorrect XSLT:

```
<xsl:text>{<xsl:value-of select="name()" />}</xsl:text>
```

A correct XSLT solution is

```
<xsl:text>{</xsl:text>
<xsl:value-of select="name()" />
<xsl:text>}</xsl:text>
```

But if the XSLT text to be added is simple, a better solution would be to use the following XSLT:

```
<xsl:value-of select="concat( '{', name(), '}')" />
```

The function `concat` is used to build a buffer that is generated. This way of coding is cleaner and more comprehensible.

OVERALL OUTPUT CONTROL

When the XSLT processor executes, it is possible to control the overall output generation using the `xsl:output` instruction. Reading the purpose of the `xsl:output` in the XSLT specification is extremely boring, and you are left scratching your head about what it means. The simplest way to illustrate what `xsl:output` represents is to consider the following XSLT:

```
<xsl:stylesheet version="1.0" xmlns:xsl="http://www.w3.org/1999/XSL/Transform">
    <xsl:output method="html" />
    <xsl:template match="*">
    <xsl:apply-templates />
        <xsl:text disable-output-escaping="yes"> &lt; node name ((</xsl:text>
            <xsl:value-of select="concat( '{', name(), '}')" />
        <xsl:text>)</xsl:text>
    </xsl:template>
    <xsl:template match="text()">
    </xsl:template>
</xsl:stylesheet>
```

Right after the `xsl:stylesheet` instruction is the `xsl:output` instruction, which has the attribute method, which has the value `html`. In all the examples shown thus far, the output method has defaulted to `xml`. This time the output should be generated for `html`. When the XSLT document is executed, the following output is generated:

```
< node name ((elements}) < node name ((child}) < node name ((elements}) < node
name ((sub}) < node name ((elements}) < node name ((data})
```

What is apparent is that the XML prolog is missing. That makes sense because an HTML document has no idea what to do with the `xml` prolog. This is a simple example of the purpose of the `xsl:output` instruction. The following attributes can defined when using `xsl:output`:

- ◆ `method`: Specifies how the XSL generated content should be output. Possible options are `xml`, `html`, `text`, `qname`.

- ◆ `version`: Specifies the version of the output method.

- ◆ `encoding`: Specifies the preferred output encoding that the XSLT processor should use to encode the data. In the case of HTML, that could mean escaping text from a Unicode source to a Central European language.

- ◆ `standalone`: Specifies whether the output document should have a standalone declaration within the document.

◆ `omit-xml-declaration`: Removes the XML declaration at the top of the generated XML buffer.

◆ `doctype-public`: Specifies the system identifier to be used in the document type declaration.

◆ `doctype-system`: Specifies the public identifier to be used in the document type declaration.

◆ `cdata-section-elements`: Specific identifiers that appear in the output in CDATA sections.

◆ `indent`: Specifies whether XSLT processor should add additional whitespace indents in the output.

◆ `media-type`: Specifies the MIME content type of the output to be sent.

In the `xsl:output` the attributes encoding and `cdata-section-elements` are useful because they allow fine-tuning of the output data. To show how the `cdata-section-elements` functions consider the following XSLT:

```
<xsl:stylesheet version="1.0" xmlns:xsl="http://www.w3.org/1999/XSL/Transform">
    <xsl:output method="xml" cdata-section-elements="true" />
    <xsl:template match="elements">
       <xsl:apply-templates />
       <xsl:element name="{@haselements}">hello</xsl:element>
    </xsl:template>
    <xsl:template match="text()">
    </xsl:template>
</xsl:stylesheet>
```

When the XSLT document is executed, the following output is generated:

```
<?xml version="1.0" encoding="UTF-
8"?><false>hello</false><false>hello</false><true><![CDATA[hello]]></true>
```

Looking at the original declaration of the `xsl:output` instruction, the attribute `cdata-section-elements` has a value of true. That value is not a `true` in the Boolean sense, but a string `true` value. And the attribute value says that whenever `true` as a node appears, put a CDATA section around the embedded text. If you look in the output, you see that did indeed occur.

To show how the encoding example functions, the XML document needs to be rewritten to the following:

```
<?xml version="1.0" encoding="ISO-8859-1"?>
<data>
<html>
    <head>
```

```
        <title>HTMLOutput</title>
    </head>
    <body>
        Stündlich
    </body>
</html>
</data>
```

Notice in this text the special Western European character, which is the u with umlaut. Now consider the following XSLT that takes the original node and copies the node to the output using xsl:copy-of instruction:

```
<xsl:stylesheet version = '1.0'
    xmlns:xsl='http://www.w3.org/1999/XSL/Transform'>
    <xsl:output method="html" encoding="UTF-8"/>
    <xsl:template match="/">
        <xsl:copy-of select="/data/*"/>
    </xsl:template>
</xsl:stylesheet>
```

When the XSLT document is executed, the following output is generated:

```
<html><head><META http-equiv="Content-Type" content="text/html;
charset=UTF-8"><title>HTMLOutput</title></head><body>
        StÃ¹/₄ndlich
    </body></html>
```

Notice how the Stündlich text has been changed to the text StÃ¹/₄ndlich. This would appear to be an error, but is not. The original encoding of the XML document was ISO-8859-1, which is Western European encoding. To convert that encoding to UTF-8, as per the xsl:output instruction, the text is converted, and the HTML meta tag is added with the encoding. The browser will then load the content and interpret it properly as per the original XML document.

A new XSLT instruction used in the example was xsl:output. The xsl:output instruction copies a selected node to the destination buffer. In this example, it is especially important because a copy operation does not change any of the values.

Summary

The focus of this chapter is on understanding the essence of XSLT. By understanding the essence, you will find it simpler to write scripts that do what you want them to do. This chapter covered these topics:

◆ The XMLSPY XSLT debugger

◆ XSLT as a transformation language first and a programming language second

◆ How to reference XML elements using either the abbreviated syntax or using axis specifiers

◆ Scripts that can iterate data, make decisions, and generate data

The next chapter covers more complex XSLT topics and some practical applications of XSLT.

Chapter 7

Advanced XSLT

IN THIS CHAPTER

- ◆ XSLT template calls
- ◆ Functions to help you understand more about XSLT
- ◆ Tips to solve common problems

XSLT INCLUDES FUNCTIONS AND MORE COMPLEX DEVELOPMENT CONSTRUCTS, but you have to know how to call them and use them effectively. The first section in this chapter deals with the more complex XSLT topics of user functions and templates. The second section helps you understand how to apply the knowledge you gained in Chapter 6 and in the first part of this chapter. The main purpose of this chapter is to introduce programming techniques that can help you solve daily XSLT development tasks.

Functions, Variables, and Imports

When developing complex XSLT applications, writing all the XSLT instructions in one document becomes very tedious. It's more useful to break the XSLT into separate function calls, which can either be defined in the same document or in another document. By breaking the XSLT into smaller chunks, it is simpler to maintain and develop the code. The following XML code is used as a basis for all the XSLT examples in this chapter:

```
<data>
    <child>
        <elements index="1">Hello</elements>
    </child>
    <elements index="2">
        <sub>
            <elements index="3"> Embedded</elements>
        </sub>
    </elements>
</data>
```

Creating variables

When you make an XSLT function call, the state of the specific value needs to be stored somewhere temporarily. In XSLT, as in other programming languages, that somewhere is in a *variable*. Unlike in other programming languages, however, variables in XSLT are read-only. This means that after a value is assigned to an XSLT variable, it can never be changed. Probably, at this point, many readers are thinking sarcastically, "Which genius came up with that brilliant idea?" The answer is that it is necessary to make the variables read-only so that the XSLT transformation process doesn't become inconsistent. Consider the following number sequence:

```
1,5,6,89,91
```

Assume that a query executes, selects the number 6 and 91, and stores them in a variable. Then another query executes on the variable and selects the number 6. Finally, at some point in time, the original query executes a change and sets the numbers to 5 and 89. What happens to the second query? Does it execute again to build another node set? It can be argued that specific rules could be introduced to handle this situation. But XSLT is a transformation language that changes data from one form to another. Even in SQL, where data is transformed and manipulated in a way similar to XSLT, the selected data sets are typically static data sets. Once selected, the value never changes (unless you requery the SQL data). The XSLT group decided to keep things simple and say that data is read-only once assigned.

To create a variable, you use the xsl:variable instruction as shown in the following example:

```
<xsl:stylesheet version="1.0" xmlns:xsl="http://www.w3.org/1999/XSL/Transform">
    <xsl:template match="elements">
        <xsl:apply-templates />
        <xsl:variable name="var1" select="text()" />
        <xsl:value-of select="$var1" />
    </xsl:template>
    <xsl:template match="text()">
    </xsl:template>
</xsl:stylesheet>
```

The xsl:variable instruction has two attributes: name and select. The name attribute is the identifier of the variable, which in this case is var1, a case-sensitive variable. The select attribute selects the data that is to be assigned to the variable. The selection could be any XPath that results in a simple text or a node set select. After the variable has been assigned, it is possible to use it by referencing the variable using the special dollar character prepended to the variable name (var1), as illustrated by the xsl:value-of instruction. Note that the select attribute in the xsl:variable could have been directly inserted into the xsl:value-of select attribute. We did not use that method because it would not have shown you how to use a variable.

It is possible to assign a variable using literal values as in the following example:

```
<xsl:variable name="var1" select="2" />
```

The variable var1 has a value of 2. Another example is as follows:

```
<xsl:variable name="var1" select="Genf" />
```

In this case, you might assume that the variable var1 has been assigned the string Genf. That assumption is incorrect. The variable var1 has been assigned the Genf XML node. To assign a string variable to variable var1, the following xsl:variable instruction has to be used:

```
<xsl:variable name="var1" select="'Genf'" />
```

EMBEDDING VARIABLE DECLARATION

The xsl:variable select is optional because, unlike the xsl:value-of instruction, the selection can be a combination of multiple data items, as shown in the following example:

```
<xsl:stylesheet version="1.0"  xmlns:xsl="http://www.w3.org/1999/XSL/Transform">
    <xsl:template match="elements">
        <xsl:apply-templates />
        <xsl:variable name="var1" >
            My value is (<xsl:value-of select="text()" />)
        </xsl:variable>
        <xsl:value-of select="$var1" />
    </xsl:template>
    <xsl:template match="text()">
    </xsl:template>
</xsl:stylesheet>
```

The xsl:variable instruction still has the name attribute, but the value of the var1 variable is based on the instructions contained. In this example, the value of the variable is the text My Value is concatenated with the value of the xsl:value-of instruction. A variable can be the result of a loop, template call, or whatever else is legal in XSLT.

Embedding values using this technique could be useful when you are building literal strings manually. There is a catch, however, because embedding variables means creating node sets and not literal values, as shown in the following example:

```
<xsl:stylesheet version="1.0"  xmlns:xsl="http://www.w3.org/1999/
XSL/Transform">
    <xsl:template match="elements">
        <xsl:apply-templates />
```

```
            <xsl:variable name="temp">1</xsl:variable>
            <xsl:variable name="var1" >
                    My value is (<xsl:value-of select="parent::*" />)
            </xsl:variable>
            (<xsl:value-of select="text()" />)
            (<xsl:value-of select="@index" />)
            (<xsl:value-of select="child::*[$temp]" />)
        </xsl:template>
        <xsl:template match="text()">
        </xsl:template>
</xsl:stylesheet>
```

The purpose of this XSLT sheet is to output a specific child element, whenever an element is found. In this case, the child element index is in the variable $temp. Executing this XSLT sheet on the original XML document results in the following:

```
<?xml version="1.0" encoding="UTF-8"?>
        (Hello)
        (1)
        ()

        (Embedded)
        (3)
        ()

        ()
        (2)
        (Embedded)
```

The result is correct because only the elements XML node with an index of 2 has a child with index 1. If you try out another index value, such as the second child index, you need to make the following XSLT changes:

```
<xsl:apply-templates />
<xsl:variable name="temp">2</xsl:variable>
<xsl:variable name="var1" >
     My value is (<xsl:value-of select="parent::*" />)
```

Executing the modified XSLT document gives the following result:

```
<?xml version="1.0" encoding="UTF-8"?>
        (Hello)
        (1)
        ()
```

```
(Embedded)
(3)
()


()
(2)
(Embedded)
```

This is a puzzling result because the index modification changed nothing. The answer to the puzzle is that the $temp variable is not a literal value, but a node set value. To retrieve the correct position, the XSLT code has to be modified to the following:

```
    (<xsl:value-of select="@index" />)
    (<xsl:value-of select="child::*[position() = $temp]" />)
</xsl:template>
```

Running the modified XSLT document gives the following result:

```
<?xml version="1.0" encoding="UTF-8"?>
        (Hello)
        (1)
        ()

        (Embedded)
        (3)
        ()

        ()
        (2)
        ()
```

This is the correct result because there is no second child XML node below any of the elements XML nodes. The reason this modification works is because the $temp variable is converted to a data type that is identical to the function position(), which is a numeric.

HOW VARIABLES ARE SCOPED

In the previous examples, all of the variables declared were at the xsl:template scope level. But there is a catch. The scope of variables in a contained XSLT statement changes how a variable can be referenced. Consider the scope change of the variable var2 in the following example:

```
<xsl:template match="elements">
    <xsl:apply-templates />
```

```
    <xsl:variable name="var1" >
        <xsl:variable name="var2" select="text()" />
        My value is (<xsl:value-of select="parent::*" />)
    </xsl:variable>
    <xsl:value-of select="$var1" />
    <xsl:value-of select="$var2" />
</xsl:template>
```

In this example, the variable var2 is declared within the declaration of var1. Outside of the variable var1, declaration var2 is not visible. The xsl:value-of that references the var2 variable generates an exception because the variable is not declared.

To declare a variable at the global-scope level, you add xsl:variable after the xsl:stylesheet instruction, as shown in the following example:

```
<xsl:stylesheet version="1.0"  xmlns:xsl="http://www.w3.org/1999/XSL/Transform">
    <xsl:variable name="globalVariable" select="/" />
    <xsl:template match="elements">
    </xsl:template>
    <xsl:template match="text()">
    </xsl:template>
</xsl:stylesheet>
```

The variable globalVariable is visible to the templates elements and text(). The only requirement with the variable globalVariable is that the XPath or embedded variable declaration needs to be absolute. The XPath cannot resolve to an element that will be matched like the xsl:template instruction.

Global variables can be hidden from a particular scope if a local variable with the same name is declared, as in the following example:

```
<xsl:stylesheet version="1.0"  xmlns:xsl="http://www.w3.org/1999/XSL/Transform">
    <xsl:variable name="globalVariable" select="/" />
    <xsl:template match="elements">
        <xsl:variable name="globalVariable" select="//elements" />
    </xsl:template>
    <xsl:template match="text()">
    </xsl:template>
</xsl:stylesheet>
```

Applying templates

Thus far, the templates presented have had an embedded xsl:apply-templates to process all the subnodes. The xsl:apply-templates instruction, as presented, processes all child nodes. It is possible to either filter or pass on extra data, as shown in the following example:

```
<xsl:stylesheet version="1.0"  xmlns:xsl="http://www.w3.org/1999/XSL/Transform">
    <xsl:template match="sub">
        <xsl:param name="functionName" />
        [<xsl:value-of select="$functionName" />]
    </xsl:template>
    <xsl:template match="elements">
        <xsl:apply-templates>
            <xsl:with-param name="functionName" select="'Hello'"/>
        </xsl:apply-templates>
    </xsl:template>
    <xsl:template match="text()">
    </xsl:template>
</xsl:stylesheet>
```

This example includes an additional xsl:template instruction that matches the XML subnode. Directly after the xsl:template instruction declaration is the xsl:param instruction. The xsl:param instruction is used to declare a parameter. It is like the xsl:variable parameter, except that the value is bound to the xsl:template instruction.

This is a change that requires a higher-level xsl:template match to create a variable. The variable is created by the xsl:template match of the elements XML node. Within that template is an xsl:apply-templates instruction with an embedded xsl:with-param instruction. The xsl:with-param instruction declares a parameter that is to be passed on whenever the xsl:apply-templates matches an XML node. In this example, all child nodes of the current context will have an additional parameter. The xsl:with-param instruction has two attributes: name and select. The name attribute identifies the parameter to define, which must be the same as the associated xsl:param instruction of the xsl:template instruction. The select attribute functions similarly to the way it was used in other XSLT instructions. It is possible to embed content within the xslt:with-param instruction similar to the way it is embedded in the xsl:variable instruction.

Executing the XSLT document on the defined XML document results in the following output:

```
<?xml version="1.0" encoding="UTF-8"?>
        [Hello]
```

This is the output that we are expecting.

The xsl:apply-templates instruction can also be used to filter which child objects get executed, as the following example shows:

```
<xsl:apply-templates select="sub">
    <xsl:with-param name="functionName" select="'Hello'"/>
</xsl:apply-templates>
```

In this example, the sub-elements have been filtered to execute only the XML subelements. If this were to execute on the example XML document, you would generate the same result as you got from the previous XSLT.

The other XSLT instruction that can be embedded within the `xsl:apply-templates` instruction is the `xsl:sort` instruction.

See Chapter 6 for details about the `xsl:sort` instruction.

Calling templates

If you know how to pass parameters to templates, it is very easy to call templates. The only difference between passing and calling is the use of the `xsl:call-template` instruction instead of the `xsl:apply-templates` instruction. To see how simple it is, consider the following modification of the previous XSLT:

```
<xsl:stylesheet version="1.0"  xmlns:xsl="http://www.w3.org/1999/XSL/Transform">
    <xsl:variable name="globalVariable" select="/" />
    <xsl:template match="sub" name="sub">
       <xsl:param name="functionName" />
          [<xsl:value-of select="$functionName" />]
    </xsl:template>
    <xsl:template match="elements">
        <xsl:apply-templates />
        <xsl:call-template name="sub">
            <xsl:with-param name="functionName" select="'Hello'"/>
        </xsl:call-template>
    </xsl:template>
    <xsl:template match="text()">
    </xsl:template>
</xsl:stylesheet>
```

A few changes have been made. The `xsl:template` match for the XML subnode has the `name` attribute associated with it. The `name` attribute identifies the name of the template, which exposes the template as an XSLT function. In the example, both the match and name are identical, which is okay, but not necessary. Within the boundary of the `xsl:template` match for `elements` XML nodes, there is an `xsl:call-template` instruction. The `xsl:call-template` instruction has the `name` attribute, which identifies the name of the template that is called. Embedded within the `xsl:call-template` instruction are the parameters, as in the previous `xsl:apply-templates` XSLT example. If this XSLT were executed on the original XML document, the result would be as follows:

```
<?xml version="1.0" encoding="UTF-8"?>
        [Hello]


        []


        [Hello]
```

SOME ODD QUIRKS AND HOW TO SOLVE THEM

The output shown in the preceding code block is a bit peculiar because there are two square brackets that contain the Hello text and one square bracket without any generated text. This is an odd result because there should be three cases of the Hello text being generated. This odd result occurs because of the additional xsl:template match of sub. Ignoring the explicit template call, the elements XML nodes that will be matched have the indices of 1 and 2 only. The elements XML node with an index of 3 is not matched because the parent XML subnode has been matched. Within the xsl:template match sub, there is no explicit call to xsl:apply-templates, which means that the XSLT processor considers all child elements as processed.

This is a side effect that we did not want. The remedy to this side effect is to consider your XML data. If the XML data specification has embedded matching tags, as in the case of the elements XML node, then within each xsl:template should be an xsl:apply-templates instruction, as shown by the following modified example:

```
<xsl:template match="sub" name="sub">
   <xsl:apply-templates />
   <xsl:param name="functionName" />
     [<xsl:value-of select="$functionName" />]
</xsl:template>
```

When you execute this modified XSLT document, the following output is generated:

```
<?xml version="1.0" encoding="UTF-8"?>
        [Hello]

        [Hello]

        []

        [Hello]

        []

        [Hello]
```

This output, although better, is a bit too good and generates too many embedded Hello texts and empty texts. The fix that we wanted has generated a new set of problems. This is where an XSLT debugger is absolutely vital. What has happened in this example is that the xsl:apply-templates instruction has executed specific XML nodes in the XML document twice. This is a very good example of the reader needing to use the integrated XML XSLT debugger to see why the nodes are selected again. To solve the double selection problem, consider the following modified XSLT:

```
<xsl:template match="sub" name="sub">
    <xsl:param name="functionName" />
    <xsl:if test="not($functionName)">
        <xsl:apply-templates select="child::*"/>
    </xsl:if>
     [<xsl:value-of select="$functionName" />]
</xsl:template>
```

The reason for the double selection is that the same template is referenced both from a method call and from a template match. This means that when you use the xsl:call-template instruction, the children are also iterated and matched. This causes the double iteration. To stop the double iteration, an xsl:if instruction can be used to test if the call is a result of a xsl:apply-templates or xsl:call-template. Depending on the test result, the xsl:apply-templates instruction is called. Remember that this only works because xsl:apply-templates is not called with a parameter. Had there been a parameter, it would be impossible to know whether the call was made by xsl:apply-templates or xsl:call-template.

After I say that, some could argue that a check can be made for the current context, or something else. My rebuttal is: Sure. Why not? But then other problems arise. The point is that there is no simple single solution to this problem. The simplest solution is to have two different templates with different identifiers. But then you might have to write two routines to do almost the same thing. The key thing to remember is that XSLT allows a template to be called using two different techniques, and the developer should be aware of that.

Using modes

To further complicate how templates are called, it is possible to introduce something called a *mode*. A mode makes it possible to call a specific function in a specific context. Consider the following XSLT that uses modes:

```
<xsl:stylesheet version="1.0"  xmlns:xsl="http://www.w3.org/1999/XSL/Transform">
    <xsl:template match="elements" mode="embedded">
        <xsl:apply-templates mode="embedded"/>
          Mode Embedded (<xsl:value-of select="text()" />)
    </xsl:template>
```

```
   <xsl:template match="elements">
       <xsl:apply-templates mode="embedded"/>
       (<xsl:value-of select="text()" />)
   </xsl:template>
   <xsl:template match="text()">
   </xsl:template>
</xsl:stylesheet>
```

In the example XSLT template, there are two xsl:template instructions with an identical match of elements XML nodes. The way that XSLT matches these nodes is to search for a match without a mode because, by default, XSLT has no modes to match on. Therefore, for the higher-level elements XML nodes without a mode, the xsl:template will be matched. After an elements XML node is matched, the xsl:apply-templates instruction is called with the mode attribute set to embedded. Whenever any matches are attempted, the mode embedded must also be present. In this example XSLT, this is the case because there is an elements match with a mode of Embedded. Executing the XSLT document on the original XML document generates the following output:

```
<?xml version="1.0" encoding="UTF-8"?>Hello
        (Hello)
    Embedded
        Mode Embedded (Embedded)


        ()
```

Everything seems okay in the output except for one extra piece of information. The Embedded text on the third line of the output is out of place. There should be a bracket around the text. This text is generated because the xsl:template with match elements and mode of embedded has an embedded xsl:apply-templates with a mode of embedded. If you inspect the original XML document, you see the elements XML node with an identifier attribute of 3 has an embedded text node. Because a switch of modes has been defined, the xsl:template instruction with a match of text() has no mode defined and, therefore, is not called. To solve this problem, consider the built-in template xsl:template definition and modify the original XSLT to the following:

```
<xsl:template match="text()" mode="?">
</xsl:template>
```

The mode definition set to the question mark indicates that any particular mode is okay when attempting to match this node.

Importing XSLT documents

XSLT would not be a complete programming language if it did not include a mechanism to include other XSLT documents. This makes it possible to modularize your XSLT documents. There are two different instructions needed to include another XSLT document, xsl:include and xsl:import. In either instruction, there exists an XSLT document that will be inserted into the parent document. In the simplest case, consider the following already-existing XSLT document:

```
<xsl:stylesheet version="1.0" xmlns:xsl="http://www.w3.org/1999/
XSL/Transform" xmlns:fo="http://www.w3.org/1999/XSL/Format">
    <xsl:template match="elements" mode="embedded">
        <xsl:apply-templates mode="embedded"/>
         Included (<xsl:value-of select="text()" />)
    </xsl:template>
</xsl:stylesheet>
```

This document is called included.xsl and can be imported as shown in the following example:

```
<xsl:stylesheet version="1.0"  xmlns:xsl="http://www.w3.org/1999/
XSL/Transform">
    <xsl:import href="included.xsl"/>
    <xsl:template match="elements">
        <xsl:apply-templates mode="embedded"/>
         (<xsl:value-of select="text()" />)
    </xsl:template>
    <xsl:template match="text()" mode="?">
    </xsl:template>
</xsl:stylesheet>
```

This example is a modification of the mode example, where the mode-based xsl:template has been moved into its own XSLT file. The xsl:import instruction is a top-level instruction. A top-level instruction is an instruction that must be a direct child of the xsl:stylesheet instruction. In the case of the xsl:import instruction, it must also be directly after the xsl:stylesheet instruction. The xsl:import instruction has the href attribute, which specifies the location of the file to import. The value is a URI, which means the reference could be downloaded from a server. Executing the XSLT document will generate the following output:

```
<?xml version="1.0" encoding="UTF-8"?>
        (Hello)

        Included (Embedded)

        ()
```

If the XSLT document doing the importing has a locally defined template match, that template match takes precedence over the one defined within the imported XSLT document. Importing documents doesn't give you much control in overriding specific templates. However, this method of overriding templates is useful when you want to ensure that local implementations are executed before imported implementations.

If the total override of a template match is not desirable, it is possible to call both the imported version of the template match and the local version. An example of this is in the following modified XSLT document doing the importing:

```
<xsl:stylesheet version="1.0"  xmlns:xsl="http://www.w3.org/1999/XSL/Transform">
    <xsl:import href="included.xsl"/>
    <xsl:template match="elements" mode="embedded">
        <xsl:apply-templates mode="embedded"/>
        Mode Embedded (<xsl:value-of select="text()" />)
    </xsl:template>
    <xsl:template match="elements">
        <xsl:apply-imports />
        <xsl:apply-templates mode="embedded"/>
        (<xsl:value-of select="text()" />)
    </xsl:template>
    <xsl:template match="text()" mode="?">
    </xsl:template>
</xsl:stylesheet>
```

In the modified XSLT document, the original xsl:template instruction with a match of elements in mode embedded is added to the XSLT document. Now, with both matches present to be able to execute both templates, an xsl:apply-modes instruction is added. This instruction is similar in action to the xsl:apply-templates instruction, except that it applies to all the xsl:template instructions. Executing this modified XSLT document will result in the following output:

```
<?xml version="1.0" encoding="UTF-8"?>
        Included (Hello)

        (Hello)

        Mode Embedded (Embedded)

        Included ()

        Mode Embedded (Embedded)

        ()
```

The downside to using this functionality is that all matching xsl:templates are called. Therefore, the objective of using this functionality is to extend existing template actions. Also be aware that in the example XSLT, the xsl:apply-imports instruction was before the xsl:apply-templates instruction. If the positions are reversed, the output is slightly modified as well.

Including XSLT documents

Importing XSLT documents gives only a specific amount of control. It is possible to get more control of which xsl:template is viewed and how it is viewed by using the xsl:include instruction. To continue the example from the preceding section, consider the following XSLT, which uses the xsl:include instruction:

```
<xsl:stylesheet version="1.0"  xmlns:xsl="http://www.w3.org/1999/XSL/Transform">
    <xsl:include href="included.xsl"/>
    <xsl:template match="elements" mode="embedded">
        <xsl:apply-templates mode="embedded"/>
        Mode Embedded (<xsl:value-of select="text()" />)
    </xsl:template>
    <xsl:template match="elements">
        <xsl:apply-templates mode="embedded"/>
        Top level (<xsl:value-of select="text()" />)
    </xsl:template>
    <xsl:template match="text()" mode="?">
    </xsl:template>
</xsl:stylesheet>
```

Executing this XSLT results in the following output:

```
<?xml version="1.0" encoding="UTF-8"?>
        Top level (Hello)

        Mode Embedded (Embedded)

        Top level ()
```

This output is no surprise because it is identical to the xsl:import instruction. In this simple example, xsl:include does indeed act like xsl:import. Consider the following XSLT document that has moved the xsl:include instruction to a farther-removed location in the XSLT document:

```
<xsl:stylesheet version="1.0"  xmlns:xsl="http://www.w3.org/1999/XSL/Transform">
    <xsl:template match="elements" mode="embedded">
        <xsl:apply-templates mode="embedded"/>
        Mode Embedded (<xsl:value-of select="text()" />)
    </xsl:template>
    <xsl:include href="included.xsl"/>
    <xsl:template match="elements">
        <xsl:apply-templates mode="embedded"/>
        Top level (<xsl:value-of select="text()" />)
    </xsl:template>
    <xsl:template match="text()" mode="?">
    </xsl:template>
</xsl:stylesheet>
```

Executing this XSLT results in the following output:

```
<?xml version="1.0" encoding="UTF-8"?>
        Top level (Hello)

        Included (Embedded)

        Top level ()
```

In this output, the included xsl:template that has the same match overrides the xsl:template instruction defined locally. By moving the xsl:include instruction, it shows that the xsl:include instruction can be a top-level child element anywhere in the document. It shows that depending on the location of the xsl:include statement, specific output can be generated.

Another way of controlling which xsl:template is matched by the XSLT processor when evaluating the XML document nodes is to use the priority attribute on the xsl:template instruction. Consider the following modification to the included XSLT document:

```
<xsl:template match="elements" mode="embedded" priority="2">
    <xsl:apply-templates mode="embedded"/>
      Included (<xsl:value-of select="text()" />)
</xsl:template>
```

The `xsl:template` instruction has the added attribute `priority` that is set to a value of 2. Now consider the modified XSLT document that includes the previous XSLT document:

```
<xsl:template match="elements" mode="embedded" priority="3">
    <xsl:apply-templates mode="embedded"/>
      Mode Embedded (<xsl:value-of select="text()" />)
</xsl:template>
```

In this example, the priority is set to 3, which is one higher than the included `priority` value. Executing the XSLT documents results in the following output:

```
<?xml version="1.0" encoding="UTF-8"?>
        Top level (Hello)

        Mode Embedded (Embedded)

        Top level ()
```

The output has changed from the previous output, with only the change in the priority of the template. A higher priority means higher precedence. Because the locally defined template priority is higher than the included defined template, the locally defined template is matched.

Priorities are useful because they allow you to include various templates and to make sure a specific template is called, regardless of how it is included. If a template does not have priority and another does, the template without a priority is considered to have a priority value of zero.

Functions and XSLT

In this chapter and in Chapter 6, I have used XPath functions such as `position` without much explanation. In XPath there are a number of functions that perform specific operations. When writing XPath, you need to know what the functions are and what they can do. The XPath functions can be broken into the following groups: node-set, string, Boolean, number, and XSLT-defined functions. These functions are discussed in the following sections.

XSLT data types and conversion

XML works because XML is based on text that can be either eight bit or Unicode. But in either case, it is still text. Text is a better approach because you don't have to worry about computer translation errors. Not all operations in XSLT, however, are based on text. XSLT includes five different data types:

- **Boolean:** A `true` or `false` value

- **Number:** A double precision floating-point number

- **String:** A sequence of ASCII or Unicode characters

- **Node-set:** A set of XML nodes from the original XML document

- **External object:** Anything that doesn't fit into one of the previous four data types. This data type is specifically geared toward the integration of external objects and references. This is made possible by the XSLT specification that allows the referencing of external functions.

Depending on the function or context, XSLT automatically converts a data from one type to another.

Node-set functions

The node-set functions enable you to know what node-set is being managed. This is important when using repetitive XSLT instructions. The following list provides the instructions that you can use to figure out the properties of a node-set:

- `number last()`: Returns the last position of the current context node-set as a number, which is the same as the node-set size.

- `number position()`: Returns the current position of the current context node-set as a number.

- `number count( node-set)`: Returns the total number of nodes in the node-set passed in as a parameter.

- `node-set id( object)`: Retrieves the unique identifier of the individual XML nodes. However, in all the examples used thus far in the book, the `id` function did not work. The `id` function requires a DTD of the ID attribute. This means that if the `ID` attribute exists, but no DTD is referenced, the `id` function will return an empty string. If `ID`s are active in the document, no XML node can have the same `ID`. IDs must be unique; and if they are not, the XML parser will return an error.

- `string local-name( node-set)`: Retrieves the local name of the first node of the node-set.

◆ `string namespace-uri( node-set)`: Retrieves the namespace of the first node of the node-set. If there is no namespace, an empty string is returned.

◆ `string name( node-set)`: Retrieves the `QName` of the first node of the node-set. A `QName` is the combination of the namespace and name of the node. A catch, though, is that the returned name may not be the name that you expected. For example, if an XSL document is being transformed, the `xsl:value-of` node is not a `QName` because the xsl prefix has not been expanded. The `QName` would be `www.w3.org/1999/XSL/Transform:value-of`.

String functions

The following string functions enable you to manipulate strings by extracting sub-strings or building new strings:

◆ `string string( object)`: Converts an object to a string using the following conversions:

  ■ `Nodeset`: Converts the nodes into a string value using default processing rules.

  ■ `Number`: Converted using the following notations:

   • Nan is converted to the string NaN.

   • Negative/positive zero is converted to string 0.

   • Positive infinity is converted to string infinity.

   • Negative infinity is converted to string –infinity.

   • Integer-based number is converted to a number with no decimal points and no leading zeros. A negative integer has a minus sign prepended.

   • All other numbers are converted to a string with decimal points and a negative sign if necessary.

  ■ Boolean true value is converted to the string `true`, and `false` value is converted to the string `false`.

  ■ Object type is converted to a string, but the exact format of the string is dependent on the implementation of the object.

◆ `string concat( string, string, string...)`: Combines various strings. The `concat` function can, in theory, have as many parameters as needed. These are then combined into one large string.

◆ `boolean starts-with( string, string)`: Tests the first parameter string to see if it starts with the second parameter string. A return value of `true` indicates that the first parameter string does contain the second parameter string. Otherwise a `false` value is returned.

◆ `boolean contains( string, string)`: Tests the first parameter string to see if it contains the second parameter string. A return value of `true` indicates that the first parameter string contains the second parameter string. Otherwise a `false` value is returned.

◆ `string substring-before( string, string)`: Returns a substring of the first parameter string that is before the found occurrence of the second string. For example, if the first parameter string is `"hello world how are you"` and the second parameter string is `"world"`, then the return value is `"hello "` (notice the included space).

◆ `string substring-after( string, string)`: Returns a substring of the first parameter string that is after the found occurrence of the second string. For example, if the first parameter string is `"hello world how are you"` and the second parameter string is `"world"`, then the return value is `" how are you "` (notice the included space).

◆ `string substring( string, number, number)`: Returns a substring of the first parameter based on the indices of the start point of the second parameter and the length of the third parameter. For example, if the first parameter is `"12345"`, the second parameter is `"3"`, and the third parameter `"3"`, the return value is `"345"`. The second parameter is an index, where the string buffer starts with an index of `"1"`. If the third parameter is not specified, the buffer starting at the second parameter and ending with the end of the buffer is returned.

◆ `number string-length( string)`: Returns the length of string. If the first parameter is not passed in, the function defaults to the current context buffer.

◆ `string normalize-space( string)`: A useful function that strips extra spaces from the start of the buffer and the end of the buffer. If, within the buffer, there are multiple space sequences, they are replaced with a single space. If the first parameter is not passed in, the function defaults to the current context buffer.

◆ `string translate( string, string, string)`: An odd function that replaces text according to a pattern. If the first parameter is `"hello"` and the second parameter `"l"` and the third parameter `"w"`, the return value is `"hewwo"`. The function does a character-by-character comparison of the first parameter with the characters of the second parameter. If a character in the second parameter is found, the character in the first parameter is replaced by the corresponding character in the third parameter. The mapping of the second parameter to the third parameter is an index. So, if in the second parameter a character corresponds to the index of two, it is replaced with the third parameter character at the index of two. If a character is found in the second parameter buffer, which does not have a corresponding index in the third parameter, that character is deleted from the first parameter buffer. This can occur because the second parameter buffer is longer than the third parameter buffer.

Boolean functions

The following Boolean functions enable you to manipulate Boolean values.

- `boolean boolean( object)`: Converts the argument to a Boolean using the following conversions:
  - `number`: Converted to `false` if the number is either positive or negative, zero or a NaN; otherwise, it is converted to `true`.
  - `node-set`: Converted to `true` if node-set is non-empty, otherwise converted to `false`.
  - `string`: Converted to `true` if string set is non-empty, otherwise converted to `false`.
  - `object`: State of either `true` or `false` is dependent on the implementation of the object.

- `boolean not( boolean)`: Inverts the Boolean value, which means a `true` will be turned into a `false` and a `false` into a `true`.

- `boolean true()`: Function that returns the value `true`. A good use of this function is when a test against a `true` value is needed or a `true` value is needed.

- `boolean false()`: Function that returns the value `false`. A good use of this function is when a test against a `false` value is needed or a `false` value is needed.

- `boolean lang( string)`: Tests to see if the current context node is a specific language as specified by the `xml:lang` attribute. For example, if the following XML were used as a basis

  ```
  <data xml:lang="en" />
  ```

  and the function `lang( "en")` were called, a `true` return value would result.

Number functions

The following number functions enable you to manipulate numbers and figure out what a number represents:

- ◆ `number number( object)`: Converts the argument to a number using the following conversions:

  - ▪ `string`: Converted to a number if the string is a number like 1, –1.1, or 0.1. Otherwise a NaN is generated.

  - ▪ `boolean`: A `true` value is converted zero and a `false` value is converted to the value 1.

  - ▪ `node-set`: A double conversion occurs. The first conversion is to a string and the next is to a number, as per the string to number conversion rule.

  - ▪ `object`: Value of the number is dependent on the implementation of the object.

- ◆ `number sum( node-set)`: Returns the sum of the nodes in the argument `node-set`. The numbers are generated by converting each node into a string, and the strings are converted to numbers. These numbers are added together. An example of adding numbers would be as follows:

```
<nums>
  <val>2</val>
  <val>2</val>
  <val>2</val>
  <val>2</val>
</nums>
```

and the XSLT:

```
<xsl:template match="nums">
  Sum (<xsl:value-of select="sum( child::*)" />)
</xsl:template>
```

If any of the nodes in the XML result in a NaN, the addition is also a NaN.

- ◆ `number floor( number)`: Returns the largest integer value of a number, without being larger than the original number. If the number were 2.345, then the function floor would return 2. But if the number were –2.345, then the floor would return –3. The negative value is correct, and a quick think validates it.

- ◆ `number ceiling( number)`: Returns the smallest number that is not less than the original number and is an integer. If the number were 2.345, then the function floor would return 3. But if the number were –2.345, then the floor would return –2.

- ◆ `number round( number)`: Returns the number that is closest to the argument and is an integer. If the number is on a split (for example, 0.5), then the integer closest to positive infinity is used. Therefore, a round of 1.5 is 2, and round of –1.5 is –1. If the number is 0 a round is 0, and if the number is –0 a round is –0. If the number is –0.5, then a round is –0.

Additional XSLT functions

The additional XSLT functions are functions that are not part of the XPath specification but are part of the XSLT specification. Typically, these functions are very specific to XSLT and are shown in the following list:

- ◆ `node-set document( object, node-set)`: Allows access to XML documents other than the main source document. For example, if the first parameter were a string, the string would be treated as a URI that references another XML document.

- ◆ `node-set key( string, object)`: The XPath id function is interesting in that it makes it possible to uniquely identify a node. But as was stated in the section defining the id function, this only works if the DTD and ID specifications are present. An XSLT processor is not required to recognize DTDs. This means that using the ID identifier is prone to error. Another way of declaring unique identifiers is to use a key. An XSL key is more flexible because it does not rely on a specific attribute. If we go back to the original XML document, the elements nodes had index attributes used to represent a unique element. Using the xsl:key instruction, a definition of a key would be as follows:

```
<xsl:key name="element-identifier" match="elements"
use="@index" />
```

  In this declaration, there is the name of the key as defined by the name attribute. The match attribute defines which XML nodes are to be matched, and the use attributes define which item are defined to contain a unique key. The unique key is referenced using the following notation:

```
key( 'element-identifier', .)
```

  What is returned is a node-set that contains all nodes containing a unique key, as per our key definition.

- ◆ `string format-number( number, string, string)`: The format number function converts the first argument into a string using the format specified by the second and third parameters.

- ◆ `node-set current()`: Returns the current context node and has the same functionality as the period abbreviated operator. However, the current context node will shift as an XPath is written.

- ◆ `string unparsed-entity-uri( string)`: Returns the URI of the unparsed entity with a specific name in the document of the context node.

- ◆ `string generate-id( node-set)`: Generates a unique identifier for a specific node in the node-set. The XSLT processor is free to generate any type of unique identifier.

- `object system-property( string)`: Retrieves information specific to the XSLT processor:

  - `xsl:version`: Returns a version number of the XSLT implemented

  - `xsl:vendor`: Returns a string identifying the vendor. The XSLT processor for XMLSPY is identified as follows: Altova GmbH & Altova, Inc.

  - `xsl:vendor-url`: Returns a string that contains the URL of the vendor of the XSLT processor.

- `boolean element-available( string)`: When using extensions within the XSLT processor, it is often necessary to test if an element is available. The element represents an instruction, much like XSL, except that it is specific to the extension. The parameter input is a `QName` that represents an instruction. If the instruction can be processed, the return value is `true`; otherwise, a `false` value is returned.

- `boolean function-available( string)`: This function is identical in purpose to the `element-available` function, except that the test is for a function and not for an instruction. If the function can be processed, a return value of `true` is generated; otherwise, `false` is returned.

XSLT Tips

By now, you have been introduced to the XSLT basics and even some of the more advanced topics. One of the challenges in working with XSLT, however, is deciding the best route to take when you want to solve a problem. In this section, I provide some tips to help you solve some common XSLT problems.

Generating content in specialized ways

When content is generated, a generic content stream is generated. Using the `xsl:output`, specific modifiers can be added and removed to generate correctly formatted data. But with XSLT, it is also possible to generate specific content like comments. To generate a comment, the following XSLT can be used:

```
<xsl:template match="*">
    <xsl:comment>My Comment</xsl:comment>
</xsl:template>
```

When the XSLT is executed, the following content is generated:

```
<?xml version="1.0" encoding="UTF-8"?><!--My Comment-->
```

Notice how the `xsl:comment` instruction has been converted to `<!-- -->`. For XML this is a correct way of specifying a comment. But when generating generic text it might not be the correct way. You manage the generic generation process by using the `xsl:output` instruction. The advantage of using the `xsl:comment` instruction is that it is generic, and the `xsl:output` generates the correct comment.

It is also possible to generate processing instructions using the following sample XSLT document:

```
<xsl:template match="*">
    <xsl:processing-instruction name="special">action="do
action"</xsl:processing-instruction>
</xsl:template>
```

When the XSLT is executed, the following content is generated:

```
<?xml version="1.0" encoding="UTF-8"?><?special action="do action"?>
```

Parsing keys in attributes

Consider the following XML:

```
<child colors="red green blue">
    <elements index="1">Hello</elements>
</child>
```

The problem is that the attribute `colors` has three keys that need to be split apart. Some XSLT processors have specific *tokenize* functions that can split apart the list into the individual data sets. But the task is to solve this problem using standard XSLT. In a traditional programming approach, the developer uses a loop and then finds each token. This is not easy to do in XSLT because looping requires a child node. The actual solution is shown in the following XSLT document:

```
<xsl:stylesheet version="1.0" xmlns:xsl="http://www.w3.org/1999/XSL/Transform">
    <xsl:template name="ExtractColors">
        <xsl:param name="allColors" />
        <xsl:choose>
            <xsl:when test="contains( $allColors, ' ') ">
                Found(
                <xsl:value-of select="substring-before( $allColors, ' ')" />
                )
                <xsl:call-template name="ExtractColors">
                    <xsl:with-param name="allColors"
                        select="substring-after(    $allColors, ' ')"/>
                </xsl:call-template>
            </xsl:when>
```

```
            <xsl:when test="string-length( $allColors) > 0">
                Found(
                <xsl:value-of select="$allColors" />
                )
                <xsl:call-template name="ExtractColors">
                    <xsl:with-param name="allColors"
                        select="substring-after(    $allColors, ' ')"/>
                </xsl:call-template>
            </xsl:when>
        </xsl:choose>
    </xsl:template>
    <xsl:template match="child">
        <xsl:variable name="colors">
            <xsl:call-template name="ExtractColors">
                <xsl:with-param name="allColors" select="@colors"/>
            </xsl:call-template>
        </xsl:variable>
        Found Colors {{<xsl:value-of select="$colors" />}}
        <element>
            <xsl:value-of select="text()" />
        </element>
        <xsl:apply-templates />
    </xsl:template>
    <xsl:template match="/">
        <data>
            <xsl:apply-templates />
        </data>
    </xsl:template>
    <xsl:template match="text()" mode="?">
    </xsl:template>
</xsl:stylesheet>
```

Looping on something other than node-sets is best handled using a recursive template call. To split apart the colors, the best approach is to generate an XML stream of nodes that are then assigned to a variable. In the XSLT document, the xsl:template match child has a child xsl:variable that calls the template ExtractColors. The template ExtractColors then makes use of the substring-before and substring-after functions to split apart the string. The recursion takes place when a substring-before function finds something and recursively calls itself, but the data passed in is substring-after.

Remember that looping can often be solved by using recursion, especially when doing string tokenization. Another way of doing looping is by using something called the Piez method, but it relies on tricking the XSLT processor. Although this technique works, I do not recommend it because it makes debugging and figuring out problems more difficult. This means maintenance and extensions could be difficult to program.

Counting attribute items

Instead of splitting the individual attribute items into a number of tokens, you can count how many tokens there are without actually performing a tokenization. Consider, again, the XML code introduced in the preceding section:

```
<child colors="red green blue">
    <elements index="1">Hello</elements>
</child>
```

The problem now is to figure out how many colors are available. The solution is provided in the following XSLT document:

```
<xsl:template match="child">
   Count(
   <xsl:value-of select=
      "string-length(@colors) - string-length(translate(@colors,' ', '')) + 1"/>
   )
</xsl:template>
```

This a sneaky solution to the problem. What happens is that the string length before and after the translate function is calculated. The translate function removes all character sequences specified when calling the translate function, which in the example are spaces. The number of spaces plus one equals the number of tokens in the buffer. The reason this works is because a space or other defined separator are required to identify each token. Although this works generally, there are some things to watch for. In the sample XML, the spaces were evenly located one space apart. If there were extra spaces, the count would be incorrect. The way to solve this is to call the function normalize-string to remove those spaces. If you use other tokens, such as commas or colons, you won't have the problem of an incorrect count.

Generating child nodes

Consider the following XML:

```
<data>
   <text>
       Here I am <b>working</b>at a job
   </text>
</data>
```

In this XML, there is an XML node and some text, with a node embedded within. Instead of embedding the text, you should make the nodes siblings, similar to the following:

```
<data>
    <text>
        Here I am </text><b>working</b><text>at a job
    </text>
</data>
```

The solution to this problem is the following XSLT:

```
<xsl:stylesheet version="1.0" xmlns:xsl="http://www.w3.org/1999/XSL/Transform">
    <xsl:template match="data/text">
        <xsl:apply-templates />
    </xsl:template>
    <xsl:template match="data/text/text()">
        <text><xsl:value-of select="."/></text>
    </xsl:template>
    <xsl:template match="data/text/b">
        <b><xsl:value-of select="."/></b>
    </xsl:template>
    <xsl:template match="/">
        <data><xsl:apply-templates /></data>
    </xsl:template>
</xsl:stylesheet>
```

The trick that this XSLT uses is that it matches on specific text nodes using the data/text/text() XPath. This splits the parsing process into multiple chunks. Notice that the xsl:template match on every text() XPath was removed. This was done because, otherwise, the XSLT does not work properly. However, as a twist, the original xsl:template with a match on every node could have been left in if a condition were added. That condition tests the parent node and then generates the proper block.

Accessing large amounts of data quickly

Consider the following XML document:

```
<data>
    <row>something</row>
    <row>more</row>
    ...
    <row>Finally there</row>
</data>
```

This node-set is huge, and the problem is to find an element quickly without having to constantly iterate through the entire list. The solution to this problem is to set up an `xsl:key` instruction similar to the following:

```
<xsl:key name="find-fast" match="row" use="." />
```

Next, you reference an individual element by using the `key` function. Note that this approach is also very useful if you need to constantly reference a specific list. For example, you iterate a node-set in which an attribute references an item from the keyed set. The advantage of the `key` function is that it is a simple one-line solution.

Finding the parent path

Consider the following XML document:

```
<data>
    <text>
        Here I am <b>working</b>at a job
    </text>
</data>
```

At each node, you want to find the parent path and index. When you know the parent path and index, they can be used as metadata information or information for later processing. The XSLT solution is as follows:

```
<xsl:stylesheet version="1.0" xmlns:xsl="http://www.w3.org/1999/XSL/Transform">
    <xsl:template match="*">
        <xsl:for-each select="ancestor::*">
            /<xsl:value-of select="name()"/>[<xsl:number/>]
        </xsl:for-each>
        <xsl:apply-templates />
    </xsl:template>
    <xsl:template match="/">
        <xsl:apply-templates />
    </xsl:template>
</xsl:stylesheet>
```

The solution to this XSLT is that a repetition of parent selection is executed by using the XPath `ancestor::*`. The position of the node is found using the `xsl:number` instruction.

Getting more help

There are always situations when the information provided in a book isn't quite enough, and you want to ask somebody who knows. Your question most likely has already been answered, and here are two places where plenty of XSLT information is stored:

♦ **The World Wide Web Consortium (`www.w3.org`):** Offers an XSLT mailing list. You can access the mailing list archives at `www.biglist.com/lists/xsl-list/archives/`.

♦ **The XSLT FAQ (`www.dpawson.co.uk/xsl/xslfaq.html`):** Provides the answers to many of the most frequently asked questions about XSLT.

Building Web Sites with Authentic and Cocoon

Building Web sites is what preoccupied the industry throughout the nineties. There were various techniques that used technologies such as PHP, ASP, or JSP. In each approach, there was a traditional programming language that was responsible for the business logic and generation of the HTML or XML content. But with XMLSPY, there is another way of building an application, which is illustrated in Figure 7-1.

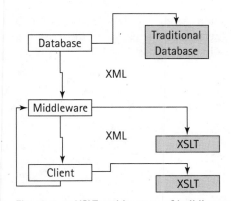

Figure 7-1: XSLT architecture of building applications.

In the architecture shown in Figure 7-1, the data is kept in a traditional database; but from there on, it is an XML document from the backend to the client and back again. In both the middleware and client layers, XSLT modifies the XML data. To illustrate such an architecture, I use the Cocoon subproject and the Authentic control. Cocoon serves as an example of how the middleware can be programmed. Cocoon is a Java-based framework used to simplify server-side content generation. The focus is on the Authentic toolkit and the XSLT Designer. Authentic is a set of tools created by Altova (makers of XMLSPY) that focuses on using XSLT to generate content.

An introduction to Cocoon and Authentic

Cocoon is an Apache subproject that uses XSLT as its core architecture to build applications. The focus of Cocoon is to build an architecture in which the style, business logic, and data are separate (see Figure 7-2).

Figure 7-2: The Cocoon separation of logic, content, and style.

The Authentic control is similar to Cocoon, except that XSLT and XML are combined to produce HTML output displayed in a browser. The advantage of the Authentic control is that a user can edit the HTML like an XML form. In architectural terms, Authentic is illustrated in Figure 7-3.

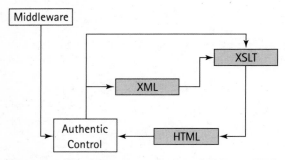

Figure 7-3: The Authentic separation of XML and XSLT to produce HTML.

The application

The application that you are going to build here is based on the original XML document presented at the beginning of this chapter. The application has two steps associated with it. The first step is to clean up the XML document to make it resemble data a bit simpler to process. The second step is to take the modified data and display it in the Authentic browser.

SETTING UP THE DATA

You may recall that in Chapter 6 I used a specific XML document throughout most of the examples to illustrate how XSL works. But in all frankness, the design and structure of that XML document leaves much to be desired. Consider the original XML:

```
<data>
    <child>
        <elements index="1">Hello</elements>
    </child>
    <elements index="2"><sub>
            <elements index="3">World</elements>
        </sub></elements>
</data>
```

The problem with this XML is that the `elements` XML node is incorrectly named and should be called `element`. The other aspect is that the important data is scattered throughout the XML document. When deciding how to move data from the middleware to the client, keep the following design guidelines in mind:

◆ **Use a schema.** A schema is useful because it ensures that the data is formatted a specific way.

◆ **Keep the XML data as simple as possible.** This means not embedding elements within elements.

◆ **Use tags that actually mean something.** For example, `elements` should be called `element`.

◆ **Use namespaces.** I have avoided them here to keep things simple.

◆ **Do not store your data as attributes.** Attributes are descriptors of the data, similar to the way adjectives describe nouns.

The purpose of the middleware is to clean up the XML into something that can be processed by the client. The XSLT document that will manage this is as follows:

```
<xsl:stylesheet version="1.0" xmlns:xsl="http://www.w3.org/1999/XSL/Transform">
    <xsl:template match="elements">
        <element>
            <xsl:value-of select="text()" />
        </element>
        <xsl:apply-templates />
    </xsl:template>
    <xsl:template match="/">
        <data>
            <xsl:apply-templates />
        </data>
    </xsl:template>
    <xsl:template match="text()" mode="?">
    </xsl:template>
</xsl:stylesheet>
```

In this XML document an `xsl:template` with match of / exists. The output stream in a properly formatted XML document needs to be generated. Notice the placement of the `xsl:apply-templates` instruction, which is placed between the `data` XML nodes. After an `elements` XML node has been found, the value of the node is output. Notice the placement of the `xsl:apply-templates` in this case. It has been placed after the `element` XML node. This is done so that nested `elements` nodes are normalized. Executing the XSLT document generates the following output:

```
<?xml version="1.0" encoding="UTF-8"?><data><element>Hello</element>
<element>World</element><element></element></data>
```

This new document serves as the basis of the data for the client-side processing using the Authentic plugin. But before we can use the Authentic plugin, a schema has to be defined for the new data. The simplest way to do this would be to use XMLSPY to generate a schema for you automatically. Doing that would result in the following schema definition:

```
<?xml version="1.0" encoding="UTF-8"?>
<!--W3C Schema generated by XMLSPY v5 U (http://www.xmlspy.com)-->
<xs:schema xmlns:xs="http://www.w3.org/2001/XMLSchema"
elementFormDefault="qualified">
    <xs:element name="data">
        <xs:complexType>
            <xs:sequence>
                <xs:element ref="element" maxOccurs="unbounded"/>
            </xs:sequence>
        </xs:complexType>
    </xs:element>
    <xs:element name="element">
        <xs:simpleType>
            <xs:restriction base="xs:string">
                <xs:enumeration value="Hello"/>
                <xs:enumeration value="World"/>
            </xs:restriction>
        </xs:simpleType>
    </xs:element>
</xs:schema>
```

This is a very simple schema that defines the two different elements used in the XML document. The only change that has to be made is to remove the `xs:enumeration` instructions because they will cause problems when validating real test data.

GENERATING THE DATA USING COCOON

The focus of this book is not Cocoon, so I'm keeping the details simple. I want you to focus on how the XML document is generated. I simply use Cocoon here because it's an outstanding XML/XSLT platform and is available for free with source code from `http://xml.apache.org`.

In Cocoon, the transformation process is controlled using a pattern match and transformation metaphor. In the example of generating the improved XML data, the following entry is made to the Cocoon execution map:

```
<map:match pattern="output.xml">
    <map:generate src="content/helloworld.xml"/>
    <map:transform src="stylesheets/middleware.xsl"/>
    <map:serialize type="xml"/>
</map:match>
```

Therefore, when the client makes a method call using http for the document `output.xml`, Cocoon automatically associates the `helloworld.xml` document with the `middleware.xsl` XSLT document and generates XML output.

The client

Now assuming that the content has been sent to the client, the Authentic plugin can consume the XML data and apply its own XSLT document to generate HTML output. Unlike in previous steps, the new XSLT document is not generated by the XMLSPY IDE, but by the XSLT designer environment. Stylesheet Designer is a tool that makes it simple to create XSLT documents. When Stylesheet Designer is started, it looks like the screen shown in Figure 7-4.

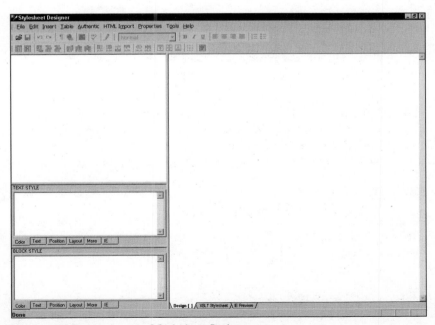

Figure 7-4: Startup image of Stylesheet Designer.

If you attempt to open a dialog box within the Stylesheet Designer, the first surprising thing you realize is that it is not possible to edit an XSLT file directly. This restriction is not without purpose. Stylesheet Designer is not a tool geared toward editing XSLT documents; it's intended for editing applications that happen to involve generating XSLT documents.

When the previously defined schema document is opened in Stylesheet Designer, your screen resembles Figure 7-5.

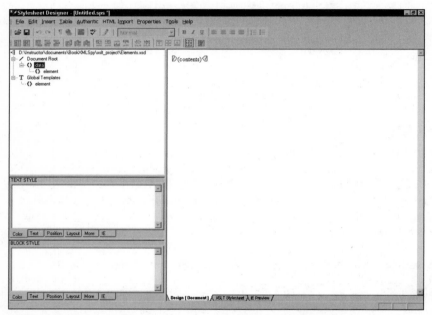

Figure 7-5: Image of Stylesheet Designer with a loaded Schema document.

In the upper-left corner of the screen is an example XML document structure based on the schema document that you just loaded. In the right-hand window is an XSLT sheet that, when transformed, results in the HTML shown. The XSLT document is defined when you click the tab XSLT Stylesheet (see Figure 7-5).

```
<?xml version="1.0" encoding="UTF-8"?>
<xsl:stylesheet version="1.0" xmlns:xsl="http://www.w3.org/1999/
XSL/Transform" xmlns:xs="http://www.w3.org/2001/XMLSchema">
    <xsl:template match="/">
        <html>
            <head />
            <body>
                <xsl:apply-templates />
            </body>
```

```
      </html>
    </xsl:template>
</xsl:stylesheet>
```

Notice that this XSLT document includes an `xsl:template` with a match of the root node. This is the place where the basis of the HTML page is generated.

The objective of the Stylesheet Designer tool is to take an XML stream and an XSLT document and combine them into a generated HTML document that can be viewed in the browser. The viewing part is available with every browser, but only the Authentic plugin makes it possible to edit the content.

When the XSLT document is saved, an `.sps` file is generated. The `.sps` file serves as the basis of the transformation. The original XML document is modified to the following:

```
<?xml version="1.0" encoding="UTF-8"?>
<?xmlspysps D:\Instructor\documents\BookXMLSpy\xslt_project\
Client.sps?>
<data xmlns:xsi="http://www.w3.org/2001/XMLSchema-instance"
xsi:noNamespaceSchemaLocation="D:\Instructor\documents\BookXMLSpy\
xslt_project\Elements.xsd">
    <element>Hello</element>
    <element>Worldfgd</element>
    <element></element>
</data>
```

There are two major changes to the original XML document. The first is the addition of the `xmlns:xsi` instruction, which references the schema file created for the XML data. The second change is the addition of the `xmlspysps` processing instruction. This processing instruction indicates to XMLSPY that, when this XML document is loaded, it should be presented as using the defined `.sps` file. If you load the XML document and activate the Large Tags feature from the toolbar, XML-SPY IDE gives you a screen that resembles Figure 7-6. (The Large Tags button is the one with a red *A*. Enabling this feature makes it easier to read the XML content.)

Notice that the tags are labeled identically to the XML document. This correlation is not accidental because the output is the XML document. To really show off how this works, look at the last element node, which is empty. Move your cursor to that node and click. Type **Bonjour** and switch to Text view. Your XML document should look like the following:

```
<?xml version="1.0" encoding="UTF-8"?>
<?xmlspysps D:\Instructor\documents\BookXMLSpy\xslt_project\
Client.sps?>
<data xmlns:xsi="http://www.w3.org/2001/XMLSchema-instance"
xsi:noNamespaceSchemaLocation="D:\Instructor\documents\BookXMLSpy\
xslt_project\Elements.xsd">
```

```
        <element>Hello</element>
        <element>World</element>
        <element>Bonjour</element>
</data>
```

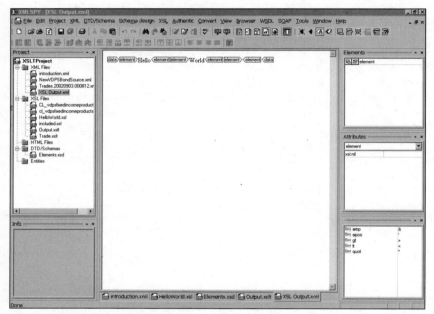

Figure 7-6: XMLSPY IDE with the XML document loaded.

The amazing bit here is that the XML has been modified, even though the HTML page is the result of an XSLT transformation. This makes building form applications much simpler.

To test the validation, add the following XSD instructions to the schema used to validate the document (to generate the XSD instructions, you use the Auto Schema generation feature available in XMLSPY):

```
<xs:restriction base="xs:string">
    <xs:enumeration value="Hello"/>
    <xs:enumeration value="World"/>
    <xs:enumeration value="Bonjour"/>
</xs:restriction>
```

Reload the document in the Authentic viewer and attempt to modify any field. The modifications should result in some red text appearing, as shown in Figure 7-7.

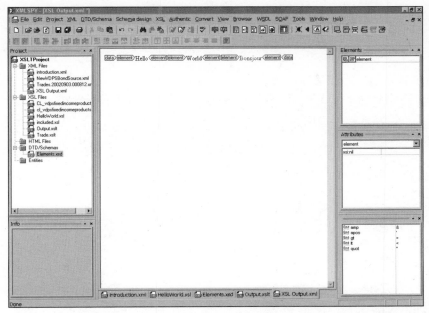

Figure 7-7: XMLSPY with the XML document loaded; an error is represented by red text.

The red text represents an error in the schema validation, which means that the XML document cannot be saved. This typically is handled using HTML and JavaScript; but with XML Schema, this operation is more consistent and maintainable.

Summary

This chapter examined what XSLT can do and how to solve specific problems that arise when you are using it. This chapter covered these topics:

◆ Calling templates and using modes and priorities

◆ Determining the various XSLT functions at your disposal

◆ Identifying techniques to help you start your XSLT coding

◆ Applying XSLT by using Cocoon and XMLSPY Authentic

In the next chapter, the discussion focuses on the Web services, SOAP and WSDL. I show you how you can use XMLSPY to generate WSDL code and how to monitor SOAP messages.

Chapter 8

Introduction to SOAP and WSDL

IN THIS CHAPTER

◆ Introducing SOAP

◆ Introducing the XSLT by using XMLSPY

◆ Writing XSLT scripts

◆ Referencing XML elements

CONSIDER THE FOLLOWING PHRASES: *Guten Tag, Tach, Moin Moin, Gruess Gott, Gruess Dich, Gruezti, Sali, Glueck Auf.* All these phrases are greetings in the Germanic language. The difference among the various greetings is that each greeting comes from a different region of the Germanic world. Yet the people in the different regions understand that all these phrases are greetings. How is that? The answer is that the phrases are based on the concept of a greeting.

Now consider a Web service. A Web service sends out data, and (you hope) the other end of the Web service picks up this data. How do the two ends of the Web service understand the data? The answer is a Web Services Description Language (WSDL) file. The WSDL file defines what a Web service is and what it represents. Consider a WSDL file as the dictionary and grammar engine of Web services. In this chapter, I try to help you understand SOAP and WSDL and how to use them. Specifically, I discuss how to create and design a WSDL service, as well as how to debug a Web service.

SOAP Theory

Simple Object Access Protocol (SOAP) was developed several years ago — specifically, in December 1999 the W3C organized the XML protocol discussion mailing list. SOAP, in its first incarnation, was a simple specification used to specify how two computers can share information using an XML message. Before SOAP applications, developers had applications communicate with each other by using technologies such as DCOM (Distributed Component Object Model), CORBA (Common Object Request Broker Architecture), IIOP (Internet Inter-ORB Protocol), and Java RMI (Remote Method

251

Invocation). The problem with these technologies is that they are specific and not one of them is a universal protocol. Therefore, to permit Internet and extranet (and not just intranet) communications, the individual parties had to agree to use a specific technology. With SOAP, the parties still need to communicate about the messages they are exchanging, but the parties do not need to discuss the technologies used.

The purpose of SOAP is to allow any computer to exchange information with another computer using any protocol. What SOAP brings to the table is a way of structuring a message so that the receiving computer can use it. For example, you decide to pass along a stack of paper to a coworker in your office. The coworker looks at you and asks, "Okay, so what do I do with this stack of paper?" If you were using the SOAP approach, you would have handed off the stack of papers wrapped in associated folders marked with sticky notes describing the purpose of the enclosed documents. SOAP, in combination with XML Schemas and WSDL, doesn't attempt to decipher the message. Instead, it provides information on how the message should be handled.

The SOAP specification in a nutshell

In its simplest form, a SOAP message looks like the following:

```
<Envelope>
    <Header>...</Header>
    <Body>...</Body>
</Envelope>
```

The SOAP message has three basic XML tags:

- ◆ Envelope: A wrapper for the SOAP message that provides the root node element

- ◆ Header: A tag used to contain information about how to route, process, or manipulate the SOAP contents; content within the Header tag is used solely by the SOAP infrastructure

- ◆ Body: A tag used to contain the actual message that will be used in an application. The contained message is constructed using XML.

The previous SOAP message is the simplest example, but the SOAP message may look more like this:

```
<?xml version="1.0" ?>
<env:Envelope xmlns:env="http://www.w3.org/2001/12/soap-envelope">
    <env:Header> ... </env:Header>
    <env:Body> ... </env:Body>
</env:Envelope>
```

The reason you are more likely to see SOAP messages that resemble this second example is because most SOAP messages contain XML namespaces. SOAP has undergone some version changes, and the way that specific XML tags are interpreted may have changed. Hence, by using a specific namespace URI identifier, it is possible to accept or reject SOAP messages. The acceptance or rejection of the SOAP message could be a SOAP gateway, or it could be the SOAP processor itself. The `env` namespace identifier specifies the version of the SOAP message.

To generate or process a message, the application looks for content between the XML `Body` tag. The content within the `Body` tag must have its own root. The best way to understand this is to consider SOAP as either a single XML document or multiple documents embedded within the SOAP XML document.

Consider the following SOAP message:

```
<Envelope>
    <Header>...</Header>
    <Body>
        <item>something</item>
        <item>another thing</item>
    </Body>
</Envelope>
```

In terms of an XML document, in which there is only one root node, it appears that the `Body` tag is the root document node for the `item` tag nodes. In fact, what is happening here is that there is no single child XML document, but multiple child documents with each child document being the `item` tag.

Must there be either a single child node or multiple child nodes? The answer is *no* because SOAP is a flexible architecture that requires the XML tags to adhere to the SOAP specification. The only requirement that has been proposed in the SOAP 1.2 specification is that each child element must have its own namespace. This makes it possible to separate the SOAP message from the XML document contained within it. In a bigger picture, this makes it possible to manipulate documents without requiring the XML document or the SOAP message to know about the other.

The details of the SOAP specification

Now that you've had a look at SOAP at its simplest level, this section walks you through the details. SOAP, by its nature, is an abstract communication mechanism without specification. In the past, and still today, the most common scenario is to send the SOAP message using the HTTP protocol. But you can also send SOAP messages by using SMTP (Simple Mail Transfer Protocol) or any other protocol. SOAP is, by its nature, stateless, meaning that a SOAP message sent at one moment in time has no recollection of an associated SOAP message sent at another period of time.

The SOAP specification does not specify how to communicate. To compare this to a language, you could say that SOAP specifies that there are words, but not how the words are put together to form a language. It would seem that SOAP is useless without this additional functionality. On the contrary, SOAP focuses on one thing and does that one thing well. The focus of SOAP is making it possible to exchange a message with another entity. In SOAP terms, there is the sender that sends the message and the receiver that receives the message. The sender may only send a single message and not receive a response, in which case the SOAP message was a *one-way* message. If the sender sends a message and the receiver sends a response to the SOAP message, a *send response* SOAP exchange occurred. Both scenarios are part of the SOAP specification.

SENDING A SOAP MESSAGE

In both a one-way and a send response message exchange, the sender must send a SOAP message. A typical SOAP message is as follows:

```
<?xml version="1.0" ?>
<env:Envelope xmlns:env="http://www.w3.org/2001/12/soap-envelope">
    <env:Header>
        <th:transaction
          xmlns:th="http://www.transaction.org/2001/12/transaction">
            123
        </th:transaction>
    </env:Header>
    <env:Body>
        <math:add xmlns:math="http://www.devspace.com/2002/1/math">
            <math:num>1</math:num>
            <math:num>1</math:num>
        </math:add>
    </env:Body>
</env:Envelope>
```

One item of interest in this message example is that XML namespaces are used everywhere. This is an important feature of SOAP that has been highlighted in the SOAP 1.2 specification. Namespaces make it possible to break a document into separate processing segments without actually destroying the format of the document.

SOAP AND NAMESPACES

The typical SOAP message just shown has three different namespaces: env, th, and math. The env namespace is part of the SOAP specification. The th namespace is a fictitious namespace that references a transaction specification. The math namespace references a namespace defined by the author to perform mathematical additions. In each of the examples, the namespace references a URI. You may think that if you typed the URI into your browser, something would be returned. Namespace identifiers don't work that way, however. The URI, in this case, is simply an identifier.

Standard XML parsers use namespace identifiers as a mechanism to group XML tags. A standard parser will not access the Internet to see what the namespace identifier represents. Applications use the namespace identifier to make sure that they are parsing the correct data. In all SOAP processor implementations, the namespace identifiers are used to identify the version of the SOAP and to execute the correct SOAP message. For example, the EasySOAP++ client is pre-SOAP 1.2 and does not accept SOAP 1.2 responses. EasySOAP++ can handle only SOAP 1.1 requests. Therefore, to process SOAP 1.2 messages, you would have to use Apache Axis, Microsoft .NET, or something similar.

SOAP HEADERS

In the typical SOAP message example shown earlier, there was a SOAP `Header` XML tag and child `transaction` XML tag. The SOAP `Header` tag is optional and does not need to be present. The purpose of the SOAP `Header` tag is to instruct the infrastructure what to do with the message. In the case of the typical SOAP message example, the `transaction` XML tag is referencing a currently executing transaction. The transaction may or may not mean anything to the receiver that has to process the SOAP message.

In the SOAP message example, if the transaction means nothing to the receiver, the transaction is ignored and processing continues. However, if the XML-tag transaction were constructed as follows, the transaction could not be ignored:

```
<th:transaction
    xmlns:th="http://www.transaction.org/2001/12/transaction"
    env:mustUnderstand="1">
```

In the modified version of the `transaction` XML tag, an attribute `mustUnderstand` is added. The `mustUnderstand` attribute is part of the SOAP namespace (prefixed with an `env`) and is a specification. In the SOAP specification, it is stated that the receiver must understand the `mustUnderstand` attribute in a header element to be able to process the SOAP message. If the receiver cannot understand the header element, the receiver must issue a fault stating that the receiver is not able to process the header element.

In a previous paragraph, I mentioned that a SOAP header element is used to indicate how to process the SOAP headers. This is not entirely true because specific `actor` attributes can be assigned. For example, a SOAP message needs routing information that is specific to the domain where the SOAP message is being sent. At this point, a SOAP header has to be added, but the SOAP receiver will not process it. A so-called SOAP intermediary processes the SOAP message. A SOAP intermediary is a server that has the capability to receive a SOAP message and process the SOAP headers, but not the contents of the SOAP message itself. If a SOAP header has to be specifically processed by the SOAP intermediary, it is possible to assign an `actor` attribute as shown by the following example:

```
<th:some_action xmlns:th="http://www.devspace.com/2001/12/something"
env:actor="http://www.devspace.com/some_logical_machine" ..>
```

In this example, the `some_action` XML tag has an `actor` attribute, which indicates that `some_action` tag should be processed at a specific SOAP intermediary. In this case the SOAP intermediary is specified using a specific URI, which (in theory) could be the IP of some computer. However, specifying a specific IP is shortsighted, and instead the SOAP intermediary should be specified using a logical name. The logical name should reflect either the business process or the purpose of the machine. Examples could include gateway, router, firewall, and so on.

One final word on SOAP headers: if a specific header element has child elements, and the specific element was not processed, then the child elements are not processed either. When processing header elements, there is a strict parent-child relationship that cannot be broken.

SOAP BODY

Every SOAP message must have a SOAP `Body` XML tag. Within the SOAP `Body` is the data to be processed by the receiver. Any valid XML data that has an associated namespace identifier can be included. Not having a namespace identifier causes an error in the SOAP processor. Otherwise, the data does not matter to the SOAP processor and is passed on as is. Within the SOAP `Body`, there can be either one child element or multiple child elements. The significance of a single or multiple child elements is only of interest to the SOAP message processor.

SOAP ENCODING

In the SOAP 1.2 specification, the other important factor is encoding of the data. Although XML allows any type of structuring and formatting, there are encoding schemes defined. The encoding schemes are purely optional and need not necessarily apply. However, if a sender sends a message with encoding defined, the receiver should, generally, not ignore the encoding. The purpose of encoding is to make it simpler to translate a data type from one application platform to another application platform.

However, there are some things to consider regarding encoding. In previous versions of SOAP, encoding was part of the specification, but now encoding is an adjunct of the SOAP 1.2 specification. What does this mean to the average programmer? It means that the W3C standards body is starting to split SOAP into different sections and areas. The SOAP-encoding specification specifically deals with using SOAP in an RPC (Remote Procedure Context). If SOAP is used in another context, the encoding specification does not necessarily apply. But there is a generally accepted encoding that applies in all circumstances. That is XML Schema Part 2, which defines how numbers, complex structures, and other things are encoded. The SOAP encoding narrows down the specification for use in arrays and other programmer-specific items. A more detailed discussion of encoding is beyond the scope of this book.

GETTING A REPLY

When the SOAP message causes the receiver to generate a reply, the reply must take a specific form. The reply has the exact same format as the request except that the generated content is a response. With SOAP 1.2, the notion is that a reply is the same as a message sent.

GETTING AN ERROR MESSAGE

The only special type of SOAP message is a SOAP error message. The generic form of the SOAP error message is as follows:

```
<?xml version="1.0" ?>
<env:Envelope xmlns:env="http://www.w3.org/2001/12/soap-envelope">
   <env:Body>
       <env:Fault>
           <faultcode>env:Receiver</faultcode>
           <faultstring>Something happened</faultstring>
           <detail>
               <err:message
                   xmlns:err="http:www.devspace.com/errors">
                   Here is some error
               </err:message>
           </detail>
       </env:Fault>
   </env:Body>
</env:Envelope>
```

The SOAP error is a document within the SOAP `Body` tag as specified by the `Fault` XML tag. The `Fault` tag is part of the `env` namespace, which is part of the SOAP specification. What is odd about the error specification is that, within the `Fault` tag, things become a bit illogical. The SOAP specification hammers home the point of the namespace identifying all elements of the SOAP message, except within the standard `Fault` child tags. Another oddity is that the value contained within the `faultcode` tag is namespace identified. The final oddity is that the four child XML tags are all lowercase although, thus far, everything else has been defined with the first letter uppercase. Although none of these oddities is illegal XML, each is just a bit out of place with the rest of the well-designed SOAP specification.

Here are the four possible child XML tags:

◆ `faultcode`: Specifies the error that has occurred. The `faultcode` error needs to be programmatically recognizable because the SOAP processor uses this error code to display the error. There are predefined error codes as follows:

  ■ `VersionMismatch`: The SOAP Envelope message being sent does not have the same namespace identifier as was expected by the receiver.

- MustUnderstand: A SOAP Header element was passed that the SOAP receiver or intermediary does not understand. An example of this error is given in the next section

- DTDNotSupported: If a SOAP message contains a DTD description anywhere, the SOAP infrastructure will generate an error because DTDs are not supported.

- DataEncodingUnknown: An encoding is used within the SOAP message that is not supported by the SOAP infrastructure.

- Sender: An error has occurred where the SOAP sender has sent data that makes it impossible for the SOAP intermediaries or SOAP receiver to process the SOAP message.

- Receiver: An error has occurred in which the problem is not the SOAP message itself, but the processing of the SOAP message. Although this may be the same as an error in the content, it really means the error lies with a dependency caused by the SOAP message. For example, if the SOAP message causes another SOAP message call and that call has an error, this faultcode is generated.

◆ faultstring: Specifies a human-readable explanation of the error. The value for faultstring is a string as defined by the XML Schema string definition.

◆ faultactor: Specifies which node on the SOAP calling chain caused the error. Using this value, it is possible to pinpoint if the SOAP receiver was at fault or if a SOAP intermediary was at fault.

◆ detail: Specifies a more detailed error message. Unlike the faultstring, the detail part of the error message can have sub-XML elements. However, if child XML elements are defined then they must be namespace defined.

The mustUnderstand attribute specifies that the specified SOAP intermediary or SOAP receiver must know what to do with the child SOAP Header element. If, however, the child SOAP Header element is unknown, an error is generated. But the SOAP error message has an additional element within the SOAP Header collection indicating which child SOAP Header element is the problem. An example error message is as follows:

```
<?xml version="1.0" ?>
<env:Envelope
    xmlns:env="http://www.w3.org/2001/12/soap-envelope"
    xmlns:err="http://www.w3.org/2001/12/soap-faults">
    <env:Header>
        <err:Misunderstood qname=" th:transaction"
        xmlns:th="http://www.transaction.org/2001/12/transaction" />
    </env:Header>
```

```
<env:Body>
   <env:Fault>
      <faultcode>env:Receiver</faultcode>
      <faultstring>
        Could not understand SOAP Header sub-tag
      </faultstring>
   </env:Fault>
</env:Body>
</env:Envelope>
```

This SOAP error message is in reference to the SOAP message that was sent with a `transaction` header element. In this example, the unknown header element is exchanged with the SOAP `err` namespace-defined `Misunderstood` element. The attribute `qname` specifies which header element is the problem. Notice that the header element associated namespace and namespace identifier are also stored within the `Misunderstood` XML tag. Exact details of why the header element is incorrect are given within the `Fault` tag.

SOAP bindings and protocols

In previous versions of the SOAP specification, the HTTP protocol was always referenced within the specification. Starting with the SOAP 1.2 specification, this reference has changed to *transport bindings*. SOAP, from day one, has not been protocol-specific, but because HTTP was used most frequently, HTTP was referenced. Transport bindings make it possible to send a SOAP message on a variety of different protocols. SOAP 1.2 still only specifically outlines the HTTP protocol, but other protocols are in the process of being defined. For example, another place where SOAP messages can be sent is via e-mail protocols – such as SMTP (Simple Mail Transport Protocol) or POP (Post Office Protocol).

What do transport bindings mean to the SOAP specification itself? Actually, not much. SOAP can be sent on any protocol because SOAP is a self-enclosed specification. Transport bindings have significance only for those programmers who implement SOAP processors. For example, defining a SOAP transport binding for HTTP specifies that a SOAP message is not the MIME type `text/xml` but `application/soap`. This detail would never be of relevance to the application programmer.

The WSDL Specification

Let's say that you decide to tell your friend about a cool new Web site. To do that, you give the friend the URL and the reason why the Web site is interesting. In a Web services world, there is no simple way to tell a computer that a cool Web service exists at a specific location. The problem is that the computer requires specific details, and a human, typically, does not provide enough details. That is the purpose of WSDL (Web Services Description Language). WSDL makes it possible to describe a Web service so that a computer program can take the WSDL information and configure specific pieces of Web service infrastructure. WSDL is to Web services what schema information is to XML files.

WSDL basics

A WSDL document defines five aspects of the SOAP message, which are defined as follows:

- ◆ **XML types:** It is possible to define the XML type of the various elements of the SOAP message. This makes it possible to verify the correctness of the data sent and/or received.

- ◆ **Message description:** A SOAP message is concatenation of various logical message sections. Consider an individual SOAP message as a chapter in a book and the logical part as a paragraph within the chapter.

- ◆ **Port type:** As a programmer, you might think port means logical device port. Instead, the port type means a combination of input and output messages. Continuing the book metaphor, think of the port as one of the book's parts, or sections, that contains individual chapters.

- ◆ **Binding:** Defines the specific format of the port type, such as protocol or data binding. Think of the binding as the entire book, including pictures, chapters, and so on.

- ◆ **Service:** Used to define the service, which implies that the `Service` tag is the entry point and puts everything together for processing.

In a nutshell, what you need to remember is that a WSDL defines the SOAP message as an abstract entity that can be correlated to some business logic. WSDL is not just a definition of the SOAP message, because that requires only the XML types. WSDL is a way of describing what the Web service does. You could say that WSDL adds the object-oriented aspect to SOAP.

Illustrated WSDL

WSDL can become complex very quickly; therefore, the focus here is on simple WSDL. The complexity of WSDL is not algorithmic but results from information overload due to the large number of elements that can be defined. Take another look at the SOAP message shown earlier:

```
<?xml version="1.0" ?>
<env:Envelope xmlns:env="http://www.w3.org/2001/12/soap-envelope">
    <env:Body>
        <math:add xmlns:math="http://www.devspace.com/2002/1/math">
            <math:num>1</math:num>
            <math:num>1</math:num>
```

```
        </math:add>
    </env:Body>
</env:Envelope>
```

In the following sections, I use this SOAP message and show you how to create a WSDL file incrementally. This method should help you understand where to start when developing your own WSDL files.

XML TYPES

The first thing you need to do is define the various XML types present in this message. In SOAP, different encodings and XML types can be used. However, the specification clearly prefers using XML Schema data types because this ensures maximum interoperability and broadest support. Converting the previous SOAP message into WSDL type definitions yields the following XML:

```
<xs:schema xmlns:xs="http://www.w3.org/2001/XMLSchema"
    targetNamespace="http://www.devspace.com/2002/1/math"
    elementFormDefault="qualified">
    <xs:element name=" add">
        <xs:complexType>
            <xs:sequence>
                <xs:element name="num" ref="num" minOccurs="1"
                    maxOccurs="unbounded"/>
            </xs:sequence>
            <xs:attribute name=" math" type="xs:anyURI"
                use="required"/>
        </xs:complexType>
    </xs:element>
    <xs:element name=" num">
        <xs:simpleType>
            <xs:restriction base="xs:byte">
                <xs:enumeration value="1"/>
                <xs:enumeration value="2"/>
            </xs:restriction>
        </xs:simpleType>
    </xs:element>
</xs:schema>
```

The previous schema definition is a self-encapsulation section of XML and can be used to validate the XML validity of the SOAP message within the SOAP `Body` tag. Pay special attention to the `targetNamespace` attribute. Notice that it has the same value as the `math` namespace definition within the SOAP message. This is intentional and provides the cross-reference between the SOAP `Body` contents and the schema.

MESSAGES

The next item that you have to define is the message that is being sent and its logical WSDL `part`. With respect to the SOAP message, the following XML is defined:

```
<wsdl:message name="msgAdd">
    <wsdl:part name="main" element="mathxsd:add"/>
</wsdl:message>
<wsdl:message name="msgAddResponse">
    <wsdl:part name="main" element="mathxsd:addResponse"/>
</wsdl:message>
```

The XML tag message identifies that a message with the name `msgAdd` and another message with the name `msgAddResponse` are being defined. Specifically what is happening is that two SOAP messages are being defined based on the elements `mathxsd:add` and `mathxsd:addResponse`. The `element` attribute references the `mathxsd` namespace that has not yet been defined. This definition has been omitted because the various WSDL pieces have not yet been put together in one XML document. The `mathxsd` is a namespace that references the schema type information defined in previously.

In the defined message `msgAdd`, there is only one part named `main`, which is `abstract identifier`. There could be multiple parts, with each part being a separate document within the XML SOAP `Body`. Consider the following SOAP message:

```
<env:Envelope xmlns:env="http://www.w3.org/2001/12/soap-envelope">
    <env:Body>
        <math:add xmlns:math="http://www.devspace.com/2002/1/math">
            <math:num>1</math:num>
            <math:num>1</math:num>
        </math:add>
        <math:subtract
            xmlns:math="http://www.devspace.com/2002/1/math">
            <math:num>1</math:num>
            <math:num>1</math:num>
        </math:subtract>
    </env:Body>
</env:Envelope>
```

The preceding example contains two embedded XML documents. The first XML document is `math:add` and the second is `math:subtract`. In terms of a WSDL message, it could be defined as follows:

```
<wsdl:message name="formulaRequest">
    <wsdl:part name="step1" element="mathxsd:add"/>
    <wsdl:part name="step2" element="mathxsd:subtract"/>
</wsdl:message>
```

In the WSDL you add two parts to the newly defined formulaRequest message, which are add and subtract. You do this so that the infrastructure can separate the SOAP message into two sections, each of which does its own processing. In this example, the infrastructure can create an add and subtract processor.

Another way of illustrating these two parts is to collapse them into one part and then, within the XML types, define a complex schema type that is, in essence, identical to the WSDL above. This redundancy is purely logical and business-related.

PORT TYPES

The port type of a SOAP message has nothing to do with a socket port. A WSDL port type is a way of describing an interaction between the sender and receiver of the SOAP message. The SOAP specification only says there is a one-way message exchange. Sending a response just happens to be yet another message exchange. Using WSDL, it is possible to define exactly what will be sent and received. This is very important. Consider the case of sending a SOAP message using SMTP. With SMTP it is not possible to get an answer right away and, hence, a waiting SOAP sender will wait indefinitely. Using WSDL as the infrastructure, you can determine if a response will be sent and when. But do not consider the port type as a physical definition of SOAP message exchange. The port type defines an abstract message exchange mechanism. The specifics are defined in the bindings, which have not yet been discussed.

In the previous WSDL message descriptions, the methods msgAdd and msgAddResponse were defined. Both of these methods tie together to form a request and response action. In terms of a port type, the WSDL is defined as follows:

```
<wsdl:portType>
    <wsdl:operation name="portAddingNumbers">
        <wsdl:input name="Adding" message="msgAdd"/>
        <wsdl:output name="Result" message="msgAddResponse"/>
    </wsdl:operation>
</wsdl:portType >
```

The root of a port type is the operation XML tag. Within the operation XML tag are a number of input and output XML tags. The exact number is based on the operation being performed. Although XML can define many input and output operations, the WSDL specification has not yet achieved that level of complexity. Instead, the WSDL defines the following four types of logical operations that can be performed:

- ◆ **One-Way Operation:** The sender sends a SOAP message to the receiver, and does not expect a response.

- ◆ **Request-Response Operation:** The sender sends a SOAP message to the receiver, and the receiver sends a response to the message.

◆ **Solicit-Response Operation:** The receiver sends a SOAP message to the sender, and the sender sends a response. If this sounds confusing, consider this nothing more than an asynchronous callback using SOAP.

◆ **Notification Operation:** The receiver sends a SOAP message to the sender, and the receiver does not expect an answer. This could also be called a targeted broadcast in SOAP terms.

The `portAddingNumbers` port type is an example of a Request-Response Operation in that it contains an `input` and `output` XML tag. The `name` attribute defines an abstract identifier of the step being carried out. The `message` attribute is a cross-reference with a previously defined WSDL message. In the Request-Response Operation, there cannot be more `input` or `output` tags. What is optional is the `fault` XML tag. The `fault` XML tag identifies a SOAP response containing a specific fault message.

The One-Way Operation can contain only one `input` tag. The Solicit-Response Operation contains the same tags as the Request-Response Operation, except that the order is different. In the Request-Response Operation, the order of the `input` and `output` tags is `input` first and `output` second. In the Solicit-Response Operation, the order is `output` first and then an `input` tag. In either case, the `fault` tag is optional. But in the Solicit-Response Operation, the `fault` tag is generated by the sender. And in the final Notification Operation, only an `output` tag is sent by the receiver. Note that there is no optional `fault` tag with either the One-Way Operation or the Notification Operation. The message exchange, in this case, is one way, and it is assumed that the message could disappear into the never-never land.

BINDING

Binding is a bit more complicated because it throws everything into question that you have learned thus far. The binding aspect is necessary, and it needs to be kept generic, but it also means that SOAP is not part of the binding. Up to this point, the discussion has centered around SOAP being used to exchange messages. What if something else is being used? Thus far, the WSDL items, XML types, message, and port type have been defined. Could these WSDL items be used for generic XML or XML-RPC? The answer is a definite *yes* because none of these items is specific to the SOAP format. Instead, the various items refer to the abstract problems that SOAP solves.

You can define a binding element in various, nonspecific ways. Here is a simple example:

```
<binding name="BindingAddition" type="portAddingNumbers">
    <operation name="AddSomeNumbers">
        <input message="add">
        </input>
    </operation>
</binding>
```

Looking at this example, you can see something odd is occurring. The binding references the port type using the attribute type. But yet within the `binding` tag there is another `operation` tag with an `input` tag. What does this imply? Does this imply there is no need to define the port type `portAddingNumbers`? The answer is WSDL allows overloading and overriding. In the port type definition, the logical operations are defined, but in the binding the specifications regarding the operation are defined.

So for example, the following SOAP bindings could be associated with the simple binding:

```
<binding name="bindingAddition" type="portAddingNumbers">
    <soap:binding style="rpc"
        transport="http://schemas.xmlsoap.org/soap/http"/>
        <operation name="AddSomeNumbers">
            <soap:operation
                soapAction="http://www.devspace.com/add"/>
                <input message="add">
                    <soap:body use="encoded"
                        namespace="http://example.com/stockquote"
                        encodingStyle=
                        "http://schemas.xmlsoap.org/soap/encoding/"/>
                </input>
        </operation>
</binding>
```

In this case, the bindings that deal with SOAP are using the `soap` namespace. The SOAP binding is specified by adding the XML `binding` tag, with a predefined `style` attribute of `rpc` and the `transport` attribute named to HTTP. The `style` and `transport` attributes are specific to the SOAP binding and are not usually included. What you do need to specify is the XML `binding` tag. It is prefixed by the namespace of the binding, which could be SOAP or HTTP. The MIME binding is a bit of an oddity because it is usually used in conjunction with another binding. The point, though, is that the XML `binding` tag or others are linked to the namespace.

Within the WSDL `operation` tag, there is a SOAP `operation` tag. The SOAP `operation` tag has the one attribute named `soapAction`. The attribute `soapAction` is special because it is used as an HTTP header addition, which is used by the HTTP binding to identify which part of the infrastructure will process the SOAP request. Adding the `soapAction` attribute may seem redundant with the addition of namespaces to the SOAP request. But the `soapAction` attribute makes it possible for SOAP intermediaries to process part of the SOAP message without actually processing the entire SOAP message. Within the WSDL `input` tag, there is a SOAP `Body` tag. The SOAP `Body` tag is used to indicate how the message will be encoded and the namespace used to identify the SOAP message.

Now back up a bit to where the WSDL `operation` and `input` tags seemed redundant because they are already specified by the port type `portAddingNumbers`. The port type is an abstract operation, used to define how messages will be sent back and forth. But those messages can be sent using different protocols (HTTP, SMTP) and different message types (SOAP, HTTP). By adding the specifics to the port type, separating the protocol from the message type is more complicated Introducing the WSDL `binding` tag makes it possible to cross-reference a logical operation to a specific binding and Internet protocol.

SERVICES

The last item to define in a WSDL file is the service itself. The service provides the entry point to the WSDL file. From the service definition, it is possible to figure out what is being defined and how it is to be used. The following code shows a sample WSDL service definition:

```
<service name="MathService">
    <documentation>Want to add numbers?  Here it is</documentation>
    <port name="AddNumbersPort" binding="tns:bindingAddition">
        <soap:address
            location="http://www.devspace.com.com/addnums"/>
    </port>
</service>
```

The service is defined by the XML `service` tag, with the `name` attribute being a unique name to identify the Web service. The XML `documentation` tag is used for the first time. I avoided using this tag, but it is optional at every major WSDL item type. The `documentation` tag makes it possible to provide generic documentation that can be displayed using a tool. Note that the `documentation` tag should not be confused with the XML `comment` tag. The `documentation` tag is for application processing and display. Within the WSDL `service` tag is the `port` tag. The `port` tag is responsible for providing a physical binding to the binding defined by `bindingAddition`. In our binding example SOAP and HTTP were used, but the address where the service was located was not provided. The SOAP `address_location` tag provides the physical address. Again, this is an abstraction to make it simpler to separate and reuse various WSDL definitions.

WRAPPING IT UP

The individual pieces of the WSDL have been defined, and now it is time to put everything together into one WSDL file. The example is defined as follows:

```
<definitions name="MyAdditionExample"
    targetnamespace="http://www.devspace.com/addition.wsdl"
    xmlns:tns=" http://www.devspace.com/addition.wsdl"
    xmlns:xsd="http://www.w3.org/2000/10/XMLSchema"
    xmlns:xsd1=" http://www.devspace.com/2002/1/math"
    xmlns:soap="http://schemas.xmlsoap.org/wsdl/soap/"
```

```
    xmlns="http://schemas.xmlsoap.org/wsdl/">
    ...<!--Put everything in here-->
</definitions>
```

The individual elements that were defined can simply be cut and pasted into the area where the XML comment says `Put everything in here`. The only issue is to make sure that the namespaces are correct. WSDL and SOAP are very namespace heavy, so namespace accuracy requires careful attention.

To keep things simple, you should cut and paste the preceding namespaces, except for the following changes:

- ◆ `targetnamespace`: This defines the namespace of your WSDL file locally and should be a unique identifier.

- ◆ `xmlns:tns`: This is the same namespace as `targetnamespace`, except that the namespace is being assigned to a prefix.

- ◆ `xmlns:xsd`: This is the namespace definition of your types defined in terms of a schema file, as the one defined in the types section of the WSDL file.

Another thing to remember when creating WSDL files is to stick with the same namespace prefixes. This makes it simpler to create and debug the various WSDL files.

To keep smaller WSDL files and make it possible to reuse different files, import sections into your WSDL file so that the definitions do not need to be re-created. Here's an example of importing XML content into a WSDL file:

```
<definitions name="MyAdditionExample">
    <import namespace=" http://www.devspace.com/2002/1/math"
            location="http://www.devspace.com/math/math.xsd"/>
    ...
</definitions>
```

Finally, the last question is: Do you create WSDL files by hand or have a tool to generate them? The answer is: Who cares? WSDL files are going to be created once and kept forever. The one problem with SOAP is that you cannot change it. Let me explain. On another platform, there is something called *DLL hell*. DLL hell is when a program does not work after the DLL has been upgraded. DLL hell only exists on individual desktops. Imagine a popular SOAP service that, when the WSDL is changed once, causes all clients to crash. The point here is that the creation of WSDL is not a point-and-click operation; generally, pointing and clicking means that you don't have to think much. (You get too excited about getting something done quickly.)

WSDL and bindings

The last piece of WSDL that you need to consider is the bindings. You need to know what the individual tags imply. There are two major binding types – SOAP and HTTP – and they are explained in the following sections. SOAP is a binding mechanism you already know. But HTTP is different. Although SOAP can use HTTP to transport the message, the HTTP binding is aimed at solving the problem of the Web client communicating within the Web service infrastructure.

SOAP BINDING

In previous examples, I have illustrated the SOAP binding, but I discuss it again here for reference purposes:

- `soap:binding`: This tag is defined within the WSDL `binding` tag and specifies that the message is bound to the SOAP protocol. There are two attributes that can be used. The first attribute is `transport` and defines the protocol that can be used. Examples include `http://schemas.xmlsoap.org/soap/http` and `http`, `ftp`, and so on. In fact, this can be anything that the infrastructure can recognize. The second attribute is `style`, which can be either RPC or document. The `style` attribute is used for encoding purposes.

- `soap:operation`: This tag is defined within the WSDL `binding::operation` tag to indicate how to process the SOAP message. There are two attributes: `style` and `soapAction`. The `soapAction` attribute can be considered an abstract identifier used to process the SOAP message. The `style` attribute can be either RPC or document, with the same intent as defined in the `soap:binding` attribute.

- `soap:body`: This tag is the most varied and defines the encoding style of the SOAP message. For example, if the SOAP message is in RPC format, the tag order occurs in a specific pattern.

- `soap:fault`: This tag is identical in function and purpose to `soap:body`, except that the tag applies when there is an error.

- `soap:header`/`soap:headerfault`: Defines the extra SOAP headers that can be sent with the request.

- `soap:address`: Defines the actual SOAP address request where the SOAP message is to be sent, which specifies a URI. There can be only one URI.

HTTP BINDING

A client cannot use a Web browser to make SOAP calls. Writing another client so that you can make SOAP calls is just plain silly because you have the wonderful Web browser. To make the Web browser part of the Web services infrastructure, a specific binding has been developed called HTTP binding. The HTTP binding makes it possible for a Web browser to make Web service requests that are part of a bigger chain. The binding attributes are most likely added to the WSDL `binding` and `service` tags.

Here's an example of processing the `Add` request using an HTTP form and HTTP POST. The appropriate HTTP POST data is as follows:

```
http://www.devspace.com/formAdd.cgi
number1=1234&number2=2345
```

The corresponding WSDL with HTTP binding would then be as follows:

```
<binding name="WebAddNumbers" type="portAddingNumbers">
    <http:binding verb="POST"/>
    <operation name="postAdd">
        <http:operation location="/formAdd.cgi"/>
        <input>
            <mime:content
                    type="application/x-www-form-urlencoded"/>
        </input>
        <output>
            <mime:content type="text/html"/>
        </output>
    </operation>
</binding>
```

The HTTP binding is specified by the prefix `http`, and the `binding` tag has the `verb` attribute. The infrastructure uses the `verb` to know how the request will be made. In this case, it is an HTTP POST. Within the WSDL `operation` tag, the `http` operation is defined with a specific location where the request will be made. Note that the location is not an absolute address. The location is appended to the address located in the WSDL service and HTTP address definition.

What is new in this WSDL is the MIME binding type identified by the `mime` prefix. The MIME binding is not a binding in the HTTP and SOAP sense. Instead the MIME binding can be considered as a way of defining how data is encoded using something other than XML. In this case, the MIME bindings specify for the input that the data will arrive as the MIME type `application/x-www-form-urlencoded`. The output is encoded as `text/html`.

XMLSPY WSDL Editing

XMLSPY helps you to code SOAP and WSDL in multiple ways, but the two most important ways are SOAP debugging and WSDL editing. Although you could start with SOAP debugging, you need a WSDL file to debug a SOAP server. Therefore, it is better to start editing a WSDL file. The simplest way to edit a WSDL document is to choose File → New and select the WSDL file type from the list box. The resulting XMLSPY IDE state should look similar to Figure 8-1.

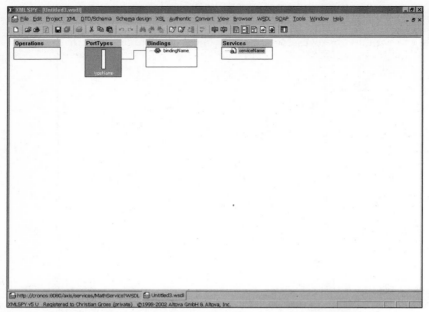

Figure 8-1: XMLSPY IDE layout after a new WSDL file has been selected.

The WSDL editor is useful, but it requires that you understand WSDL. The way to read this document is to start from the left and read to the right. If you want to edit or update this WSDL graphically, Editing view requires that you right-click to access a menu that describes the operations that can be executed at that location (see Figure 8-2).

The best strategy on coding a WSDL file is to start with a real-life scenario. For example, if you want to create a Math Service, describe the Math Service in either pseudocode or regular code, as in the following example:

```
public interface MathService {
    public int doAdd( int inp1, int inp2);
    public int doSubtract( int inp1, int inp2);
}
```

In this interface definition, there are two methods with specific parameters. This interface indicates an RPC type service. The parameter encoding could either be XML Schema or literal. The more appropriate solution would be to be to use an XML Schema because literal encoding is something from the past when there was no XML Schema. The other item to note is that the Web service has four SOAP messages, which are grouped into two sets of input and output messages. There are output messages in this example because both methods return an integer value.

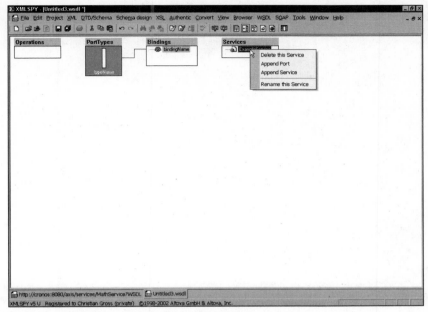

Figure 8-2: Right-click the WSDL graphical editor.

The first step is to define the operations. Right-click on the Operations GUI element and select Append Operation To Port Type from the menu. This results in the addition of an item to the Operations box. You rename that item to doAdd, which represents the name of the MathService.doAdd method. Then, right-click this item and select Add Input Element from the menu. Repeat this step, selecting Add Output Element this time. Then repeat the entire process to add the other method doSubtract. The result should look similar to Figure 8-3.

Next, you need to edit the WSDL so that messages are associated with the Operations. The way to add messages is to select the Messages tree control item, right-click, and select Append Message from the menu. The created message represents a SOAP message that is sent. The SOAP message needs parameters, which you can add by right-clicking the newly created message and selecting Add Message Part from the menu. To edit the details of the parameter, select the parameter and look at the Details window on the center right side of the XMLSPY IDE in Figure 8-3. The last step is to associate the messages with the Operations. You do this by dragging and dropping the sub-message item in the Overview window over to the correct Operation method in the Operations window. After the steps just outlined, the XMLSPY IDE should look similar to Figure 8-4.

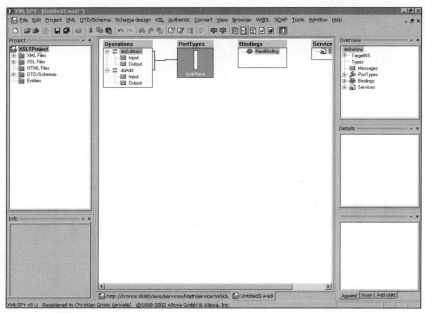

Figure 8-3: The result of editing the operations in the WSDL graphical editor.

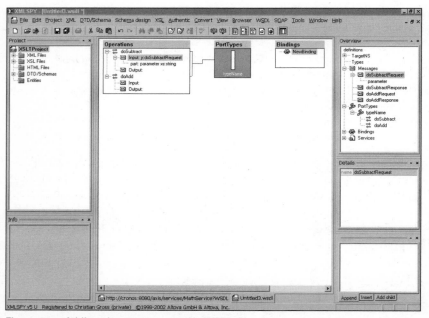

Figure 8-4: Adding the messages to the WSDL file.

The preceding steps are the hardest part of defining a Web service. The rest involve cross-referencing the already existing created messages with the ports and bindings. You select the Binding from the Overview menu items on the far-right side, and then you associate the PortType to the TypeName port and the style to RPC from the Details list box. In the Services WSDL item, you right-click and create a new service, which is bound to the NewBinding. You create the binding selection by selecting it from the Details window. When all the changes have been made, your Web service should look similar to Figure 8-5.

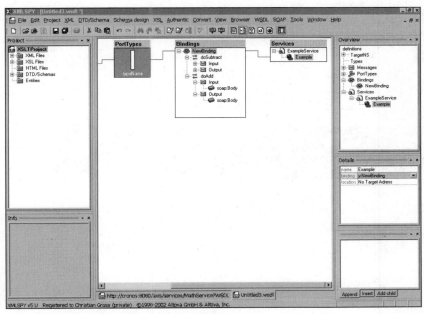

Figure 8-5: Wiring the Web service together.

You can define the rest of the details, such as URI naming, by going through the various details of each item and setting them to the appropriate value. The strategy of building the WSDL incrementally from the message to the service is the strategy that you should use. It is the simplest and most logical when you're using the XML-SPY WSDL editor. As a practice exercise, go back and cross-reference the WSDL elements defined in the WSDL graphical editor.

XMLSPY SOAP Debugging

The other way that XMLSPY helps with SOAP is in the testing of a Web service. XMLSPY helps you to code SOAP and WSDL in multiple ways, but the two most important ways are SOAP debugging and WSDL editing. To debug SOAP Service from the XMLSPY menu, choose SOAP → SOAP Debugger Session. A dialog box appears asking for a WSDL file. Before you specify the WSDL file created previously, be aware that you need a running server to test the Web service. In the case of this chapter, the sample SOAP session is based on the Java Axis server. Axis has the capability to dynamically generate a WSDL file from a Web service when given the correct URL. After the URL has been entered in the XMLSPY dialog box and the OK button is clicked, another dialog box appears asking for the server host and port id. Click OK and the XMLSPY IDE should look similar to Figure 8-6.

A copy of Apache Axis, a Java framework for constructing SOAP processors, including clients, servers, and gateways, is available on the CD that accompanies this book. Axis includes utilities for working with WSDL files, including a tool that generates Java classes from WSDL.

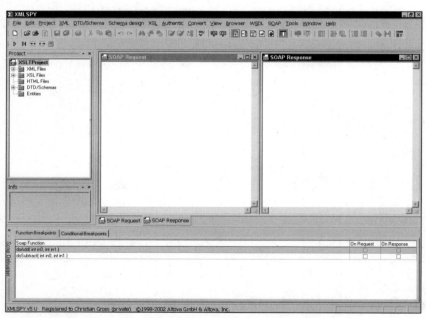

Figure 8-6: SOAP debugger XMLSPY IDE layout.

To activate the debugger, choose SOAP → GO. At that point, the SOAP debugger is running. Because there is no action, you may wonder whether anything is happening at all. The XMLSPY SOAP debugger is a proxy that intercepts SOAP requests and allows the developer to check the validity of the SOAP request. This means that to test a SOAP request, you need both a client and server application. The difference is that the client application needs to redirect the SOAP request to the XMLSPY proxy. The address of the XMLSPY proxy is the IP address where XMLSPY is executing, and the port ID is the same as the WSDL file has specified. In Figure 8-6, in the bottom window, the Function-Breakpoints tab is active. On the right side of that window, it is possible to capture SOAP requests and perform a breakpoint, as shown in Figure 8-7.

After the breakpoint has been hit, it is possible to investigate the SOAP message and test the correctness. The default view of the SOAP Request window is the graphical XML view, but you can switch to Text view and look at the SOAP request or SOAP response.

The usefulness of the SOAP debugger is not for the simple RPC SOAP requests. Where the XMLSPY SOAP debugger becomes useful is when the SOAP request is a large or complicated piece of XML. XMLSPY has built-in schema validation, and it is possible to check a specific state of the SOAP message.

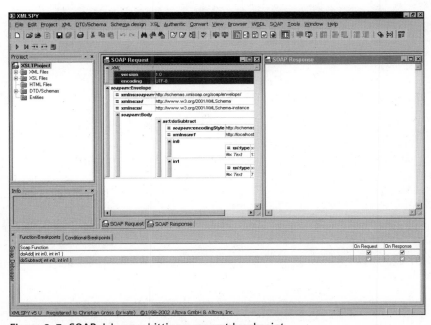

Figure 8-7: SOAP debugger hitting a request breakpoint.

Summary

The focus of this chapter was on understanding SOAP and WSDL. This chapter covered these topics:

◆ Using SOAP and WSDL to build Web services

◆ Building a WSDL file by using XMLSPY

◆ Debugging SOAP Web services with XMLSPY

Based on the material in this chapter, you should now know how to construct a WSDL file. A WSDL file is a descriptor that many will reference in building their applications, so it's important that you consider what a WSDL file is and what its ramifications are.

In the next chapter, you find out all about how to register and take the XMLSPY – XML Developer Certification exam.

Chapter 9

Altova XML Developer Certification

IN THIS CHAPTER

◆ Altova XMLSPY – XML Developer Certification exam overview

◆ How to register

◆ Sample questions

◆ Tip and strategies for test takers

ALTOVA HAS PARTNERED WITH PROMETRIC, the leading information technology education and certification company, to offer an XML certification examination. XML certification is meant as a unique challenge for XML developers to demonstrate a high level of understanding of XML technologies, and there are many advantages to acquiring the certification. This chapter covers everything you need to know about the Altova XML developer certification, including what topics are covered on the exam, how to register, pricing and availability, types of questions, and some test-taking strategies. The benefits of taking the Altova XML exam include professional recognition and gaining a competitive advantage over other XML developers.

Altova XMLSPY – XML Developer Certification Overview

The Altova XMLSPY – XML Developer Certification is designed to challenge XML developers seeking to upgrade their technical skill sets in core XML infrastructure technologies. It is not an examination about the use of XMLSPY, although a solid understanding of the XMLSPY development environment would undoubtedly be helpful in learning the subject matter. The Altova XMLSPY – XML Developer Certification is unique among XML certification course offerings in that the materials covered are truly platform- and vendor-independent, covering only standards-based W3C technologies relating to XML subject matter. The certification does not cover topics related to XML programming language bindings, such as Java APIs for XML processing or Microsoft's XML processing APIs.

Subjects covered

The Altova XMLSPY – XML Developer Certification covers the core infrastructure XML technologies. These are W3C recommendations with the notable exception of WSDL. WSDL is, however, widely implemented in its draft form and is expected to be even more widely adopted when finally released as a full W3C recommendation. The certification requires a 60-minute examination consisting of 50 multiple choice questions, each having four to five choices. An overall score of 80 percent or higher must be obtained in order to pass the examination (that means you cannot make more than 10 mistakes). The questions are practical in nature in that the subjects covered reflect XML technologies that are being used in industry software development projects across various technology platforms (for example, Microsoft .NET and J2EE). Figure 9-1 shows what subjects are covered.

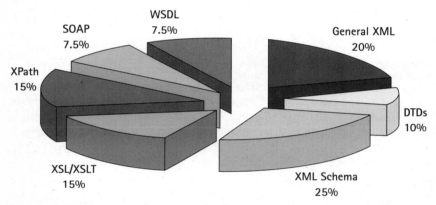

Figure 9–1: Breakdown of topics covered and the relative weight of each subject.

Benefits of certification

Earning the Altova XMLSPY – XML Developer Certification recognizes your expertise in working with XML technologies. In the information technology (IT) industry, your employer, clients, and peers will recognize this certification as a symbol of the skills and knowledge you've gained through experience and dedicated study. The Altova XMLSPY – XML Developer Certification provides the following:

◆ Industry recognition of your knowledge of and proficiency in standards-based XML technologies

◆ A logo and a certificate that identify your certification status to colleagues and clients

◆ Invitations to Altova special events, including various industry tradeshows and Webinars

Furthermore, various software industry salary studies have indicated that IT certification can potentially help you land your next job, move up a level within your organization, or earn a higher salary. Finally, it is always more enjoyable to study with a purpose, and setting a goal of becoming a certified XML developer can be a great way of motivating and challenging yourself. What are you waiting for, anyway?

Availability

The Altova XMLSPY – XML Developer Certification exam is currently offered only in the English language, and only in the U.S. and Canada. The program may be expanded to additional international testing sites at a future date. Prometric delivers Altova XMLSPY – XML Developer Certification examinations at all of the more than 1,500 Prometric testing centers in the U.S. and Canada. The cost of taking the XML Developer Certification exam is $119 (US). If you are unsuccessful in passing the examination the first try, there are no restrictions on how many additional attempts you may have to pass the examination.

How to register

Registration for the Altova XMLSPY – XML Developer Certification examination can be done either by phone, online, or in person at a local authorized Prometric testing center. To register online, please visit `www.2test.com/`. Payment can be made by phone or online using any major credit card. You have one full year from the time of payment until you must schedule an examination with a local testing center. To locate a testing center in your local area, visit `www.2test.com/tcl/ZipCode.jsp`.

Sample Questions

In this section, I cover several sample questions – drawn from all covered subject areas – to give you a general idea of the kind of questions to expect on the exam.

XML basics

This is the easiest section of the examination, covering general XML questions about syntax and concepts including elements, attributes, namespaces, well-formedness, and document validation.

QUESTIONS

Q1. In this XML fragment: `<bar:foo b="a" c="d"/>`, what is the name of the element?

(a) `bar:foo` is the name of the element

(b) `foo` is the name of the element

(c) `bar` is the name of the element

(d) `b` is the name of the element

(e) None of the above

Q2. Consider the following XML document:

```
<?xml version="1.0" encoding="UTF-8"?>
<!DOCTYPE bar SYSTEM "foo.dtd">
<bar>
<a>Some Text</a>
<b c="d" f='e'/>
<h>
<!-- foo bar -->
<g>More text</g>
</h>
</bar>
<!-- foo bar -->
```

Which of the following statements is true?

(a) This file is invalid

(b) This file is not well formed

(c) `bar` is the root element of the document

(d) All of the above

(e) None of the above

Q3. What is the correct syntax for instructing an XML parser not to process any special characters, such as elements, attributes, or entities, in a specified section of an XML document?

(a) `<PCDATA>Text goes here</PCDATA>`

(b) `<CDATA> Text goes here </CDATA>`

(c) `<!PCDATA[Text goes here]]>`

(d) `<![CDATA[Text goes here]]>`

(e) None of the above

Answers

Question 1: The correct answer is (b), *foo is the name of the element*. The section on general XML editing and validation will most certainly contain at least two or three questions on namespaces. Furthermore, knowledge of namespaces is assumed in order for you to understand some of the questions on XML Schema. So if you don't completely understand namespaces, you'll be doubly whacked. Be sure to know your namespace syntax, including how to declare and prefix namespaces. Be sure you understand the rules governing the scoping of namespaces. A suggested exercise is to design an XML Schema that properly imports different schema components. Then practice editing and validating instance documents, first using qualified element default form, and then an unqualified element default form.

Question 2: The correct answer is (c), *bar is the root element of the document*. First, this question' format – providing a small XML document and asking you to identify something inside the XML code – is a very common format for exam questions. Don't be caught off guard by strange element names such as foo and bar. They are meaningless. This question tries to test your understanding of XML document structure; the key to getting this question right is to recall that comments, parsing instructions, CDATA, and a root element are all permitted to appear at the root level of an XML document.

Question 3: The correct answer is (d), `<![CDATA[Text goes here]]>`. As with many IT certification exams, it's important to remember the basic XML syntax for important language constructs. Any content appearing within a CDATA block is treated as plain text, even if it contains special characters such as elements, attributes, or entities.

Document Type Definitions

The exam section on DTDs covers syntax, built-in element and attribute types, document type declarations, and entities. It also tests your ability to apply a simple DTD to visually perform a validation on simple instance documents.

QUESTIONS

Q1. What symbol is used to denote a parameter entity in a Document Type Definition?

(a) the * symbol

(b) the $ symbol

(c) the # symbol

(d) the @ symbol

(e) the % symbol

Q2. Consider the DTD fragment: `<!ELEMENT bar (foo?)>`. Which of the following statements is true?

(a) The `foo` element may occur zero or one time in the `bar` element

(b) The `foo` element may occur zero or more times in the `bar` element

(c) The `foo` element must occur one or more times in the `bar` element

(d) The `foo` element must occur only once in the `bar` element

(e) None of the above

ANSWERS

Question 1: The correct answer is (e), *the % symbol.* A parameter entity can be differentiated from a general entity definition in a DTD by the presence of the % sign. You need to know how to declare and reference both general and parameter entities in DTDs.

Question 2: The correct answer is (a), *The `foo` element may occur zero or one time in the `bar` element.* Know your DTD occurrence operators by heart. This question can take time to read and think through. The best strategy for answering such a question is to immediately associate the question mark operator with an element occurrence that specifies 0 or 1 times. Then simply look for the answer among the choices.

XML Schema

XML Schema is the most heavily weighted topic (25 percent) on the Altova XML-SPY – XML Developer Certification examination. This is because XML Schema development is a necessary first step in architecting any XML development project, regardless of what server, application framework, programming language, or database you choose to build your application. The XML Schema questions cover important XML Schema concepts including differences between complex types and global elements, local and global elements, and important XML Schema language constructs. The XML Schema questions also cover the more advanced topics discussed in Chapter 5, including importing XML Schema components and object-oriented XML Schema design.

QUESTIONS

Q1. Which of the following XML Schema fragments defines an element called `age` where the lowest acceptable value is 0 and the highest acceptable value is 120?

(a)

```
<xsd:element name="age" type="xsd:integer">
    <xsd:minInclusive value="0"/>
    <xsd:maxInclusive value="120"/>
</xsd:element>
```

(b)

```xsd
<xsd:element name="age" type="xsd:integer">
    <xsd:min value="0"/>
    <xsd:max value="120"/>
</xsd:element>
```

(c)

```xsd
<xsd:element name="age" type="xsd:integer">
    <xsd:simpleType>
        <xsd:minInclusive value="0"/>
        <xsd:maxInclusive value="120"/>
    </xsd:simpleType>
</xsd:element>
```

(d)

```xsd
<xsd:element name="age">
    <xsd:simpleType>
        <xsd:restriction base="xsd:integer">
            <xsd:minInclusive value="0"/>
            <xsd:maxInclusive value="120"/>
        </xsd:restriction>
    </xsd:simpleType>
</xsd:element>
```

(e)   All of the above

Q2. Consider the following schema:

```xsd
<xsd:schema xmlns:xsd="http://www.w3.org/2001/XMLSchema">
    <xsd:element name="foo">
        <xsd:complexType>
            <xsd:sequence minOccurs="2" maxOccurs="10">
                <xsd:element name="bar" type="xsd:string"
                        minOccurs="2" maxOccurs="10"/>
            </xsd:sequence>
        </xsd:complexType>
    </xsd:element>
</xs:schema>
```

What can be said of the following instance document (assume that the XML Schema Validating Processor can locate the corresponding XML Schema file):

```xml
<foo>
<bar>moo</bar>
<bar>moo</bar>
</foo>
```

(a) The instance document is valid.

(b) The instance document is invalid.

(c) The instance document is not well formed.

(d) Impossible to tell / None of the above.

Q3. Consider the following XML Schema fragment:

```
<xs:element name="foo">
  <xs:simpleType>
    <xs:restriction base="xs:string">
      <xs:pattern value="\d{4}-[a-z]-[A-Z]{3}"/>
    </xs:restriction>
  </xs:simpleType>
</xs:element>
```

Which of the following describes an acceptable range of values for the foo element?

(a) Four digits, followed by three uppercase or lowercase letters

(b) Four digits, followed by a hyphen, followed by a lowercase letter, followed by a hyphen, followed by three uppercase letters

(c) A slash followed by four instances of the letter *d*, followed by a lowercase letter, followed by three uppercase letters

(d) A slash followed by four digits, followed by a hyphen, followed by a lowercase letter, followed by three lowercase letters from *a* to *z*

(e) None of the above

ANSWERS

Question 1: The correct answer is (d). You can assume that there will be questions asking you to define and derive simple types, as well as to define and derive complex types. These questions will either be in this format or the reverse: the component definition is given, and you must explain what has been defined.

Question 2: The correct answer is (b), *The instance document is invalid.* The element bar must occur a minimum of two times, but it is nested inside of a compositor that specifies a minimum occurrence of two times. Therefore, the net result is a multiplicative effect: bar must occur a minimum of four times in an instance document. The instance document is, therefore, invalid (bar appears only twice). You can be certain that the various compositors (sequence, choice, all) will be covered in the examination.

Question 3: The correct answer is (b) *Four digits, followed by a hyphen, followed by a lowercase letter, followed by a hyphen, followed by three uppercase letters.* This question requires an understanding of regular expressions, which are described in detail in Appendix C. Regular expressions are included in the exam because they are a very frequently used means for constraining the value space of string types.

XSL/XSLT

Questions on XSL/XSLT focus on stylesheet flow control, variables, data types, and templates; the section includes questions on XSL/XSLT syntax, and questions which ask you to determine the output, given a specified input document and stylesheet.

QUESTIONS

Q1. Which element allows you to iterate through a node-set in XSLT?

(a) `xsl:while`

(b) `xsl:loop`

(c) `xsl:for-each`

(d) `xsl:repeat`

(e) `xsl:for`

Q2: How is a variable called `foo` referenced in XSLT?

(a) `#foo`

(b) `$foo`

(c) `{foo}`

(d) `(foo)`

(e) `%foo`

ANSWERS

Question 1: The correct answer is (c) `xsl:for-each`. There are numerous questions regarding syntax of XSL language constructs and so these kinds of questions are pretty much a giveaway. Where it gets tricky is that more advanced questions assume you understand these language constructs. You will be asked to mentally perform an XSLT transformation; and the specified stylesheet will, of course, use many of the basic XSLT language constructs.

Question 2: The correct answer is (b) `$foo`. The $ symbol is used to reference variables in XSLT. Again, it is imperative that you understand how to declare a variable, assign it to a parameter, and use the parameter in invoking (or calling) a specific template by name.

XPath

The XPath section is a section for picking up easy questions quickly. Most of the questions are XPath expressions that you need to evaluate in your head. Other questions are the reverse. They ask you to take an XML document and give the XPath expression to retrieve a specified node-set. The recommended exercise to study for this section is to use the XMLSPY XPath Analyzer to visualize node-sets resulting from XPath expressions. Be sure to know both the shorthand and complete ways of specifying an axis and the most common XPath functions, and data types.

QUESTIONS

Q1. Which XPath pattern selects all children nodes of the current node?

(a) `//*` selects all children of the current node

(b) `//` selects all children of the current node

(c) `..` selects all children of the current node

(c) `$` selects all children of the current node

(e) `*` selects all children of the current node

Q2. Which XPath expression selects all `foo` nodes with a `moo` attribute equal to `bar`?

(a) `//foo[moo='bar']`

(b) `//foo[@moo='bar']`

(c) `//foo/[moo='bar']`

(d) `//foo/moo/[@='bar']`

(e) `//foo/moo/['bar']`

ANSWERS

Question 1: The correct answer is (e), `*` *selects all children of the current node*. This is a simple question – just memorize the various selection operators and you can pick up some easy points.

Question 2: The correct answer is (b), `//foo[@moo='bar']`. Again, all that is required to answer this question is an understanding of how to specify axis and predicates.

WSDL

WSDL questions cover both concepts and syntax, although this section is more weighted in concepts relative to other sections. For example, consider the following two conceptual questions:

QUESTIONS

Q1. In WSDL a notification is defined as:

(a) An operation that sends a message without waiting for a response

(b) An operation that sends a message and waits for a response

(c) An operation that can receive a message without sending a response

(d) None of the above

Q2. Compared to a conventional programming language the WSDL `portType` element is roughly the same as:

(a) A function library or package

(b) A function or method

(c) A variable

(d) A function or method parameter

(e) None of the above

ANSWERS

Question 1: The correct answer is (a), *An operation that sends a message without waiting for a response*. Recall from the discussion on WSDL in Chapter 8 that you can describe various types of method invocations.

Question 2: The correct answer is (a) A *function library or package*. Again, this question tests your understanding of WSDL concepts.

Tips and Strategies

The *XMLSPY Handbook* covers all the topics covered in the Altova XMLSPY – XML Developer Certification examination, so be sure to go over the examples presented in this book. Remember that the examination is only one hour in duration, and that there are exactly 60 questions; therefore, it is advisable not to spend too much time pondering a particular question. I wrote or reviewed all the questions on the examination, and some are a bit tricky or less obvious.

Understanding the material presented in *XMLSPY Handbook* is a great way to study for the XML Developer Certification exam, but it's not the only resource available. I highly recommend checking out some of the additional resources listed in Appendixes A and B. Additionally, an online testing application with sample questions has been developed by the folks at W3Schools.com, a leading (and free) XML resource on the Web. XML standards are always evolving. See the appendixes for some great recommendations on how to stay current in this fast-paced technology area.

One final note: The test is administered by computer (no need to bring pencils or paper to the examination). If you've never taken a computer-administered test before, be sure to listen carefully to the instructions and, if you have any questions, ask the test administrator.

Summary

This chapter provided details about the Altova XMLSPY – XML Developer Certification exam offered through Prometric and offered resources to help you pass it on your first try. This chapter covered these topics:

◆ Overview of the exam format and topics covered

◆ How to register for the exam

◆ Sample questions from all topics with detailed explanations

◆ Tips on passing the examination

This chapter wraps up the discussion of XML development with XMLSPY. I covered basic XML editing and validation, content model development using DTDs and XML Schemas, transforming XML using XSLT, and transmitting information using WSDL and SOAP. The appendixes, which follow, provide some additional information on free XML resources. It is my sincere hope that the material presented in this book gives you the information you need to successfully take and pass the Altova XMLSPY – XML Developer Certification examination.

Appendix A

XMLSPY and Related Technical Resources

IN THIS APPENDIX

- ◆ XMLSPY technical resources
- ◆ External XSL/XSLT processors
- ◆ Complementary tools
- ◆ XML servers and databases

SPIES ARE RESOURCEFUL and work with a number of tools in order to successfully complete a mission. This appendix is a briefing on the vast wealth of XMLSPY technical resources available on the Web, including complementary XML processor and server technologies, as well as third-party integrated XMLSPY plugins, which greatly extend and enhance development capabilities of the XMLSPY editing environment. This appendix also covers information about XMLSPY training academies and how to obtain XMLSPY support.

XMLSPY Technical Resources

Altova has numerous developer resources available to further advance your XML development skills and offer additional information about XMLSPY and related technologies. The following is a listing of the most important XMLSPY technical resources.

Altova Developer Connection

The Altova Developer Connection is a monthly newsletter for the XMLSPY developer community to keep you up-to-date with the latest Altova product updates, new technology integrations, events calendar (tradeshows and Webinars), new tutorials, feature demonstration videos, press releases, and much more. To sign up for the newsletter, fill out the subscription form located at the bottom of Altova's main page at www.altova.com.

Altova Developer Forum

A message board that enables you to post questions about XMLSPY and related topics. Monitored by XMLSPY support and engineering staff. For more information, visit www.altova.com/forum/forums/index.asp.

XMLSPY white papers

Altova publishes roughly one white paper per quarter. These papers focus on different aspects of XML technologies and how they are being applied to solve industry-computing problems. In addition, Altova releases partner white papers, which cover various technology-integration scenarios. Several white papers are available for free download in PDF format at www.altova.com/resources_wp.html.

XMLSPY training

Although hundreds of universities and technology education companies make use of XMLSPY to teach XML technologies, at the time of this writing there are only two companies that offer courses entirely dedicated to covering the use of XMLSPY. Check the Altova Web site for additional training courses because another dozen training companies are expected to offer XMLSPY training courses in 2003. The following list describes the currently available training courses:

WestLake Internet Training: A leading IT education company with offices in Arlington, VA; Frederick, MD; Iselin, New Jersey; New York, NY; Pittsburgh, Pennsylvania; Southfield (Detroit), Michigan; and Washington, DC. On-site training is also available for companies. WestLake offers a two-day course entitled "Introduction to XMLSPY." For more information visit www.westlake.com/courses/285XMLSPY.html.

The Richard Hale Shaw Group: A professional software developer's resource for training and mentoring located near Ann Arbor, Michigan, it offers training in Microsoft .NET, C#, Visual Basic .NET, Visual Studio .NET, .NET Web services, UML, and Java Web services. The company offers a five-day XMLSPY Boot Camp roughly once per quarter, and on-site training is available. For more information visit www.xmlspybootcamp.com.

XMLSPY support

The best place to look if you have a question about XMLSPY is the FAQ site maintained by XMLSPY support engineers at www.altova.com/support_faq_ide.html. To make accessing the FAQ easier, questions and answers have been grouped into categories according to features. Altova's Web page also includes a copy of the online manual, and the entire site is searchable through a search utility located at the top-right side of every page. A fully searchable online help manual is also accessible inside the XMLSPY environment by selecting Help → Table Of Contents. Finally, a Web-based support form can be accessed at www.altova.com/support.

External XSL/XSLT Processors

XMLSPY's built-in XSLT processor is designed for testing and debugging purposes only – it cannot be used outside of the XMLSPY editing environment in a server-production environment. The key difference between the XMLSPY's XSLT processor and an external production XSLT processor, such as Apache Xalan or MSXML 4.0, is that a production XSLT processor is optimized to deliver maximum speed and concurrency. The XMLSPY processor is optimized for error reporting to facilitate XSLT-stylesheet development and debugging. XSLT stylesheets developed in XML-SPY can be run on any commercial-grade XSLT processor; however, you should always verify that XSLT stylesheet transformations work as intended on the targeted processor. This is necessary because, in practice, there are often slight differences between XSL technology implementations. This is the case for any standards-based technology. The following sections provide a partial listing of commonly used XSLT and XSL:FO processors.

MSXML 4.0

Microsoft Core XML Services (MSXML 4.0) was released March 13, 2002 – it was formerly called the Microsoft XML Parser. The new release includes support for XML Schema and offers substantially faster parsing and XSLT transformation. MSXML 4.0 SP 1 is available for Windows 95/98/ME/NT4/2000/XP and can be downloaded for free from the Microsoft Developer Network at http://msdn.microsoft.com/downloads/default.asp?url=/downloads/sample.asp?url=/msdn-files/027/001/766/msdncompositedoc.xml. The MSXML engine is supported directly within XMLSPY – to specify MSXML as the default XSLT processor, choose Tools → Options → XSL and then select the Microsoft XML Parser option.

Apache Xalan

The Apache Group's XML Project includes Apache Xalan, a powerful XSLT stylesheet processor available in Java and C++. Apache Xalan can be used from the command line or programmatically accessed inside of a Java or C++ application. Apache Xalan is available under an open source license and can, therefore, be freely embedded into an application. Source code is available at no cost.

To use Xalan Java as the XSLT processor in XMLSPY, follow these steps:

1. Download the Xalan-Java v2.4 binary distribution from http://xml.apache.org/xalan-j/.

2. All Java applications need a Java Runtime Environment, so the CD-ROM that accompanies this book includes the Java 2 Platform, Standard Edition, v1.4 for Windows. Run the installer and accept the default settings.

3. Decompress the Xalan-Java archive file and set the system path and Java classpath according to the instructions in the ReadMe file.

4. Choose Tools → Options → XSL and then select External XSLT Transformation Program. Next, type the command line for invoking the processor: **java org.apache.xalan.xslt.Process –IN %1 –XSL %3 –OUT %2.**

To use Xalan C++ as the XSLT processor in XMLSPY, follow these steps:

1. Download the Xalan C++ v1.4 binary distribution from `http://xml.apache.org/xalan-c/`.

2. Decompress the Xalan C++ archive file and set the system path according to the instructions in the ReadMe file.

3. To set Xalan C++ as the default XSLT processor in XMLSPY, choose Tools → Options → XSL and then select External XSLT Transformation Program.

4. From this same menu screen, type the command line for invoking the processor: **testXSLT –IN %1 –XSL %3 –OUT %2.**

Apache FOP

Apache FOP 0.20.3 is an open-source XSL:FO transformation engine that supports transformation to numerous output formats including PDF, PCL, PS, SVG, AWT, MIF, and TXT. The primary output target is PDF. Apache FOP is a Java application that requires a Java Runtime Environment 1.2.2 or newer. This can be downloaded from `http://java.sun.com/j2se/downloads.html`.

To perform an XML-to-PDF transformation within XMLSPY, follow these steps:

1. Decompress the binary distribution of Apache FOP, which is included on the CD-ROM that accompanies this book.

2. Choose Tools → Options → XSL and specify the path to the `fop.bat` file, which is located in the root directory of the Apache FOP binary distribution.

3. To invoke an FO transformation, open an `.fo` file from the `XMLSPY examples\tutorial` directory (such as `tiger.fo`) and press the XSL:FO button located on the main toolbar (or press Ctrl+F10). Viewing a PDF file requires Adobe's Acrobat Reader, which is also included on the CD.

For more information about Adobe Acrobat and the PDF file format, visit `www.adobe.com/products/acrobat/`.

RenderX XEP

RenderX XEP is a commercial-grade XSL:FO processor that can be invoked directly from within the XMLSPY editing environment by means of an XMLSPY plugin. RenderX's XEP for XMLSPY can convert XSL:FO documents to a printable form through XMLSPY menus and toolbars. It can also apply XSL:FO stylesheets to XML documents using an integrated XSLT transformer. The PDF output can be immediately viewed in Adobe Acrobat Reader — for more information see `www.renderx.com/~renderx/portal/xmlspy.html`.

Complementary Tools

As mentioned in Chapter 1, XMLSPY is not meant to be a replacement for your existing tool set, but rather is to be used in conjunction with other tools to help complete software development projects. The following is a listing of some of the complementary tools known to be valuable additions to XMLSPY.

XMLSPY plugin for Visual Studio .NET

Visual Studio .NET is Microsoft's newest tool set for rapidly building and integrating Web services into Microsoft Windows applications. To learn more about Microsoft Visual Studio .NET, see: `http://msdn.microsoft.com/vstudio/`. Altova XMLSPY includes a beta version of Visual Studio Integration that allows a user of Microsoft Visual Studio .NET to invoke XMLSPY editing commands from menu bars inside of the Visual Studio .NET editing environment. At the time of this writing, the plugin for Visual Studio simply launches a separate instance of XMLSPY; however, future versions of the XMLSPY plugin for Visual Studio .NET will include closer product integration. They will also allow any XMLSPY editing feature to appear directly inside Visual Studio .NET. Download the XMLSPY plugin for Visual Studio .NET at `www.altova.com/components_microsoft.html`.

Jasc WebDraw

Jasc Software, the producers of Paint Shop Pro, has recently released WebDraw 1.0, a new visual tool creating Scalable Vector Graphics (SVG) and animation. SVG is one of the newest XML standards for representing graphics and animations in an XML format. WebDraw allows you to use freehand tools to visually create graphics, and allows you to toggle back and forth to see the generated SVG code. SVG can be used to include visual elements inside of an XML document, which can then be transformed or further edited from within the XMLSPY environment. A free evaluation copy can be downloaded from `www.jasc.com/products/webdraw/`.

Microsoft Visual SourceSafe

Visual SourceSafe 6.0 is a widely used version control system for software development that is directly supported inside XMLSPY. The basic idea behind a version control system is that it enables development teams to protect and track the development of source code throughout the software lifecycle through a file-locking mechanism. This mechanism requires developers to check in and check out files from the repository, protecting files from accidental overwrite by preventing more than one user from modifying the same file at the same time. For more information on Microsoft Visual SourceSafe visit `http://msdn.microsoft.com/ssafe/`.

Jalindi Igloo

Jalindi Igloo is a software driver that allows XMLSPY to be used in conjunction with other version control systems, including the popular CVS revision control and repository system. For more information on Jalindi Igloo, visit `www.jalindi.com/igloo/`. To use XMLSPY with CVS, first install WinCVS on your computer and configure it properly to access your CVS repository. WinCVS is an open-source graphical user interface for CVS. For more information on WinCVS, visit `www.wincvs.org/`. Next install Jalindi Igloo, which enables the source control commands on the Project menu within XMLSPY and enables you to connect XMLSPY to a CVS repository for integrated check-in and check-out capabilities when you are working with your XML projects.

Apache Ant

Apache Ant is an open-source Java-based build tool that enables you to compile and archive your software application. It is functionally similar to other build tools like Make. Ant differs from other build tools in that it uses an XML-based configuration file, calling out a target tree where various tasks get executed. XMLSPY's built-in Java code generation templates autogenerate an Apache Ant build file. For more information on Apache Ant, visit `http://jakarta.apache.org/ant/`.

Forte For Java (NetBeans)

Forte For Java, also known as Sun ONE Studio 4, is an integrated development environment for Java developers. It is based entirely on the open source NetBeans Tools Platform. Sun Microsystems recently released several new Java programming APIs, including the Java API for XML Parsing, the Java API for XML Binding, the Java API for XML Messaging, and the Java API for XML Registries, all of which are supported within the Forte For Java/NetBeans Java IDE. Furthermore, XMLSPY's built-in Java code generation templates autogenerate a Forte For Java/NetBeans project file. To download the NetBeans IDE, visit `www.netbeans.org/`.

Apache AXIS

Apache AXIS is an open-source implementation of the SOAP protocol, which is a protocol for exchange of information in a decentralized, distributed environment. Apache AXIS includes a SOAP server that can operate standalone or can plug into external Servlet engines such as Tomcat. It also includes various WSDL utilities. One of the WSDL utilities can autogenerate Java classes from WSDL files. This makes it ideal to use in conjunction with XMLSPY's WSDL editor. For more information about Apache AXIS, visit http://xml.apache.org/axis/.

Global XML – XML Integration Workbench

Global XML has bundled XMLSPY 5 with its GoXML Transform product, which is a data transformation workbench and engine that enables mappings to and from XML. It has the capability to generate XML from a variety of data sources. For more information about the product bundling visit www.xmlglobal.com/prod/xmlworkbench/index.jsp.

Reliance Any2XML

Reliance's Any2XML converts any unstructured text data to XML through the use of regular expressions for pattern matching to exact data, allowing you to convert data from different sources to XML. The Any2XML Developer Edition is available as a third-party plugin for XMLSPY. It enables you to import any text document directly into XMLSPY. For more information visit http://goreliance.com/downloads/any2xmlspyplugin.

XML Databases and Repositories

XMLSPY's mission is to provide XML development support and integration with all of the leading XML databases and repositories to bridge the transition from an XML editing environment to any XML document storage and retrieval platform. The following is a listing of some of the XMLSPY integrations that have been completed in XMLSPY.

Oracle9iR2

Oracle XML DB is a new feature of Oracle9i Database Release 2; it provides a high-performance, native XML storage and retrieval technology available with Oracle9iR2. Oracle XML DB provides full support for XML Schema and implements a WebDAV repository interface. This makes Oracle9iR2 ideally suited for use in conjunction with XMLSPY to build document frameworks, which are Web-based XML content applications. An example product catalog application, including source code, can be viewed at www.altova.com/nanocatalog.html.

Oracle has recently published two technical white papers about Oracle XML DB:

Oracle XML DB: A Technical White Paper
http://technet.oracle.com/tech/xml/xmldb/pdf/xmldb_92twp.pdf

Oracle XML DB: Uniting XML Content and Data
http://technet.oracle.com/tech/xml/xmldb/pdf/xmldb_buswp.pdf

Both white papers highlight XMLSPY's authoring support for Oracle XML Schema Extensions from within XMLSPY's Schema Design view. More information on Oracle XML DB can be found at http://technet.oracle.com/tech/xml/xmldb/content.html.

Microsoft SQL Server 2000

Microsoft SQL Server 2000 supports XML technologies by means of the SQL Server 2000 Web Services Toolkit and SQLXML 3.0, which is included on the CD accompanying this book. SQLXML 3.0 includes mapping schemas, which are additional attributes under a separate namespace that are ignored by an XML validator. They contain information on how to persist an XML document into relational database tables residing in the SQL Server database. A sample News Room application (including source code) has been developed using XMLSPY and SQL Server 2000. It can be viewed at www.altova.com/nanonews.html. For more information about SQL Server 2000, visit www.microsoft.com/sql/.

Software AG Tamino XML Server

XMLSPY 5 includes integrated support for Software AG's Tamino XML Server. The XMLSPY editing environment includes the capability to search, open, edit, save, or delete XML documents to and from a Tamino XML Server. Additionally, the XMLSPY Schema Editor supports editing of Tamino Schema Definitions (TSD), conversion of XML Schemas to TSD files, and validation of XML instance documents using Tamino Schemas. Altova has partnered with Software AG to offer a product bundling of XMLSPY 5 and Tamino XML Server (limited edition, for development purposes only) — for more information visit www.softwareag.com/tamino/.

XML Servers

Altova is working with various Web services platform companies to facilitate debugging and deployment of Web service applications from the XMLSPY editing environment to any of the leading industry Web service engines. The following is a listing of some of the server products for which Altova offers bundles or provides technological integration.

BEA WebLogic Workshop

BEA WebLogic Workshop is a Web services development framework with an integrated server runtime environment that enables any application developer to prototype, test, and deploy Web service applications to the BEA WebLogic platform. Altova offers an integrated bundling with the BEA Weblogic Workshop. XMLSPY's SOAP debugger has been verified to work with BEA's SOAP servers. For more information about BEA Weblogic Workshop, visit `http://commerce.bea.com/downloads/weblogic_platform.jsp`.

Iona XMLBus

Iona's Orbix E2A XMLBus Edition is a Web services development and deployment environment for the integration of heterogeneous applications built with .NET, Java, J2EE, J2ME, and CORBA. XMLBus provides development tools, deployment infrastructure, and enterprise-class management for deployed Web services. XMLBus includes a WSDL generation utility that complements the XMLSPY WSDL editor because it is likely that Web service development will be a combination of converting existing applications into Web services and developing new Web services from scratch. The XMLSPY SOAP debugger has been tested to work with Iona's XMLBus. Altova offers a product bundling with IONA's XMLBus. For more information on XMLBus, visit `http://www.iona.com/products/webserv-xmlbus.htm`.

Appendix B

Popular XML Standards and References

IN THIS APPENDIX

- ◆ Core infrastructure standards
- ◆ Industry-specific XML standards
- ◆ Standards consortiums
- ◆ XML publications and Web sites

THIS APPENDIX IS A GUIDE to the countless XML-based standards. It highlights some of the most important or promising technologies while also categorizing the different applications of XML technologies and their relationship with other XML or related standards.

Core Infrastructure Standards

The following XML technologies are said to belong to the core XML infrastructure group because they establish the basis for all other XML-based technologies, including all the industry-specific XML vocabularies, which will be discussed in the next section.

Infrastructure technologies

The following core XML infrastructure technologies provide the technological foundation from which all other related XML technologies are derived:

- ◆ Extensible Markup Language 1.0 (www.w3.org/TR/REC-xml): The core XML specification, originally published in February 1998. A second edition was published in October 2000.

- ◆ Namespaces in XML (www.w3.org/TR/REC-xml-names/): XML namespaces provide a method for qualifying element and attribute names used in XML documents by associating them with namespaces identified by URI references. Published as a W3C recommendation in January 1999.

◆ **Document Object Model (DOM)** (www.w3.org/DOM/): A platform- and language-neutral interface to an XML document meant to provide a standardized interface by which software applications and scripts programmatically access and update the content, structure, and style of an XML document. Available in several parts: DOM Level 1 (W3C recommendation, October 1998), DOM Level 2 (W3 recommendation, November 2000), and DOM Level 3 (W3C Working Draft, April 2002).

◆ **XML Schema** (www.w3.org/XML/Schema): An XML-based vocabulary for describing families or classes of XML documents. The XML-Schema specification is comprised of two parts: XML Schema Part 1, Structures (www.w3.org/TR/xmlschema-1/), which offers facilities for describing the structure and constraining the contents of XML 1.0 documents; and XML Schema Part 2, Data Types (www.w3.org/TR/xmlschema-2/), which describes an XML-based syntax for defining data types to be used in XML Schemas, as well as other XML specifications. Published as a W3C recommendation in May 2001.

Transformation technologies

XSL Transformation (www.w3.org/TR/xslt): XSL consists of both XSLT, a language for transforming XML documents into other XML documents, and XSL:FO, a document layout and formatting language. Published as a W3C version 1.0 recommendation in November 1999.

Document searching & retrieval

XML documents contain a wealth of information that is useful only if it can be efficiently searched and its contents retrieved. The following specifications provide the means to search and retrieve the content stored in your XML documents:

◆ **XML Path Language** (www.w3.org/TR/xpath): Expressions for finding, evaluating, and extracting information from XML documents. Published as a W3C recommendation in November 1999.

◆ **XQuery** (www.w3.org/XML/Query): XML-based query language to extract data from real and virtual documents on the Web, facilitating interaction between the Web world and relational databases. Working draft in progress.

◆ **Resource Description Framework** (www.w3.org/RDF/): RDF integrates a variety of applications from library catalogs and world-wide directories to syndication and aggregation of news, software, and content to personal collections of music, photos, and events using XML as an interchange syntax, with the overall goal of providing a system for better describing and exchanging knowledge on the Web. Published as a W3C recommendation in February 1999.

Web services

Web services refers to the use of XML-based protocols to access programs (services) on the Internet. The following technologies are used to describe, locate, and invoke services in a standardized way:

- **Simple Object Access Protocol (www.w3.org/TR/SOAP/):** SOAP is a lightweight protocol for exchange of information in a decentralized, distributed environment. It is an XML-based protocol that consists of three parts: an envelope that defines a framework for describing what is in a message and how to process it; a set of encoding rules for expressing instances of application-defined data types; and a convention for representing remote procedure calls and responses. Published as a W3C note in May 2000.

- **XML Protocol (www.w3.org/2000/xp/Group):** XML Protocol is part of the Web Services group whose mission is to develop a set of technologies in order to bring Web services to their full potential. It focuses on topics such as Web services architecture. The Web Services group has numerous publications published as notes or drafts.

- **Web Service Description Language (www.w3.org/2002/ws/desc/):** An XML vocabulary for describing the interface that clients, servers, and other agents can use to interoperate. It includes a definition for the types and structures of the data being exchanged, descriptions of the sequence of operations supported by a Web service, and a mechanism for binding a protocol used by a Web service, independent of its message exchange patterns and its messages. Published as a Note by the W3C in March 2001.

- **Universal Description Discovery and Integration (www.uddi.org/):** UDDI is an XML vocabulary for describing services, discovering businesses, and integrating business services using the Internet, as well as an operational registry (or directory). The UDDI protocol is a building block that will enable businesses to quickly, easily, and dynamically find and transact with one another using their preferred applications.

Transport protocols

XML technologies were not developed in a vacuum, rather they were built on top on existing, widely supported transport and application protocols. The following is a listing of important transport protocol specifications that often come up when working on XML-application development:

- **Hypertext Transfer Protocol (www.w3.org/Protocols/):** HTTP is an application-level protocol for distributed, collaborative information systems. It is a generic, stateless protocol that can be used for many tasks beyond its use for hypertext. These include name servers and distributed object management systems through extension of its request methods, error codes, and headers. A feature of HTTP is the typing and negotiation of data representation, allowing systems to be built independently of the data being transferred.

◆ **File Transfer Protocol (`www.ietf.org/`):** FTP defines a set of commands that enable file sharing over the Internet. The FTP protocol is a primary Internet protocol that allows different machines, using different operating systems and different hardware to exchange files efficiently in a safe manner.

◆ **Web-based Distributed Authoring and Versioning (`www.webdav.org/`):** WebDAV is a set of extensions to the HTTP protocol that enables users to collaboratively edit and manage files on remote Web servers.

Industry-Specific Standards

Industry consortiums are bringing together technology and professional services companies to drive the adoption of common XML-based vocabularies to streamline information interchange among firms belonging to a particular industry. These industry-specific standards are built upon the core XML technologies listed in the previous section. XMLSPY is an extensible editor in that it automatically supports editing and validation of any of the following industry-standard XML formats because they all have a content model defined using either an XML Schema or a DTD.

Document presentation

Numerous XML technologies are dedicated to providing ways of visually displaying documents in different formats. The following standards can be grouped into the category of document presentation:

◆ **Extensible Hypertext Markup Language (`www.w3.org/TR/xhtml1`):** XHTML is a reformulation of HTML 4 as an XML 1.0–compliant vocabulary. Published as a W3C recommendation in January 2000.

◆ **Wireless Markup Language (`www.wapforum.org/`):** WML is an XML vocabulary for fast delivery of information and services to mobile users. These include handheld digital wireless devices such as mobile phones, pagers, two-way radios, smartphones, and communicators built on any operating system including PalmOS, EPOC, Windows CE, FLEXOS, OS/9, JavaOS, and so on.

◆ **Scalable Vector Graphics (`www.w3.org/TR/SVG/`):** SVG is an XML vocabulary for describing two-dimensional vector and mixed vector/raster graphics in XML. It allows for three types of graphic objects: vector graphic shapes (for example, straight and curved lines), images, and text. Graphical objects can be grouped, styled, transformed, and easily embedded into an XML document.

- Virtual Reality Modeling Language (`www.vrml.org/`): VRML is a file format for describing interactive 3D objects and worlds. VRML is designed for use on the Internet, intranets, and local client systems. VRML is also intended to be a universal interchange format for integrated 3D graphics and multimedia. VRML may be used in a variety of application areas such as engineering and scientific visualization, multimedia presentations, entertainment and educational titles, Web pages, and shared virtual worlds.

- Voice Extensible Markup Language (`www.w3.org/TR/voicexml/`): VoiceXML is designed for creating audio dialogs that feature synthesized speech, digitized audio, recognition of spoken and key input, recording of spoken input, telephony, and mixed-initiative conversations. Its major goal is to bring the advantages of Web-based development and content delivery to interactive voice response applications. It was published as a W3C Note in May 2000.

- Cascading Style Sheets (`www.w3.org/Style/CSS/`): This is a simple mechanism for adding style (for example, fonts, colors, spacing) to Web documents.

Sciences

Although scientific concepts are known to be universal, we lack a truly universal and efficient means to electronically express complicated formulas. The following standards help address this need:

- Chemical Markup Language (`www.xml-cml.org/`): XML vocabulary for representing molecular information, covering macromolecular sequences to inorganic molecules and quantum chemistry.

- Mathematical Markup Language (`www.w3.org/TR/REC-MathML/`): XML vocabulary for describing mathematical notations that enables mathematical expressions to be easily sent, received, and processed on the Web. This was a W3C recommendation, finalized July 1999.

Publishing

The publishing industry is responsible for creating volumes of useful content on a daily basis. The purpose of the following standards is to enable loosely structured documents to be expressed as XML documents:

- News Markup Language (`www.newsml.org/`): NewsML is the standard XML grammar for describing news articles for use in print or Web publishing.

- DocBook (`www.oasis-open.org/committees/docbook/`): DocBook is a popular XML content model for describing books, articles, and other prose documents such as technical documentation.

Finance

The financial industry has greatly benefited from advances in Internet technologies and is eagerly pursuing the development of standards-based XML formats for describing business processes. The following is a listing of some of the financial industry's most adopted standards:

- **Extensible Business Reporting Language** (www.xbrl.org): An XML grammar for describing financial statements of both public and private companies, used by the accounting profession, regulators, analysts, the investment community, capital markets, and lenders. It provides accurate and reliable information.

- **Research Information Exchange Markup Language** (www.rixml.org): XML standard to categorize and describe the contents of financial research reports, used to facilitate sharing of information between a financial institution and its clients.

- **Financial Products Markup Language** (www.fpml.org): FpML is the industry-standard protocol for complex financial products, describing interest rate swaps, Forward Rate Agreements, interest rates, derivatives, swaps, foreign exchange, and other financial products. It is used to automate the flow of information across financial institutions.

- **Market Data Definition Language** (www.mddl.org): Market Data Definition Language (MDDL) is an XML-based interchange format and common data dictionary on the fields needed to describe financial instruments, corporate events affecting value and tradability, and market-related, economic and industrial indicators. It enables the exchange of market data between dealers and brokers.

Life sciences

XML technologies are being employed to solve today's medical challenges. Here are some of the relevant medical standards:

- **Gene Expression Markup Language** (www.geml.org/): XML vocabulary for biological gene expression data, using bioinformatics professionals to catalog and search genetic data.

- **Health Level 7** (www.hl7.org/): HL7 is an XML vocabulary for the healthcare industry, including pharmacy, medical devices, imaging, insurance (claims processing), and both clinical and administrative data. Its purpose is to improve patient care and ensure interoperability between healthcare information systems.

Human resources

Human Resources Markup Language (www.hr-xml.org): HR-XML is an XML vocabulary for describing human-resource processes and documents, including stock options, resumes, job descriptions, benefits enrollment, background checks, time expenses, and more. It is designed to reduce paperwork and provide a standard means for companies to transmit information.

Standards Consortiums

Who is in charge of creating the above standards? Anyone can participate – typically technology or service companies pay an annual membership, which enables them to sponsor employees to serve as experts on technical committees. Furthermore, the discussions of technical committees are usually publicly archived mailing lists. The following is a listing of the most prominent standards organizations doing work related to XML technologies:

- ◆ **World Wide Web Consortium** (www.w3.org): Develops core Internet technologies to lead the Web to its full potential by means of specifications, guidelines, and reference implementations.

- ◆ **Web Service Interoperability Consortium** (www.ws-i.org): An open industry organization chartered to promote Web services interoperability across platforms, operating systems, and programming languages.

- ◆ **Internet Engineering Task Force** (www.ietf.org): The IETF is an international community of network designers, operators, vendors, and researchers working to ensure stable and robust operation of future Internet architectures.

- ◆ **Organization for the Advancement of Structured Information Standards** (www.oasis-open.org/): OASIS is a global consortium that drives the development, convergence, and adoption of e-business standards. Producing world-wide standards for security, Web services, XML conformance, business transactions, electronic publishing, and much more.

- ◆ **International Standards Organization** (www.iso.org/): The ISO is the world's largest network of national standards institutes consisting of international organizations, governments, industry, business, and consumer representatives. It works to promote the development of standardization and related activities in the world with a view to facilitating the international exchange of goods and services. It also aims to develop cooperation in the spheres of intellectual, scientific, technological, and economic activity.

XML Publications and Web Sites

The preceding listing is only a partial listing of popular XML standards and related technologies – new standards are constantly under development because XML is one of the fastest evolving technology areas. The following resources are provided to help you keep up-to-date on XML and related technologies.

XML discussion forums

The following forums offer XML-related discussions:

- Apache-FOP-User (http://xml.apache.org/fop/resources.html#)
- RDF-Interest (www.w3.org/RDF/Interest/)
- WSDL-DevelopMentor (http://discuss.develop.com/wsdl.html)
- XML-Dev (http://lists.xml.org/archives/xml-dev/)
- XML-L (http://listserv.heanet.ie/xml-l.html)
- XSL-List (www.mulberrytech.com/xsl/xsl-list/)
- XHTML-L (http://groups.yahoo.com/group/xhtml-l/)
- XML-Schema-DEV (http://lists.w3.org/Archives/Public/xmlschema-dev/)

XML-related newsgroups

Newsgroups are a great resource for XML discussions and questions. Be sure to search the newsgroup archives because it is possible that the answer you seek has already been posted. The following is a list of some recommended XML-related newsgroups:

- comp.text.xml
- microsoft.public.msdn.webservices
- microsoft.public.sqlserver.xml
- microsoft.public.xml
- microsoft.public.xml.soap
- microsoft.public.xsl
- comp.lang.java.programmer
- netscape.public.mozilla.xml
- comp.databases.oracle

XML-related software development magazines

The following is a list of recommended developer publications that are known to regularly publish XML-related technical articles:

- *ASP.NET Pro Magazine,* Informant Communications Group (www.aspnetpro.com/)

- *C/C++ Users Journal,* CMP Media (www.cuj.com/)

- *Dr. Dobbs Journal,* CMP Media (www.ddj.com/)

- *EContent Magazine,* Online Inc. (www.econtentmag.com/)

- *Java Developer Journal,* Sys-Con Media (www.sys-con.com/java/)

- *Java Pro,* Fawcette Technical Publications (www.fawcette.com/javapro/)

- *Microsoft Certified Professional,* 101 Communications (www.mcpmag.com/)

- *MSDN Magazine,* CMP Media (http://msdn.microsoft.com/msdnmag/)

- *.NET Developer Journal,* CMP Media (www.sys-con.com/dotnet)

- *.NET Magazine,* Fawcette Technical Publications (www.fawcette.com/dotnetmag/)

- *New Architect Magazine,* CMP Media (www.newarchitectmag.com/)

- *Oracle Magazine,* Oracle Publishing (www.oracle.com/oramag/)

- *SQL Server Magazine,* Penton Media (www.sqlmag.com/)

- *Visual Studio Magazine,* Fawcette Technical Publications (www.fawcette.com/vsm/)

- *Web Services Journal,* Sys-Con Media (www.sys-con.com/webservices/)

- *Windows Developer Magazine,* CMP Media (www.windevnet.com/wdm/)

- *XML-Journal,* Sys-Con Media (www.sys-con.com/xml/)

- *XML & Web Services Magazine,* Fawcette Technical Publications (www.fawcette.com/xmlmag/)

Note that many of the previously listed software-development publications offer free monthly subscriptions (print or electronic format) provided that you are working for a sufficiently large software development group. See the publisher's Web site for more detailed information on obtaining subscriptions.

XML-related Web Sites

The following is a list of recommended XML-related Web sites that are useful for staying current on the newest developments in XML products and technologies, as well as for learning XML industry news:

- **Apache XML Project** (`http://xml.apache.org`): Numerous open source XML development resources.

- **DevX XML Zone** (`www.devx.com/xml/`): Select XML news and developer articles.

- **Google News** (`http://news.google.com/news`): Most comprehensive XML News Archive, just type **XML**.

- **IBM DeveloperWorks XML Zone** (`www.ibm.com/developerworks/xml/`): IBM frequently updated articles on XML technologies.

- **Microsoft XML** (`http://msdn.microsoft.com/xml/`): The Microsoft XML main page.

- **O'Reilly XML.COM** (`www.xml.com/`): Articles about XML technologies with focus on lesser-known XML technologies and more academic uses of XML.

- **Robin Cover Pages** (`www.oasis-open.org/cover/`): Select XML news.

- **Sun Microsystems Java and XML homepage** (`http://java.sun.com/products/xml`): Describes Java-based XML APIs.

- **W3Schools** (`www.w3schools.com`): XML and related tutorials.

- **XMLHack** (`www.xmlhack.com`): News for the XML developer community.

- **XMethods** (`www.xmethods.com`): Listing of publicly available Web services, ideal for using with XMLSPY's SOAP tester and debugger.

- **XML FAQ** (`www.ucc.ie/xml/`): Frequently asked questions about XML.

- **XML.org** (`www.xml.org`): Industry news portal.

Appendix C

Regular Expression Primer

IN THIS APPENDIX

- ◆ Regular expression syntax and tutorial
- ◆ The XMLSPY Regular Expression Builder
- ◆ Regular expression examples

THE XML SCHEMA SPECIFICATION includes a pattern-matching mechanism for placing additional restrictions on the permissible value space of XML Schema elements of type xsd:string. Regular expressions are a concise and flexible way to enforce virtually any string pattern, and their use within an XML Schema can save considerable time in writing custom validation modules. This appendix contains a tutorial explaining regular expression syntax, as well as how to use the XMLSPY Regular Expression Builder. Finally, a cheat sheet is included, containing regular expression syntax examples for various commonly encountered data patterns.

Regular Expression Syntax

XML Schema regular expressions are used with the XML Schema pattern facet to place constraints or restrictions on a string of characters that conform to the defined pattern. If you recall from the discussion of XML Schemas in Chapter 5 the pattern facet is a constraint on the value space of a data type, achieved by constraining the lexical space to literals that match a specific pattern. Patterns are expressed by means of a regular expression, which is the subject of this appendix.

Regular expressions are not a programming language; rather, they constitute a concise syntax for describing character patterns, which have been widely implemented by numerous languages and tools, including any validating XML Schema processor. The syntax for the pattern-matching scheme is, for the most part, borrowed from the Perl scripting language, and a regular expression is essentially Perl regular expressions (or simply *regex* for short) with a few minor omissions and modifications. Perl stands for Practical Extraction and Report Language, and it is a great language for doing just that!

The following discussion pertains to the use of regular expressions in conjunction with validating instance documents against XML Schemas. However, many other freely available tools and APIs support the use of regular expressions,

including Python, and the Unix programs grep (Global Regular Expression Print),
sed (Stream EDitor), and egrep (Extended GREP).

Matching individual characters

If I use the value xmlspy as a regular expression to restrict a string element, I am
indicating to the XML Schema validator that the element or attribute in question
must exactly match the specified pattern of the characters x, m, l, s, p, y, consecu-
tively and in the specified case. Therefore, the smallest unit of a pattern is a single
character, and a regular expression consists of a pattern of characters. Of course, in
this example, I pre-specified exactly what the pattern value had to be equal to. A
more complex regular expression is constructed using metacharacters, which are
placeholders for a specified range of character values. Table C-1 shows a listing of
metacharacters.

TABLE C-1 METACHARACTERS FOR MATCHING INDIVIDUAL CHARACTER VALUES

Syntax Form	Description	Example	Possible Example Values
.	Any single character (except the newline or return character)	xmlspy.	xmlspyA, xmlspy4, xmlspy!
[...]	Matches any character inside the square brackets; uses a dash to indicate a range, multiple ranges are permitted.	xmlspy[1-5]	
	xmlspy1, xmlspy2 ... xmlspy5		
[^...]	Matches any character except those listed within the brackets	xmlspy[^6-9]	xmlspy1, xmlspy2 ... xmlspy5

Metacharacters are used as wildcards to specify permissible permutations inside
a pattern. The period (.) character has special meaning, representing a wildcard for
any single character. To explicitly specify that an actual period character should
appear, you need to use an escape character, which is discussed later in this
appendix. Inside a set of square brackets, you can list all the allowable characters.
For example, [12345] indicates that 1, 2, 3, 4, *or* 5 are acceptable values. You
can express this more concisely using the hyphen (-) character to specify a range of
ordinal values, as in [1-5]. The hyphen only has a special meaning if there is
exactly one alphanumerical character to the left and right of it. You can indicate
multiple ranges by separating the characters with commas. For example, [0-9,A-
Z,a-z] satisfies any alphanumerical character. Finally, you can use the caret

character (^) to denote exception and to specify the set of invalid characters. Some additional examples are provided in Table C-2.

TABLE **C-2 EXAMPLES OF CHARACTER RANGES**

Example	Possible Values	Illegal Values	Notes
0-9,A-Z,a-z	3, t, Q	#, %, $	Any number or letter
[-cde]	-, c, d, e	a, b, c	The dash has no special meaning
[cde-]	c, d, e, -	a, b, c	The dash has no special meaning

Quantifiers

The metacharacters specified in the previous section act as placeholders for a single character only; it is not allowed to pick, say, two of the values specified in the range. Metacharacters are often used in conjunction with quantifiers, which allow you to explicitly specify the number of times a particular character or metacharacter should appear. Quantifiers are listed in Table C-3.

TABLE **C-3 QUANTIFIERS FOR SPECIFYING CHARACTER OCCURRENCES**

Syntax Form	Description	Example	Possible Example Values
?	The preceding character may appear zero or one times	abc.	abc, ab
*	The preceding character may appear zero or more times	abc*	ab, abc, abccccc
+	The preceding character may appear one or more times	abc+	abc, abccccc
{x}	Matches the preceding element x times, where x is a positive integer value	abc{3}	abccc
{x, y}	Matches the preceding element at least x times, but not more than y times	abc{3,5}	abccc, abcccc, abccccc

Escape characters

So far we've been using various special characters such as asterisks, periods, dashes, braces, and so on, to specify regular expression patterns. The question naturally arises: How do you search for an actual occurrence for one of the special characters? The answer is to use an escape character, which is a backslash (\) prepended in front of special character, which removes the special meaning of the character (meaning that it is treated as a normal character instead of part of a metacharacter expression). Escape characters have the unfortunate side effect of making your regular expression rather unreadable, but they are an important aspect of properly using regular expressions. Table C-4 lists the most commonly escaped characters.

TABLE C-4 ESCAPING SPECIAL CHARACTERS

Expression	Description
\s	Any whitespace (tab, space, etc)
\n	Newline character
\r	Return character
\t	Tab character
\\	Backslash character
|	Vertical bar
\.	Period character
\-	Dash character
\^	Caret character
\?	Question mark character
*	Asterisk character
\+	Addition sign character
\{	Opening brace character
\}	Closing brace character
\[	Opening bracket character
\]	Closing bracket character
\(	Opening parenthesis character
\)	Closing parenthesis character

Alternation

Alternation is equivalent to the logical OR operation, and can be used to specify an enumeration of patterns, one of which must be satisfied. Alternation uses the vertical bar symbol (|) to indicate the logical OR operator. As an example, suppose you wanted to perform a match that allowed for both U.S. and British spellings of the word `center` or `centre`. The following regular expression could effectively allow for both spellings: `cent(re|er)`. Parentheses are used to delimit groupings, which correspond to available listing of choices separated by the OR character.

Differences compared to Perl regular expressions

If you have already used and are familiar with Perl regular expressions, be advised that although the syntax for pattern matching in XML Schema is very similar to Perl regular expressions, there are a few noteworthy exceptions. The first major difference is that XML Schema patterns are meant to match on an entire string, and not on substrings. In contrast, Perl can be used to search through multiple documents simply to try to find matching patterns. Anchor characters, like the ^ and $ are no longer used at the beginning and end of an expression to indicate the beginning or end of string (although the ^ symbol is still used in XML Schema patterns as the exception character). Another important difference is that the *zero-width* assertions, lookahead and lookbehind, and the use of backreferences are all not permitted.

The XMLSPY Regular Expression Builder

XMLSPY supports a Regular Expression Builder in XML Schema Design view. To access this functionality, select an XML Schema element of type `string` in the graphical design page. Then, go to the Facets Window and choose the Patterns tab. Click the Insert New Pattern button, which is located in the top-left corner of the Facets window. Click the down arrow on the new row that you created. A drop-down list of common regular expressions appears, as shown in Figure C-1.

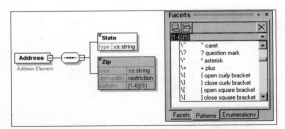

Figure C-1: The XMLSPY Regular Expression Builder.

In XML Schema, a string element can contain multiple patterns, and a data element is considered to be valid if it satisfies any one of the specified regular expression patterns. To add an additional pattern constraint, click the Insert button.

Character Class Escape Sequences

Some escape sequences, called *character class escape sequences,* can be used to specify multiple characters at one location. Table C-5 lists some character class escape sequences that you can use as shortcuts for commonly matched character groupings when you're building custom regular expressions.

TABLE C-5 SHORTHAND NOTATIONS FOR COMMON CHARACTER GROUPS

Expression	Description
\d	Any digit
\D	Any non-digit
\p{L}	Any letter
\p{Lu}	Any lowercase letter
\p{Ll}	Any uppercase letter
\p{N}	Any number
\p{P}	Any punctuation
\p{Z}	Any separator character

Appendix D

What's on the CD-ROM

IN THIS APPENDIX

◆ System requirements

◆ Using the CD with Microsoft Windows

◆ The contents of the CD

◆ Troubleshooting

System Requirements

Make sure that your computer meets the minimum system requirements listed in this section. If your computer doesn't match up to most of these requirements, you may have a problem using the contents of the CD.

◆ Microsoft Windows 9x, 2000, NT4 (with SP4 or later), Me, or XP

◆ Pentium processor running at 120 MHz or faster

◆ At least 32MB of total RAM installed on your computer; for best performance, we recommend at least 64MB or more

◆ A CD-ROM drive

◆ An Internet connection to obtain a software key code and an e-mail address that the key can be mailed to (an Internet connection is not required after you obtain the key code)

Using the CD with Windows

To install the items from the CD to your hard drive, follow these steps:

1. Insert the CD into your computer's CD-ROM drive.

2. A window appears with the following options: Install, Explore, and Exit.

   Install: Gives you the option to install the supplied software and/or the author-created samples on the CD-ROM.

Explore: Enables you to view the contents of the CD-ROM in its directory structure.

Exit: Closes the autorun window.

If you do not have autorun enabled, or if the autorun window does not appear, follow these steps to access the CD:

1. Choose Start → Run.

2. In the dialog box that appears, type **d:\setup.exe**, where *d* is the letter of your CD-ROM drive. This brings up the autorun window described in the preceding set of steps.

3. Choose the Install, Explore, or Exit option from the menu. (See Step 2 in the preceding list for a description of these options.)

4. To install XMLSPY 5, please follow the detailed instructions located in Chapter 1 of the book.

The Contents of the CD

The following sections provide a summary of the software and other materials you'll find on the CD.

Author-created materials

All source code examples used throughout this book will automatically install themselves when you run the XMLSPY 5 installer. You can access them via the default project when you first start XMLSPY 5. Chapter 2 explains how to use the XMLSPY Project view in detail. As an additional convenience, all author-created material from the book, including code listings and samples, are also located on the CD in the folder named Author.

Applications

The following sections describe the applications available on the CD-ROM.

ACROBAT READER

From Adobe Systems, Inc. Freeware product for Microsoft Windows. Adobe Acrobat Reader is an application for reading Portable Document Format (PDF). PDF has become a standard electronic format for representing any document. PDF helps ensure that a document prints out in the same way that it is displayed on the screen. For more information, check out www.adobe.com/acrofamily/.

JAVA 2 PLATFORM, STANDARD EDITION, V1.4 FOR WINDOWS

From Sun Microsystems, Inc. Commercial product for Microsoft Windows. The Java 2 Platform, Standard Edition is both a set of Application Program Interfaces (APIs) for writing Java Programs and a Java Runtime Environment (a virtual operating system) that enables you to execute Java applications on the Windows Operating System. For more information, check out http://java.sun.com/j2se/.

APACHE AXIS

From Apache Software Foundation. Open-source software utility written in Java and supported on all platforms. AXIS is a Java framework for constructing SOAP processors including clients, servers, gateways, and so on. AXIS, formerly IBM's SOAP4J, includes a SOAP server that can operate as a standalone or in conjunction with a Java Servlet Engine, such as Apache Tomcat. It also has utilities for working with Web Service Description Language (WSDL) files, including a tool that generates Java classes from WSDL. For more information, check out http://xml.apache.org/axis/.

APACHE FOP

From Apache Software Foundation. Open-source software utility written in Java and supported on all platforms. FOP stands for Formatting Objects Processor. It is a Java-based print formatter for XSL formatting objects that can be used to render an XML file containing XSL formatting objects (XSL:FO) into a page layout. Apache FOP is most commonly used for XML-to-PDF transformations and can be invoked from within the XMLSPY editing environment. For more information, check out http://xml.apache.org/fop/.

SQLXML 3.0 SP1

From Microsoft Corporation. Commercial product for Microsoft Windows. SQLXML enables XML support for your SQL Server 2000 Database. It allows developers to create XML views of relational data so that you can work with the data as if it were an XML file. For more information, check out http://msdn.microsoft.com/library/default.asp?url=/nhp/Default.asp?contentid=28001300.

XMLSPY 5 ENTERPRISE EDITION

From Altova, Inc. Exclusive 90-day trial version for Microsoft Windows. XMLSPY is an XML development environment with graphical utilities for editing, validating, and debugging any XML document, including XML Schema, XSL/XSLT, DTDs, WSDL, and many others. For more information, check out www.altova.com.

Shareware programs are fully functional, trial versions of copyrighted pro-grams. If you like particular programs, register with their authors for a nomi-nal fee and receive licenses, enhanced versions, and technical support. *Freeware programs* are copyrighted games, applications, and utilities that are free for personal use. Unlike shareware, these programs do not require a fee or provide technical support. *GNU software* is governed by its own license, which is included inside the folder of the GNU product. See the GNU license for more details.

Trial, demo, or evaluation versions are usually limited either by time or func-tionality (such as being unable to save projects). Some trial versions are very sensitive to system date changes. If you alter your computer's date, programs may "time out" and no longer be functional.

Troubleshooting

If you have difficulty installing or using any of the materials on the companion CD, try the following solutions:

◆ **Turn off any anti-virus software that you may have running.** Installers sometimes mimic virus activity and can make your computer incorrectly believe that it is being infected by a virus. (Be sure to turn the anti-virus software back on later.)

◆ **Close all running programs.** The more programs you're running, the less memory is available to other programs. Installers also typically update files and programs; if you keep other programs running, installation may not work properly.

◆ **Reference the ReadMe:** Please refer to the ReadMe file located at the root of the CD-ROM for the latest product information at the time of publication.

If you still have trouble with the CD, please call the Customer Care phone num-ber: (800) 762-2974. Outside the United States, call 1 (317) 572-3994. You can also contact Customer Service by e-mail at techsupdum@wiley.com. Wiley Publishing, Inc. will provide technical support only for installation and other general quality control items; for technical support on the applications themselves, consult the pro-gram's vendor or author.

Index

A

abbreviated syntax, axis specifiers and, 192-193

abstract types, XML Schema groups, 158-160

Access, 41

Acrobat Reader, CD-ROM bundle and, 316

all compositors, XML Schemas, 143-144

all groups, XML Schemas, 149-151

alternation, regular expressions, 313

Altova Developer Connection newsletter, 289

Altova Developer Forum message board, 290

Altova XML developer certification

    availability, 279

    benefits, 278

    coverage, 278

    registration, 279

    sample questions, 279-287

    tips and strategies, 287

    usefulness of, 277

anonymous types (XML Schemas), defining, 121-122

Any2XML (Reliance), 295

Apache Ant, 294

Apache AXIS, 295

    CD-ROM bundle and, 317

Apache FOP, 292

    CD-ROM bundle, 317

Apache Xalan, 291-292

applications

    CD-ROM bundle, 316-317

    database integration, 6

attributes, 20

    DTDs and, 66

        declaration simplified, 69-70

        defaults, 68-69

        types, 67-68

    Grid view

        editing, 31-33

        inserting, 31-33

        moving, 33-34

        renaming, 34

        switching with elements, 34

    quotation marks and, 22

    Schema elements, displaying, 91

    XML Schemas, 115-117

    xsl, variable instruction, 214

    XSLT

        counting tokens in, 238

        parsing keys in, 236-237

Attributes window, 78

Authentic, 242

AXIS (Apache), 295

    CD-ROM bundle, 317

axis specifiers, XPath expressions, 187-192

    abbreviated syntax and, 192-193

B

BEA WebLogic Workshop, 297

bindings

    SOAP, 259

    WSDL, 264-268

        HTTP binding, 268-269

        SOAP binding, 268

boolean data type, 229

boolean element available function, 235

boolean function available function, 235

Boolean functions, 232

building Schemas, 98-106

business objects, Schema Designer and, 93

C

calling XSLT templates, 220

CD-ROM, 315

    contents, 316-317

    system requirements, 315

    troubleshooting, 318

    Windows and, 315

CDATA (character data), 25-67

319

continued

continued

Sun Microsystems, Inc.
Binary Code License Agreement

READ THE TERMS OF THIS AGREEMENT AND ANY PROVIDED SUPPLEMENTAL LICENSE TERMS (COLLECTIVELY "AGREEMENT") CAREFULLY BEFORE OPENING THE SOFTWARE MEDIA PACKAGE. BY OPENING THE SOFTWARE MEDIA PACKAGE, YOU AGREE TO THE TERMS OF THIS AGREEMENT. IF YOU ARE ACCESSING THE SOFTWARE ELECTRONICALLY, INDICATE YOUR ACCEPTANCE OF THESE TERMS BY SELECTING THE "ACCEPT" BUTTON AT THE END OF THIS AGREEMENT. IF YOU DO NOT AGREE TO ALL THESE TERMS, PROMPTLY RETURN THE UNUSED SOFTWARE TO YOUR PLACE OF PURCHASE FOR A REFUND OR, IF THE SOFTWARE IS ACCESSED ELECTRONICALLY, SELECT THE "DECLINE" BUTTON AT THE END OF THIS AGREEMENT.

1. **LICENSE TO USE.** Sun grants you a non-exclusive and non-transferable license for the internal use only of the accompanying software and documentation and any error corrections provided by Sun (collectively "Software"), by the number of users and the class of computer hardware for which the corresponding fee has been paid.

2. **RESTRICTIONS.** Software is confidential and copyrighted. Title to Software and all associated intellectual property rights is retained by Sun and/or its licensors. Except as specifically authorized in any Supplemental License Terms, you may not make copies of Software, other than a single copy of Software for archival purposes. Unless enforcement is prohibited by applicable law, you may not modify, decompile, or reverse engineer Software. Licensee acknowledges that Licensed Software is not designed or intended for use in the design, construction, operation or maintenance of any nuclear facility. Sun Microsystems, Inc. disclaims any express or implied warranty of fitness for such uses. No right, title or interest in or to any trademark, service mark, logo or trade name of Sun or its licensors is granted under this Agreement.

3. **LIMITED WARRANTY.** Sun warrants to you that for a period of ninety (90) days from the date of purchase, as evidenced by a copy of the receipt, the media on which Software is furnished (if any) will be free of defects in materials and workmanship under normal use. Except for the foregoing, Software is provided "AS IS". Your exclusive remedy and Sun's entire liability under this limited warranty will be at Sun's option to replace Software media or refund the fee paid for Software.

4. **DISCLAIMER OF WARRANTY.** UNLESS SPECIFIED IN THIS AGREEMENT, ALL EXPRESS OR IMPLIED CONDITIONS, REPRESENTATIONS AND WARRANTIES, INCLUDING ANY IMPLIED WARRANTY OF MERCHANTABILITY, FITNESS FOR A PARTICULAR PURPOSE OR

NON-INFRINGEMENT ARE DISCLAIMED, EXCEPT TO THE EXTENT THAT THESE DISCLAIMERS ARE HELD TO BE LEGALLY INVALID.

5. **LIMITATION OF LIABILITY.** TO THE EXTENT NOT PROHIBITED BY LAW, IN NO EVENT WILL SUN OR ITS LICENSORS BE LIABLE FOR ANY LOST REVENUE, PROFIT OR DATA, OR FOR SPECIAL, INDIRECT, CONSEQUEN-TIAL, INCIDENTAL OR PUNITIVE DAMAGES, HOWEVER CAUSED REGARDLESS OF THE THEORY OF LIABILITY, ARISING OUT OF OR RELATED TO THE USE OF OR INABILITY TO USE SOFTWARE, EVEN IF SUN HAS BEEN ADVISED OF THE POSSIBILITY OF SUCH DAMAGES. In no event will Sun's liability to you, whether in contract, tort (including negligence), or otherwise, exceed the amount paid by you for Software under this Agreement. The foregoing limitations will apply even if the above stated warranty fails of its essential purpose.

6. **Termination.** This Agreement is effective until terminated. You may ter-minate this Agreement at any time by destroying all copies of Software. This Agreement will terminate immediately without notice from Sun if you fail to comply with any provision of this Agreement. Upon Termination, you must destroy all copies of Software.

7. **Export Regulations.** All Software and technical data delivered under this Agreement are subject to US export control laws and may be subject to export or import regulations in other countries. You agree to comply strictly with all such laws and regulations and acknowledge that you have the responsibility to obtain such licenses to export, re-export, or import as may be required after delivery to you.

8. **U.S. Government Restricted Rights.** If Software is being acquired by or on behalf of the U.S. Government or by a U.S. Government prime con-tractor or subcontractor (at any tier), then the Government's rights in Software and accompanying documentation will be only as set forth in this Agreement; this is in accordance with 48 CFR 227.7201 through 227.7202-4 (for Department of Defense (DOD) acquisitions) and with 48 CFR 2.101 and 12.212 (for non-DOD acquisitions).

9. **Governing Law.** Any action related to this Agreement will be governed by California law and controlling U.S. federal law. No choice of law rules of any jurisdiction will apply.

10. **Severability.** If any provision of this Agreement is held to be unenforce-able, this Agreement will remain in effect with the provision omitted, unless omission would frustrate the intent of the parties, in which case this Agreement will immediately terminate.

11. **Integration.** This Agreement is the entire agreement between you and Sun relating to its subject matter. It supersedes all prior or contempora-neous oral or written communications, proposals, representations and

warranties and prevails over any conflicting or additional terms of any quote, order, acknowledgment, or other communication between the parties relating to its subject matter during the term of this Agreement. No modification of this Agreement will be binding, unless in writing and signed by an authorized representative of each party.

Java™ 2 Software Development Kit (J2SDK), Standard Edition, Version 1.4.X Supplemental License Terms

These supplemental license terms ("Supplemental Terms") add to or modify the terms of the Binary Code License Agreement (collectively, the "Agreement"). Capitalized terms not defined in these Supplemental Terms shall have the same meanings ascribed to them in the Agreement. These Supplemental Terms shall supersede any inconsistent or conflicting terms in the Agreement, or in any license contained within the Software.

1. **Software Internal Use and Development License Grant.** Subject to the terms and conditions of this Agreement, including, but not limited to Section 4 (Java Technology Restrictions) of these Supplemental Terms, Sun grants you a non-exclusive, non-transferable, limited license to reproduce internally and use internally the binary form of the Software complete and unmodified for the sole purpose of designing, developing and testing your Java applets and applications intended to run on the Java platform ("Programs").

2. **License to Distribute Software.** Subject to the terms and conditions of this Agreement, including, but not limited to Section 4 (Java Technology Restrictions) of these Supplemental Terms, Sun grants you a non-exclusive, non-transferable, limited license to reproduce and distribute the Software, provided that (i) you distribute the Software complete and unmodified (unless otherwise specified in the applicable README file) and only bundled as part of, and for the sole purpose of running, your Programs, (ii) the Programs add significant and primary functionality to the Software, (iii) you do not distribute additional software intended to replace any component(s) of the Software (unless otherwise specified in the applicable README file), (iv) you do not remove or alter any proprietary legends or notices contained in the Software, (v) you only distribute the Software subject to a license agreement that protects Sun's interests consistent with the terms contained in this Agreement, and (vi) you agree to defend and indemnify Sun and its licensors from and against any damages, costs, liabilities, settlement amounts and/or expenses (including attorneys' fees) incurred in connection with any claim, lawsuit or action by any third party that arises or results from the use or distribution of any

and all Programs and/or Software. (vi) include the following statement as part of product documentation (whether hard copy or electronic), as a part of a copyright page or proprietary rights notice page, in an "About" box or in any other form reasonably designed to make the statement visible to users of the Software: "This product includes code licensed from RSA Security, Inc.", and (vii) include the statement, "Some portions licensed from IBM are available at http://oss.software.ibm.com/icu4j/".

3. **License to Distribute Redistributables.** Subject to the terms and conditions of this Agreement, including but not limited to Section 4 (Java Technology Restrictions) of these Supplemental Terms, Sun grants you a non-exclusive, non-transferable, limited license to reproduce and distribute those files specifically identified as redistributable in the Software "README" file ("Redistributables") provided that: (i) you distribute the Redistributables complete and unmodified (unless otherwise specified in the applicable README file), and only bundled as part of Programs, (ii) you do not distribute additional software intended to supersede any component(s) of the Redistributables (unless otherwise specified in the applicable README file), (iii) you do not remove or alter any proprietary legends or notices contained in or on the Redistributables, (iv) you only distribute the Redistributables pursuant to a license agreement that protects Sun's interests consistent with the terms contained in the Agreement, (v) you agree to defend and indemnify Sun and its licensors from and against any damages, costs, liabilities, settlement amounts and/or expenses (including attorneys' fees) incurred in connection with any claim, lawsuit or action by any third party that arises or results from the use or distribution of any and all Programs and/or Software, (vi) include the following statement as part of product documentation (whether hard copy or electronic), as a part of a copyright page or proprietary rights notice page, in an "About" box or in any other form reasonably designed to make the statement visible to users of the Software: "This product includes code licensed from RSA Security, Inc.", and (vii) include the statement, "Some portions licensed from IBM are available at http://oss.software.ibm.com/icu4j/".

4. **Java Technology Restrictions.** You may not modify the Java Platform Interface ("JPI", identified as classes contained within the "java" package or any subpackages of the "java" package), by creating additional classes within the JPI or otherwise causing the addition to or modification of the classes in the JPI. In the event that you create an additional class and associated API(s) which (i) extends the functionality of the Java platform, and (ii) is exposed to third party software developers for the purpose of developing additional software which invokes such additional API, you must promptly publish broadly an accurate specification for such API for free use by all developers. You may not create, or authorize your licensees to create, additional classes, interfaces, or subpackages that are

in any way identified as "java", "javax", "sun" or similar convention as specified by Sun in any naming convention designation.

5. **Notice of Automatic Software Updates from Sun.** You acknowledge that the Software may automatically download, install, and execute applets, applications, software extensions, and updated versions of the Software from Sun ("Software Updates"), which may require you to accept updated terms and conditions for installation. If additional terms and conditions are not presented on installation, the Software Updates will be considered part of the Software and subject to the terms and conditions of the Agreement.

6. **Notice of Automatic Downloads.** You acknowledge that, by your use of the Software and/or by requesting services that require use of the Software, the Software may automatically download, install, and execute software applications from sources other than Sun ("Other Software"). Sun makes no representations of a relationship of any kind to licensors of Other Software. TO THE EXTENT NOT PROHIBITED BY LAW, IN NO EVENT WILL SUN OR ITS LICENSORS BE LIABLE FOR ANY LOST REVENUE, PROFIT OR DATA, OR FOR SPECIAL, INDIRECT, CONSEQUENTIAL, INCIDENTAL OR PUNITIVE DAMAGES, HOWEVER CAUSED REGARDLESS OF THE THEORY OF LIABILITY, ARISING OUT OF OR RELATED TO THE USE OF OR INABILITY TO USE OTHER SOFTWARE, EVEN IF SUN HAS BEEN ADVISED OF THE POSSIBILITY OF SUCH DAMAGES.

7. **Trademarks and Logos.** You acknowledge and agree as between you and Sun that Sun owns the SUN, SOLARIS, JAVA, JINI, FORTE, and iPLANET trademarks and all SUN, SOLARIS, JAVA, JINI, FORTE, and iPLANET-related trademarks, service marks, logos and other brand designations ("Sun Marks"), and you agree to comply with the Sun Trademark and Logo Usage Requirements currently located at http://www.sun.com/policies/trademarks. Any use you make of the Sun Marks inures to Sun's benefit.

8. **Source Code.** Software may contain source code that is provided solely for reference purposes pursuant to the terms of this Agreement. Source code may not be redistributed unless expressly provided for in this Agreement.

9. **Termination for Infringement.** Either party may terminate this Agreement immediately should any Software become, or in either party's opinion be likely to become, the subject of a claim of infringement of any intellectual property right.

For inquiries please contact: Sun Microsystems, Inc., 4150 Network Circle, Santa Clara, California 95054, U.S.A.
(LFI#113729/Form ID#011801)

Wiley Publishing, Inc.
End–User License Agreement

the "What's on the CD-ROM" appendix of this Book. These limitations are also contained in the individual license agreements recorded on the Software Media. These limitations may include a requirement that after using the program for a specified period of time, the user must pay a registration fee or discontinue use. By opening the Software packet(s), you will be agreeing to abide by the licenses and restrictions for these individual programs that are detailed in the About the CD-ROM appendix and on the Software Media. None of the material on this Software Media or listed in this Book may ever be redistributed, in original or modified form, for commercial purposes.

5. **Limited Warranty.**

(a) WPI warrants that the Software and Software Media are free from defects in materials and workmanship under normal use for a period of sixty (60) days from the date of purchase of this Book. If WPI receives notification within the warranty period of defects in materials or workmanship, WPI will replace the defective Software Media.

(b) WPI AND THE AUTHOR OF THE BOOK DISCLAIM ALL OTHER WARRANTIES, EXPRESS OR IMPLIED, INCLUDING WITHOUT LIMITATION IMPLIED WARRANTIES OF MERCHANTABILITY AND FITNESS FOR A PARTICULAR PURPOSE, WITH RESPECT TO THE SOFTWARE, THE PROGRAMS, THE SOURCE CODE CONTAINED THEREIN, AND/OR THE TECHNIQUES DESCRIBED IN THIS BOOK. WPI DOES NOT WARRANT THAT THE FUNCTIONS CONTAINED IN THE SOFTWARE WILL MEET YOUR REQUIREMENTS OR THAT THE OPERATION OF THE SOFTWARE WILL BE ERROR FREE.

(c) This limited warranty gives you specific legal rights, and you may have other rights that vary from jurisdiction to jurisdiction.

6. **Remedies.**

(a) WPI's entire liability and your exclusive remedy for defects in materials and workmanship shall be limited to replacement of the Software Media, which may be returned to WPI with a copy of your receipt at the following address: Software Media Fulfillment Department, Attn.: XMLSPY Handbook, Wiley Publishing, Inc., 10475 Crosspoint Blvd., Indianapolis, IN 46256, or call 1-800-762-2974. Please allow four to six weeks for delivery. This Limited Warranty is void if failure of the Software Media has resulted from accident, abuse, or misapplication. Any replacement Software Media will be warranted for the remainder of the original warranty period or thirty (30) days, whichever is longer.

(b) In no event shall WPI or the author be liable for any damages whatsoever (including without limitation damages for loss of business profits, business interruption, loss of business information, or any other pecuniary loss) arising from the use of or inability to use the Book or the Software, even if WPI has been advised of the possibility of such damages.

(c) Because some jurisdictions do not allow the exclusion or limitation of liability for consequential or incidental damages, the above limitation or exclusion may not apply to you.

7. **U.S. Government Restricted Rights.** Use, duplication, or disclosure of the Software for or on behalf of the United States of America, its agencies and/or instrumentalities "U.S. Government" is subject to restrictions as stated in paragraph (c)(1)(ii) of the Rights in Technical Data and Computer Software clause of DFARS 252.227-7013, or subparagraphs (c) (1) and (2) of the Commercial Computer Software - Restricted Rights clause at FAR 52.227-19, and in similar clauses in the NASA FAR supplement, as applicable.

8. **General.** This Agreement constitutes the entire understanding of the parties and revokes and supersedes all prior agreements, oral or written, between them and may not be modified or amended except in a writing signed by both parties hereto that specifically refers to this Agreement. This Agreement shall take precedence over any other documents that may be in conflict herewith. If any one or more provisions contained in this Agreement are held by any court or tribunal to be invalid, illegal, or otherwise unenforceable, each and every other provision shall remain in full force and effect.